WHEN SHE WAS WAS
WHITE

WHEN SHE WAS WHITE

THE TRUE STORY OF
A FAMILY DIVIDED BY RACE

Judith Stone

miramax books

HYPERION

NEW YORK

ISBN 0-7868-6898-8

First Edition
10 9 8 7 6 5 4 3 2 1

To my parents,
Natalie and Rudyard Stone, with love

The past itself is constantly restructured by the present.
—Jean Piaget, *The Child and Reality*

People are trapped in history and history is trapped in them.
—James Baldwin, *Notes of a Native Son*

. . . i'm wearing
white history
but there's no future
in those clothes
so I take them off and
wake up
dancing.
—Lucille Clifton, "my dream about being white"

ACKNOWLEDGMENTS

A huge and heartfelt *dankie, siyabonga, ke a leboha,* thank you to Sandra Laing, and to her family: Johannes Motlaung, Henry and Sharon Laing, Elsie and Jafta Allies, Prins Laing, Anthony Laing, Steve Laing, the late Stiena Nkosi, Jenny Zwane, the late Lisa Zwane and Lucas Zwane. *Baie dankie* to Leon Laing, who didn't want to talk about the past, but did.

I am deeply grateful to the MacDowell Colony for bestowing the peace of mind that allowed me to finish this book.

Many thanks to Anthony Fabian for his perspicacity and tenacity, Elize Lötter for her generosity and vision, Karien van der Merwe for her energy and enthusiasm, and for wise guidance from the get-go, Jonathan Burnham, Amy Gross, my agent Gail Hochman, and my editor, the kind and imperturbable JillEllyn Riley. Susan Frisbie, PhD (and pal), senior lecturer in the department of English, Santa Clara University, offered extraordinarily insightful and helpful early (and late) readings of the manuscript; Dianne Armer and Carroll Johnson of the Bo Ek Foundation for the Floundering provided vital moral and material support.

The expertise of the following people was tremendously helpful (and any interpretive blunders are all mine): Ashwell Adriaan, curatorial consultant at the Apartheid Museum, Johannesburg; Sarron Goldman, PhD, lecturer, department of psychiatry and Clinical Neurosciences, University of Western Australia. Wilmot

James, PhD, executive director of the Africa Genome Education Institute; Trefor Jenkins, MD, professor emeritus, Department of Human Genetics of the South African Institute of Medical Research, University of the Witwatersrand; Stephen Karakashian, PhD, associate for development and training, Institute for Healing of Memories, Cape Town; Anthony Minnaar, professor of criminal justice studies, College of Law, University of South Africa, Pretoria; and the staff of the South African Institute on Race Relations, Johannesburg.

For their invaluable assistance I thank Graeme Bloch, Connie Carelse, Cheryl Carolus, Isabeau Coetze, Mildred Fredericks, Amina Frense, Rita Joubert, Anita Marsili, Anna Marsili, Emilia Marsili, Willy Meyer, Kobus Meyer, Simon Mlotha, Danie Nortje, Johann Potgieter, the late Njanja Rampuru, Jane Raphaely, Anco Steyn, Dianne Steyn, Helen Suzman, Alan Swerdlow, Antony Thomas, David Zeffertt, and Maja Kriel Zeffertt.

For their spirited support and sapience I salute Carol Adair, Jim Anderson, Lucy Anderson, Cliff Burnstein, Judy Coyne, Lesley Dormen, Rosemary Ellis, Nicole Gregory, Dalma Heyn, Evan Imber-Black, Joan Konner, Sara Nelson, Christy Platt, Andrew Postman, Karen Pritzker, Jamie Raab, Clarence Reynolds, Kathy Rich, Kay Ryan, Elaine Segal, Willa Shalit, Aviva Slessin, a pile of Stones—Natalie, Rudyard, Esther, Larry, Lisa, Jessica, Meredith, and Jordan—Sabra Turnbull, Pegi Vail, Melanie Wyler, Joey Xanders, and Pamela Yates.

Special thanks to Sechaba Africa Travel.

WHEN SHE WAS WHITE

1

REMOVED

S ANDRA LAING WAS TEN WHEN THE POLICE TOOK HER away. Not long after the teacher led morning prayers, the principal sent a boy to say that Sandra was wanted immediately. She sat quietly doing sums, one of the few classroom tasks that brought her peace or pleasure. She liked the tidiness and predictability of numbers.

The other children, sitting in pairs, giggled and whispered as Sandra rose from the little two-person desk she shared with no one and left without looking at them. The air was mild, with the hint of bite that marks a South African summer easing into autumn. Sandra crossed a central courtyard to the administrative wing of Piet Retief Laerskool Primary, a public elementary school for white children, most of them Afrikaners, descendants of the nation's first white settlers. A secretary pointed Sandra toward the door of Principal J. P. Schwartz's office. She knocked and entered.

The principal sat at his desk as usual, but behind him stood two khaki-uniformed policemen, a thin one and a wide one, their arms crossed. The sight of them sped the little girl's heart. "Sandra," Schwartz said in Afrikaans, "*Ek is bevrees jy sal ons moet verlaat.* I'm afraid you're going to have to leave us. Go with these officers to fetch your things. They will take you home." She wondered what she could have done that was bad enough to get her expelled. She hadn't socked anyone in donkey's years, or accused the other children of stealing her sweets, or complained of being called ugly names. Was it because she wet the bed and vomited nearly every night? Could the cops toss you in the chokey for that? "Why must I leave?" she asked Schwartz, surprised at the sound of her own voice. Usually when he summoned her, she'd look at the floor and pretend to be a tree. But the appearance of policemen suggested discipline of a disturbing new order and made her bold. "You will have to ask your father," the principal said. "Now please go with these gentlemen."

The thin policeman gently touched her shoulder. "Come," he said. She trotted after the men, a small but solid girl in summer uniform, a skirt and tunic of muted green. Recalling that day, Sandra thinks she might have stared at the stitching in the leather holsters at the officers' waists, although she's not absolutely certain they wore guns. She wanted her brother Leon, but he was at the high school, two miles away. And what could he do if he saw his little sister being hauled off by the *polisie*, except burn with shame? What would her parents say? Her mouth soured and she grew ill picturing her father's face when the officers deposited her at his doorstep. But then, as she'd taught herself to do whenever something was too painful or terrifying to think about, she willed a sort of thick, soft humming to fill her ears, the sound fog would make if it sang. She'd hit on that technique not long after she arrived at school and the trouble started. When her worries seemed so loud in her head that she was sure people could hear them grinding like a gearbox, the fog seemed to cool and blunt her hot, sharp thoughts. Her breathing slowed.

The policemen escorted her out the front gate of the school, beneath the painted sign that read *Arbeid Oorwin*—Work Conquers—and to their car. "Why am I being kicked out?" Sandra asked the officers, addressing their boots. "We don't know," the thin one said. "We've just been told to take you home. Your pa can explain."

Slowly they drove the mile or so to the hostel, the dormitory for boarding students. The only witnesses to their short journey were a few black gardeners tending yards on a quiet street in Piet

Retief, a small farming and timber community two hundred miles southeast of Johannesburg. The town was named in honor of a nineteenth-century Afrikaner pioneer murdered, Sandra's teacher told the children, by double-crossing Zulu barbarians. A proper name for a proper *verkrampte*, conservative, Afrikaner enclave. It was March 10, 1966. The week before, John Lennon had declared the Beatles more popular than Jesus, and their records would soon be banned in South Africa. On Robben Island, in the sea off Cape Town, Nelson Mandela was serving the second year of a life sentence for sabotage. These matters lay as far from Sandra's knowing, she says, as the back of the moon. She was also unaware of the fact that for more than four years, Principal Schwartz and a determined group of teachers, parents, and public officials had worked hard to force Sandra's removal from school, while her mother and father had struggled to prevent it.

The teacher in charge of boarding students, Johannes Van Tonder, tall and soldier-straight, waited at the front door of the hostel. The sight of him—his scowl, the stick he always carried—twisted Sandra's insides. He clearly despised her, but she wasn't entirely sure why. She knew, and she didn't know—that's what the fog in her head was good for. He marched her to the unadorned room she shared with nine other little girls and watched while she packed the suitcase stowed in her closet. Later that day, Van Tonder told Sandra's two close friends, Emilia and Elize, that she'd left school for good, but he never told them the reason.

The policemen flanked Sandra on the front seat of their sedan. They didn't say a word during the forty-minute ride up the narrow road to Panbult, where her father ran one of two general stores he and his wife owned in the southeastern corner of what is now the province of Mpumalanga, then the Eastern Transvaal. The familiar route cut through the heart of the highveld, South Africa's fertile central plateau, past fields of wheat and corn, rolling pastures where cows grazed, dirt-road turnoffs that led to coal mines, and vast plantations of pine, eucalyptus, and acacia trees. In occasional clearings ringed by piles of downed logs, big hive-shaped ovens roasted wood into charcoal.

Panbult was even smaller than Piet Retief: a few concrete grain silos, a railroad siding where coal was transferred from mine trucks to freight trains, a sawmill, a petrol station, and her father's tin-roofed general store. Abraham must have spotted the police car that day through the door of the shop. By the time Sandra slid out across the plastic-covered seat of the sedan, he'd planted himself on the wooden front *stoep* with his legs apart and his fists on his hips. Abraham Laing, forty-nine then, compact and balding, looked pained but not surprised to see the police delivering his daughter, like a man who opens a newspaper to find grim tidings he expected but hoped would never come. "Are you Abraham Laing?" one policeman asked. Sandra's father nodded. She went to him and he put an arm around her. "It's all right, my *skat*," he said. Then he gave those policemen hell. "They needed two big men to shift a tiny child? Was she too much for one? The devil take you! Get out! *Voetsek!*" As if they were dogs. Abraham's temper, which usually unsettled Sandra, was a balm that day. He wasn't angry at her, but at them.

"Man, pull yourself together," the officer said calmly. "We're just doing what we were told. Call the school inspector if you're unhappy."

"You can be sure I will," Abraham Laing shouted. The policemen drove off.

"Papa," Sandra said, "why can't I go to school anymore?" They watched the police car until it was a speck. Abraham was silent. She asked again. Usually, such persistence would earn a scolding. This time, her father began to weep, digging his fingers into Sandra's shoulder. She had never seen him cry before, and this response was more alarming than yelling would have been. Still, he didn't answer.

He told her to hop into the *bakkie*, the pickup, parked in front of the shop, and called to his black helper to lock up early for lunch. Abraham and Sandra headed down the reddish dirt road that led through grassland and stands of pine to their home in Brereton Park, twelve miles away, where Sandra's mother, Sannie Laing, kept the family's other general store. The road was empty except for the occasional coal or timber truck raising clouds of russet dust.

Brereton Park, designated by the government a white area like Piet Retief and Panbult, was an isolated crossroads on the crest of a gentle hill, where the dirt road from Panbult intersected another, became a gravel driveway, then dwindled to a rutted track with a grass strip down the middle. The whole place consisted of the Laing's thatch-roofed stone house, shielded from the road by a row of acacia trees, and their shop, shaded by eucalyptus and jacaranda, just a few yards away across the grassy track. Brereton Park General Dealers, a combination store, post office, and petrol station, served Driefontein, a black township three miles farther along the track. Behind the shop lay an open field where cows browsed, white tickbirds riding their backs, and beyond that, commercial pine forests owned by timber companies and maintained by black laborers. The Laings were the only white family for miles around: Sannie and Abraham, Sandra, her brother Leon, who was almost seven years older than she, and her new little brother Adriaan, four months old.

Sannie Laing, forty-five, ran out of the shop, her good face red, alarmed to see her husband home so early in the day. Adriaan was in the house with Nora, the black nanny who had cared for Sandra since she was a baby. "What is it, Abraham?" Sannie Laing said. "What has happened?" Sandra thought she saw a secret message fly between them. "Ma," Sandra said, fitting herself to the curve of her mother's warm side, "why must I come home? Why can't I go to school?" Sannie Laing, aproned and ample, began to weep, as her husband had. She wouldn't answer Sandra either, only cried and cried. The child thought how horrible her crime must be if her father and mother couldn't bear to utter the words for it.

Sandra Laing says today that her parents never told her why she was kicked out of school. Eventually she learned what happened, but she doesn't remember when or how she pieced together the details of the events that transformed her life. It bothers her that she can't reconstruct the precise moment she became conscious of her changed fate. She's dead certain, however, that on the day the police brought her home from Piet Retief Primary and for nearly two years after that, while she was at the center of a legal and political battle followed closely by the South African and international press, she convinced herself she'd been expelled from school for punching the arms of classmates who taunted her relentlessly.

Later, Sandra came to understand that she'd been forced to leave Piet Retief Primary because only white children were legally allowed to attend the school, and the government of South Africa had officially declared her to be no longer white.

The Population Registration Act of 1950 required that the Department of the Census assign everyone in South Africa to one of three racial categories: European, changed in 1960 to White, for the heirs of the Dutch, French, German, and, later, English who colonized the country; Coloured, for people of mixed race, a complex grouping with seven subdesignations, one of which, Asian (also referred to as Indian), later became a fourth category; and Native (later Bantu), for the black majority, with nine subdivisions based on historical tribal affiliations. Classification was essential for assuring segregation and white supremacy, the explicit goals of apartheid—the word means "apartness" in Afrikaans—the most restrictive system of legalized racial discrimination in recent history. Imposed by the Afrikaner-led National Party government in 1948, apartheid was a harsher and more pervasive form of the social and political system that had prevailed since white colonists first claimed South Africa in the mid-seventeenth century and subjugated the original inhabitants.

Each racial classification opened a door into a very different existence. Under apartheid, South Africa's white minority—about 3.5 million citizens in 1966—controlled the lives of some 15 million disenfranchised and dispossessed nonwhites, determining where they lived and worked, how well they ate, whom they could marry, when and where they might travel, whether they received decent or substandard—or any—schooling and health care, and, in essence, the age at which they were likely to expire.

Since both of Sandra Laing's parents were white, she'd been propelled at birth through the portals of white privilege and guaranteed the relatively pleasant and comfortable life of a middle-class Afrikaner child. Her birth certificate records the date she entered the world, November 26, 1955; her Christian name, Susanna Magrietha, the same as her mother's; her sex; and her color: *Blanke*, White.

But because of her frizzy hair and light brown skin, variously described in newspapers as toffee, tawny, honey, and sallow, the director of the Census had officially changed Sandra's classification to coloured. Now she couldn't legally enter a restaurant or movie theater with her parents or brothers; share a bus seat, a park bench, or a church pew; swim at the same beach, visit the same clinic, or be buried in the same cemetery. According to the letter of the law, she could no longer live with her white family, except as a servant.

2

GOGGAS

U NTIL SHE WAS SENT TO SCHOOL IN PIET RETIEF AT THE age of six, Sandra insists, she had no idea she looked different from the rest of her family. Her parents never mentioned the color of her skin, unless you counted the times her mother declared approvingly, as they worked side by side in the garden, "You have green hands." The customers at the general store, all of them black, said nothing about Sandra's appearance, and the Laings had no white neighbors to comment. On the rare occasions that the family drove to Piet Retief to visit the doctor or dentist, say, and then stopped afterward to eat an ice cream in the park, perhaps some white citizen looked meaningfully from Sandra to the sign on the bench that said *Net Blanke*, Whites Only. But the child couldn't read yet. "On the day that my mum and I came to town to buy my school uniform," Sandra says, "the lady at the shop kept asking my mum, 'Are you sure you want a uniform for *this* little girl?' I thought she meant I was too young to leave home."

Photographs from Sandra's school days show a lively, smiling child with her mother's upturned, Dutch-girl nose and slightly canted brown eyes. Sandra sees in her younger self the stubborn set of her father's jaw and a softer, fuller version of his resolute mouth. But while her parents appear to be as pale as milk in these black-and-white pictures, Sandra's skin reads as the light brown of barely steeped tea, and her short, tight, dark curls look exuberantly African.

The Laing family set off to register Sandra at boarding school on the last Sunday in January 1962. She was excited about wearing a uniform, curious to see the hostel where she'd be living, and anxious at the thought of being separated from her mother and her nanny, Nora. On the drive to Piet Retief, she sat in the backseat of the family's blue Volkswagen Beetle with her brother Leon, who was beginning his final year at the elementary school. He was nearly thirteen, a bespectacled, brown-haired boy with a pleasant, oblong face. They bounced over the dirt road corrugated by the brief but mighty afternoon rains that slam the highveld during summer. The last of the season's wildflowers remained, their shapes, but not their names, familiar to Sandra—yellow stars, silver spears, red droplets, purple fountains. Termite castles rose among the flowers, some of them higher than a man's head, towers of red earth constructed with extraordinary will and enterprise, Abraham Laing pointed out to his children, by mere tiny *goggas*, insects.

When they arrived at Piet Retief Primary, Abraham and Leon waited in the car while Sandra and her mother went inside to register. They hadn't met Principal Schwartz in person yet; the Laings had mailed in Sandra's application and a copy of her birth certificate. When Sannie finished filling out forms, the family drove to the Deborah Retief Hostel, named for pioneer Piet's daughter. A two-story brick building surrounded by green lawns and a wire fence that kept out the neighbors' cows, the hostel was divided into a girls' and a boys' side, each with dormitory rooms, bathrooms, and a separate playground. All the children, nearly two hundred of them, shared a study hall and dining room, and the supervising teachers lived in small, ground-floor apartments. The black people who cooked, cleaned, laundered, and gardened lived out of sight on the edge of Piet Retief in the townships, also called native locations, reserved for them by law.

Abraham took Leon to the boys' side of the hostel while Sannie settled Sandra into a long, plain room with big windows, divided nearly in half by a row of wooden wardrobes. On either side was a

line of five narrow metal beds, and next to each a little wooden chair
with a hinged seat that opened to reveal a space where the children
could put their shoes, polish, and a shoebrush. Sannie busied herself hanging clothes in the wardrobe. Sandra doesn't remember meeting the little girl, a few months younger than she, who was to become
her closest friend at school; she doesn't, in fact, remember knowing
her. Emilia Marsili came, as did many of the kids in the hostel, from
an Afrikaner community in the small neighboring nation of Swaziland, then a British protectorate nominally ruled by a black king.
Piet Retief was only thirty miles from the border.

    Emilia's mother, Anna Marsili, now in her eighties, has never
forgotten her first glimpse of Sandra. "We stood outside in the cor-
ridor, waiting to register Emilia, and I saw Mrs. Laing and Sandra inside the office," she recalls. "She was a dear little thing, all smiling,
and I thought to myself, oh, this poor girl's going to have a hell of a
time. I told Emilia, 'You must be especially nice to her.' I said to my
husband, 'She's going to have a bad time; watch out.'"

    Two weeks after Sandra's arrival at school, Principal Schwartz
wrote the following letter, here translated from Afrikaans:

*Confidential Letter to the Inspector of Education from the
Principal of Piet Retief Primary*

30 January 1962

RE: ADMITTANCE OF PUPIL: SUSANNA
MAGRIETHA LAING

Dear Sir:

    I hereby wish to inform you that I admitted the above-
mentioned pupil to my school on the grounds that I received
a birth certificate (No. 55957—entry 52/55—issued by the
District Registrar at Amersfoort on 12/6/61) from the pupil's
parents. This birth certificate indicates that said child has
been registered and classifed as being of the White race.

. . . I saw the child for the first time when her mother brought her to the school.

The impression that I and several teachers got, as well as parents of some of the other children who saw the child, is that this child could possibly be of mixed blood or race (coloured). The above-mentioned teachers and parents have discussed the case with me. I explained that because the birth certificate, which was submitted to me, indicates that the child is of the white race, I had no choice but to admit the child to my school.

For your information, I wish to provide you with the following description of the child:

1. The little eyes are dark brown, almost black.
2. The general impression one gets from the complexion and the form of the face is that this child is of mixed blood.
3. The lips stand out somewhat (are thick) as in the case of a person with mixed blood.
4. The color of the skin also correlates with that of a person with mixed blood—i.e., yellow brown.
5. In my opinion, anyone who saw the child would without a doubt classify this child as a non-White.
6. On the very first day that this child was admitted to the hostel it was brought to my attention that the native servants working in the hostel were very surprised to see this child in a white hostel and they have already started talking about the situation among one another.
7. Personnel members at the hostel have also informed me that the hostel children noticed the child's appearance and complexion from the very first day and have been talking about it since.

Furthermore, I would like to inform you that the child does not speak Afrikaans, although she seems to understand it. The language she speaks is Zulu.

It is my personal opinion that this child should not be admitted to a white school or a white hostel in the Republic of South Africa.

It will be highly appreciated if you could bring this matter to the attention of the Director of Education since I am expecting that some of the parents who have children attending my school will rebel.

Therefore, it will also be appreciated if you could treat this case as an exceptionally urgent matter.

Thanking you in advance.

Dutifully Yours,
J. P. Schwartz, Principal

3

HIDDEN HISTORY

P RINCIPAL SCHWARTZ WAS WRONG ABOUT THE ZULU. IT'S true that Sandra knew a bit of siSwati, the language of the Swazi people, which sounds much like isiZulu; she'd picked it up from her nanny, Nora. But her mother tongue was indisputably Afrikaans, the language that evolved from the Dutch spoken by South Africa's first white settlers, enriched by tangy borrowings from the people here when they arrived and the slaves they imported from elsewhere in Africa, and from India and Indonesia. Sannie Laing's people, and perhaps half of Abraham's, were Afrikaners, descendants of those settlers. When she was older, Sandra's life would change in ways that required her to become fluent in Zulu and Swazi, and proficient in English. But when Mr. Schwartz met her, she was an Afrikaans speaker, like any other Boer child. *Boer* is what Afrikaners still proudly call themselves. It means, simply, "farmer" in Dutch and Afrikaans. Used disparagingly by nineteenth-century British settlers but long since reclaimed, the word connotes self-reliance, plain speaking, pig-headedness, piety, and some share of nostalgia for the covenant that Afrikaner pioneers made with the Almighty to assume stewardship of a land they considered rightfully theirs. The word is used by black Africans, in another tone entirely, as slang for white policemen and for bigoted whites in general.

More than four decades after Mr. Schwartz confidently but incorrectly declared Sandra a Zulu speaker, people are still passing judgment on her with great assurance and varying degrees of accuracy. I wasn't surprised to find that South Africans are familiar with the story of Sandra Laing. She has, after all, been in the news, off and on, since soon after she was expelled from school. The public avidly followed press coverage of Sannie and Abraham Laing's fight to keep their daughter white. Newspapers carried the details of their declaration before God and a magistrate that Sandra was their biological child and not the product of interracial adultery, their famous loss in the Supreme Court, the surprising legal twist that followed, and the dramatic decision Sandra made as a teenager that led to estrangement from her parents and a future far different from the one they'd planned for her. Two television documentaries chronicled Sandra's life, and magazine articles explained the genetic mechanism that could account for her appearance in a white family. Over the years, reporters sometimes sought her out for "Where is she now?" pieces; anti-apartheid activists cited her case as a grim and vivid example of the arbitrariness, cruelty, and lunacy of racial classification laws. And at the turn of the millennium, nearly a decade after those laws were abolished and six years after apartheid was officially dismantled, Sandra again made headlines because of another seismic—and public—shift in her relationship with her family.

What I didn't expect was the number of people who insisted they knew the *real* story of Sandra Laing—the hidden history, the secret truth. "We heard the rumor that for a fact Sandra's father was the African man who worked in her parents' shop," said an Afrikaner woman in her seventies whose children went to school with Sandra. A gynecologist using the computer next to mine at an Internet café in a Johannesburg suburb, a black man who'd studied in the United States, announced he had inside information. "I'll tell you about Sandra Laing," he said, when he learned that I was working on a book about her. "I'll tell you what actually happened."

"So you know that her parents were white, and she—"

"Don't be naïve," he said. "A friend of mine is from Piet Retief and knew the family. The mother is black and that's why Sandra came out the way she did."

"I never heard that from anyone in town," I said. "I've spent a lot of time talking to people, black and white, who knew Sandra as a child."

"Well, it's true. The mother had a sister who was very dark, and the family paid her to leave town." His source had, unfortunately, emigrated to New Zealand and couldn't be reached for corroboration, but the doctor's faith in her account remained unshakable.

"It is without question something genetic," declared Anco Steyn, a former classmate of Sandra's who installs electronic gates and burglar alarms, a good choice of occupation in greater Johannesburg, where an average of 174 armed robberies a day are reported to the police. The topic of Sandra's appearance came up at a sundowner, a twilight cocktail party. Blacks and whites had been crossing the color line and creating children for nearly three hundred years, said Anco, an Afrikaner who was raised in Swaziland. "We're all mixed blood here, so what does it matter?" A revolutionary statement not likely to have been uttered by many men of his class and clan before the end of apartheid—or after it.

Attending the same party was one of Sandra's roommates during her last year at Piet Retief Primary. Elize Lötter, a childhood friend of Anco's, had become a corporate trainer, teaching people how to deal with workplace diversity in the new South Africa, and helping narrow a skills gap created by fifty years of deliberately inferior education for black students. Elize reported a conversation she'd had with a black executive in his late thirties, a man whose education and bespoke tailoring were British. He felt certain that Sannie Laing had fooled around. "It was often the case that white women kept a black male servant as a sex slave," he told Elize. She found that notion simultaneously heartbreaking and hilarious, recalling her own few glimpses of matronly Sannie Laing, and newspaper photos of her in plain housedresses and sensible glasses. Of course there were such liaisons, Elize acknowledged, and of course a temptress and transgressor can come unfashionably packaged. But she thought Sannie Laing's publicly professed and privately observed adherence to the separatist racial policies of the National Party made the sex-slave hypothesis highly unlikely.

The person most tentative about the ultimate truth of the Sandra Laing case is Sandra herself. She struggles daily to recover a life story interrupted by trauma and loss, at times usurped by the press, and occasionally warped by the interpretations and interventions, both well-meaning and self-serving, of people with varying ideas about what her ordeal symbolizes. Each of her families—the one she was born to, the one that took her in, and the one she's created—seems to need her story to mean something different.

The first time Sandra and I discussed the day she'd awakened a member of one race and gone to bed assigned to another, she was pained by the extent of the gaps in her memory. In November 2001, two weeks before her forty-sixth birthday, Sandra invited me to sit on a peacock-blue, plush love seat while she took the matching chair, both bought on credit and crammed into a living room barely big enough to hold them. She'd also managed to squeeze in a couple of end tables and a wall unit that held a television, stereo, family photographs, potted plants, and two fake Staffordshire china spaniels meant to convey European elegance, but so shoddily produced that they looked faintly similan. More family photos hung on the walls, along with a group shot of Bafana Bafana, the national soccer team; a clock shaped like an oversized wristwatch; and a reproduction of the Last Supper on a rectangle of wood. The floor was covered with linoleum simulating parquet.

Sandra and her family rented this tiny, two-bedroom house in Tsakane, a black township in the East Rand, an industrial district twenty-five miles southeast of Johannesburg. The East Rand was once rich in mines—gold, coal, uranium, and platinum—but most have shut down, leaving behind patches of poisoned soil and at least 40 percent unemployment in a cluster of townships that is home to nearly a million people of color. Outside, on the pitted, unpaved street set with brick houses identical to Sandra's, a spring breeze raised dust devils laced with fine siftings of toxic metals blown from a range of slag piles a mile away, high, flat-topped heaps of mine waste a dull yellow-brown, the color of a headache.

Sandra shared the house with her common-law husband, Johannes Motlaung, their son Steve, then thirteen, and two of Sandra's four older children. Prins, who was twenty-one, and eighteen-year-old Anthony slept in one minuscule bedroom, decorated with posters of Britney Spears and Tupac Shakur. Johannes, Sandra, and Steve slept in the other. Sandra's eldest son, Henry, twenty-nine, and daughter, Elsie, twenty-eight, lived with their spouses not far from Sandra in two different coloured townships.

De facto segregation still exists in the new South Africa, preserved not by law but by economics. Though many admirable improvements have been made since 1994, when Nelson Mandela was elected president and the nonwhite majority took control of the government in the nation's first democratic, multiracial election, most of the wealth is still in the hands of whites and most of the poor are black. But for the first time in three hundred years, a nonracial constitution offers the hope of justice for all and the legal means to achieve it.

Sandra, shy but friendly, sat beneath the last photograph ever taken of her mother. Speaking softly, she occasionally wept when she recounted an especially painful event from her past, but even then kept her lovely face still. Much of the time she gazed at the floor, looking up briefly for emphasis. Plump as a pomegranate, with a cap of close-cropped curls, she looked girlishly, vulnerably young, although she'd recently become a grandmother. The skin that has caused her so much trouble over the years was unlined and unblemished.

We were alone in the usually crowded house. Johannes was at his job, driving a truck for a munitions company. Prins and Anthony had gone off to play video games at a sports bar, bankrolled by their mother since both were jobless. They hailed one of the packed minivan taxis, called combis, that ply the townships honking for customers, painted with mottoes on the bumpers and back windows: Only God Can Judge Me and Too Much Is Never Enough. Steve and his two best friends, out in the yard, shrieked with laughter as they took turns rolling each other up in an old bedspread.

Often people meeting Sandra for the first time peg her as uncannily serene, unless they notice how thoroughly her nails are gnawed. "I eat my fingers," she said with a small smile that first day, hiding her hands in the folds of her skirt.

The year before, in 2000, Sandra had come to the attention of Anthony Fabian, a British filmmaker, who was moved by an interview she gave on BBC radio and thought her experiences would make a wonderful feature film, his first. He raised development funds, tracked Sandra down in Tsakane, offered a substantial sum of money for the rights to her life story, and commissioned a screenplay from a white South African writer living in Los Angeles, who came home to meet Sandra. So many people asked Tony Fabian whether he was adapting the film from a book, he says, that a year into revising the script, he spoke to publishers and discovered there was indeed interest in a book about the Sandra Laing case. The editor who bought the book felt that Sandra's story could best be reported by an observer from outside South African culture. That's how I came to be sitting in the parlor of a house in Tsakane asking Sandra Laing to reconstruct her life, the first in a series of conversations that would continue for five years.

I soon saw that my task would involve not just gathering Sandra's testimony, but also tracking down information to fill gaps in her story—things she'd forgotten, and things she'd never known. Sandra apologized for not remembering more. She told me that although she could picture some parts of her early life as clearly as video, many later events—great expanses of experience—were gone. "Why do you think I've forgotten so much?" she asked.

"Why do *you* think?"

She sighed. "Too painful."

To fill in those blanks, we used official documents, government records, library archives, and interviews with Sandra's friends, family, neighbors, former classmates, and the parents of children who attended Piet Retief Primary in the 1960s. I also consulted various experts, among them lawyers, historians, geneticists, sociologists, psychologists, and some of the South African journalists who'd covered her story over the years. When the testimony of eyewitnesses didn't jibe with Sandra's description of an event, or with one another's, I talked with her about what the discrepancies might mean. The *Rashomon* effect is inevitable any time several people recount the same incident, but especially in South Africa, where previously suppressed versions of history were publicly acknowledged—and the public record altered to include them—through the Truth and Reconciliation Commission hearings of 1996, designed to allow victims of apartheid to tell, finally, their silenced stories.

We were helped greatly by the small support community that had coalesced around Sandra by the time that I met her, among them an Afrikaner television producer who'd been assigned by the South African Broadcasting Company (SABC) to cover Sandra's story and had become a close friend; a former classmate, also an Afrikaner, who defied her *volk*, her people, to marry outside her race; a coloured therapist whose own painful racial secrets resonate with Sandra's, for good and ill; and a bent Swazi woman in her eighties, living without running water or electricity in hills a billion years old, who played a crucial role in Sandra's survival.

Sandra speaks Afrikaans, Swazi, Zulu, and English; I'm limited to the last. Sometimes when we were in the presence of another Afrikaans speaker whose English Sandra considered better than hers, she'd answer my questions in Afrikaans and then ask the other person to translate. With her children, Sandra speaks Afrikaans, her mother tongue and theirs, although she says she feels most relaxed speaking Zulu, which is what she and Johannes use with each other. When she tells a joke it's in Zulu. When she counts or talks to God it's in Afrikaans.

At first, the answer Sandra gave most often to questions about her past was, "I don't remember." Of course, "I don't remember" can also mean "I don't wish to remember," or "I remember, but I won't tell you," or "I remember, and I may tell you later if I trust you." I was aware that as a visiting white American, I might be toting less historical baggage than a white South African, but I benefited from just as much unearned privilege. This was driven home early in my first trip, when the power conferred by my skin color led to my accidentally committing a crime.

Tony Fabian and I planned to visit Clarens, a rural village in Free State, one of nine provinces in the Republic of South Africa, prized for its beautifully craggy setting and for being a hip, artsy outpost in a notably conservative area. A Johannesburg friend, a law professor, asked us to bring back some files from his country house there. We'd find no street sign, he said, but he gave detailed directions.

At a stone house with green trim and a chain-link fence, as described, we asked a black gardener mowing the lawn if we could pick up a few things for the owner of the house. The man, who introduced himself as Jacob, said he didn't have a key, but offered to fetch a neighbor who did. He left by the same gate we'd walked through to find him and pedaled off on a bicycle. A white man of perhaps seventy soon drove up, and we explained our mission. He pulled a ring of keys from his pocket and cheerfully commenced probing a huge padlock on a thick chain wrapped several times around the post of a double gate across the driveway, a few feet from where we'd entered the yard. "Oh, you don't have to bother," I said. "The gate's open right over there." The man looked at me with narrowed eyes, and then laughed. "That's Jacob's gate," he said, and went back to work on the padlock.

He let us into the house, where we searched desk drawers and closets for the files, all the while exchanging pleasantries with the keeper of the keys, who said he was the owner's brother-in-law. But while Tony and I called the owner David, he seemed to be talking about a Robert. After a fruitless hunt for the files, it dawned on Tony and me at about the same time that we had just broken into a stranger's house. Mortified, we thanked the man, said the papers must not be there after all, and tried not to dissolve into hysterical laughter until we hit the car. But it wasn't funny, really. As white visitors, we were granted license, no questions asked, to enter the home of a stranger and rifle through his belongings. And we'd just witnessed a small but telling example of the lingering social deformities of apartheid: a man had gone to enormous trouble rather than walk through a convenient gate he considered tainted and unworthy of a white.

Sandra and I were attempting a candid conversation in a country where race and class differences have skewed the distribution of power for more than three hundred years. That was bound to affect how she told her story, and how I heard it. If you believe, as do some post-colonial theorists, that in the very act of telling Sandra's story I am appropriating it, that any intercultural translation is ipso facto a betrayal, then you'd say we were screwed from the start. But Sandra and I thought that since we liked each other and were both committed to the same goal—telling her story in a way that she feels accurately presents her views and those of others involved in her life—then if I pledged to try to remain conscious of my cultural assumptions, things might work out.

Over time, Sandra began to recall, or reveal, more and more. Sometimes her memory was jogged by visits with people from the old days or a document from her previously unavailable government file; sometimes she retrieved memories when she was strong enough to withstand them. In time, she was able to reconstruct more fully her journeys back and forth across the color line—the government ultimately changed her race classification three times—and occasionally offered startling revisions. Her struggle to face a difficult past, to take painful but ultimately rewarding steps toward repairing the damage done to her (and the damage she's done to herself), to reclaim the story of her life and to find meaning, peace, and even joy in it, is also the struggle of a post-apartheid South Africa coming to terms with its own hidden history.

Very early in this process, I had to decide how, or whether, to assign racial labels to people. Though race classification no longer exists, I can remember few conversations in South Africa in which the subject of race didn't come up, sometimes unexpectedly. For example, talking with an Afrikaner travel agent in Johannesburg, I said, "I can see that your colleague is—"

"Coloured, yes."

"Um, I was going to say I can see that he's very creative."

Most scientists agree that race isn't a biologically meaningful concept. Of the 25,000 or so genes that determine heritable characteristics—whether each of us is tall, shy, pudgy, arthritic, fleet-footed, or brilliant—only a tiny fraction have to do with skin color, hair texture, and the shape of eyes or noses. To put it another way: Sandra's DNA is 99.9 percent identical to Principal Schwartz's and that of every other person on the planet. And only 15 percent of the differences in that remaining 0.1 percent have anything to do with the visible markers of race.

Still, in daily life, what most people understand as race matters; and in South Africa, it matters terribly. (I find useful the working definition of race offered by the sociologist Pierre L. van den Bergh: "a group that is socially defined, but on the basis of physical criteria.") Even sixteen years after the abolition of race classification, and thirteen years after the fall of apartheid, race remains a central issue in the lives of South Africa's 47.4 million citizens—79 percent of them black, 9.6 percent white, 8.9 percent coloured, and 2.5 percent Indian/Asian, according to 2006 estimates. Race still determines for many of them (de facto, if not de jure) the level and quality of their employment, housing, education, and health care, their safety from violent crime, and their life expectancy.

Revealing a person's race conveys something, but not everything, about the way she or he has experienced life in South Africa. But which descriptive words are appropriate? Many of the terms used by apartheid-era government officials and scientists are now considered derogatory, but the people who deplore them don't always agree on what should take their place. For example, South Africans of mixed racial origin, formerly classified by the government as coloured, now call themselves coloured, "coloured," so-called coloured, brown, and black. Zimitri Erasmus, a sociology professor at the University of Cape Town, writes that she refers to herself as "culturally coloured and politically black." To the first European settlers of South Africa, to Sandra's father, and to many of his contemporaries, anyone not officially white was black, no matter what the genetic ingredients or color gradient.

In this book, when I'm quoting from or referring to historical documents, I use the words that had legal and social meaning during the apartheid era: *white, coloured* (and its subcategories, including *Asian,* generally applied to Indian descendants of indentured servants and slaves, or of a small merchant class) and *black, native,* or *Bantu.* The last is a word originally used by white anthropologists to label a Southern African language group. It means simply "person" or "human" in tribal languages comprising the Bantu group. But clearly it was intended to mean "not quite human" by apartheid bureaucrats who decided to use *native* and *Bantu* rather than *African* as the official label for black people because they wanted only Afrikaners to bear a name suggesting entitlement to the land. I sometimes use the term *nonwhite* to refer to black people, rather than calling white people *non-black*. This choice privileges, you should pardon the expression, whiteness as the norm—but accurately reflects the realities of Sandra Laing's life.

When a present-day reference to race is necessary for clarity, I use the terms *white, coloured,* and *black* for contemporary individuals, unless they call themselves something else. (What does Sandra Laing call herself? Different things at different times.) Ultimately I'd prefer the simple taxonomy proposed by American psychologist Linda James Myers: Given what paleontologists and geneticists tell us about human origins—that our earliest ancestor emerged in Southern Africa around 120,000 years ago—the world's people can be sensibly divided into only two groups: those who acknowledge their African descent and those who don't.

4

GLAD AS A BIRD

I WAS OVER THE MOON WHEN MY DAUGHTER WAS BORN," Sannie Laing is quoted as saying in an interview that ran in the August 13, 2000, issue of the London *Times Sunday Magazine.* She was eighty-one then, a fragile, stroke-wracked woman whose path had diverged from her daughter's many years before, in ways that confounded and burdened them both.

I immediately noticed that the color of Sandra's skin was darker. But it did not affect my joy at her arrival. If my husband was alarmed at her skin color at first sight, he did not show it. The nursing staff did not react either.

We were members of South Africa's Nationalist Party and Dutch Reformed Church. We lived for our country, church and family. My husband and I discussed Sandra and the color issue, but we just assumed it had something to do with what happened in previous generations. During the 1950s and '60s, a few cases of genetic kickbacks occurred. Abraham and I traced our family trees back to our great great grandparents. Nowhere could we find a marriage between two different races. It became an impossible task to find out why this had happened to us. But I never looked at Sandra as any different. She was our daughter, and blood is thicker than water.

Sandra Laing was born at a hospital for whites only in Amers-foort, a village of sheep farmers about fifty miles from Brereton Park. Her parents kept a general store in Balmoral, an even smaller *dorp,* rural village, outside Amersfoort. When I met Sandra, she knew little about her ancestors, not even the names of her grand-parents. A check of public records showed that Sannie Laing was the daughter of Jan Adriaan Roux and his wife Susanna Magrietha, nee Veldman. The name Roux appears on the roster of the first per-manent white settlers who arrived at the Cape of Good Hope in 1652, as employees of the Dutch East India Company. Most of them, including the Roux family, were French Huguenots, Protes-tants who'd fled to the Netherlands from Catholic France in the early seventeenth century to escape persecution. Sandra's Roux grandparents had a farm near an Eastern Transvaal dorp called Am-sterdam, where Sannie was born in 1920, the youngest of three sis-ters. Sandra remembers only Tannie (Aunt) Marie, who had an orchard and helped Sandra pick peaches and plums when she was a toddler. "She loved me," Sandra says. There were some older cousins; one of them, Tannie Marie's daughter, still lives in Amsterdam but has refused to speak to Sandra since 1991. Tannie Marie never said anything to suggest her niece was different from the rest of the fam-ily, Sandra says, and neither did her *ouma*, Granny Roux. "I don't re-member her much, but she was all right with me; she also loved me," Sandra says. "She never said anything about my color."

Abraham's father, Alfred Laing, was born in 1874 in Memel, Germany, near the Lithuanian border, and emigrated to South Africa in 1900; available records don't say where his wife Sophia was born, and Sandra doesn't know. Piet Retief and neighboring Wakker-stroom attracted a community of Germans who'd come to the East-ern Transvaal as missionaries, woodcutters, carpenters, and tradesmen in the mid-nineteenth century. Later, a number of them switched to farming corn, wheat, and tobacco. Alfred Laing was a shopkeeper. He may originally have been a Lutheran, like most members of the Eastern Transvaal's German community. But his son Abraham born in Wakkerstroom in 1916 was raised in the Dutch Reformed Church, similar to the Lutheran faith in its stern Calvinism, although more emphatic in its insistence on the depravity of all humankind, and more enthusiastic in the quest for biblical proof that blacks were inferior and that apartheid was ordained by God. *Ouma* Laing died before Sandra was born. Sandra recalls once meeting an elderly uncle who lived in Wakkerstroom; records show that a John Henry Laing bought an early discharge from the police force in 1919 and died in 1967. He may have been Abraham's brother, or Alfred's.

Sannie and Abraham married in May 1943 in Amsterdam; Leon was born six years later. Sandra knows Sannie and Abraham met in Johannesburg, but not what they were doing there. Her parents' early lives are a mystery to her. "I never asked my mum or dad about their growing-up years," she says. "They never told me anything about themselves as kids." By the time she felt able to ask, it was too late; everyone who knew her family history was gone.

Apart from the rarely seen older cousins, Leon was the only white child Sandra knew before she went away to school. Her best friends were three Swazi girls from the black township of Drie-fontein. Two of them, one her age and one a few years younger, were, she thinks, the daughters of Nora—Sandra doesn't remember her last name—the housekeeper and nanny who came every day to cook, clean, and look after the Laing children. The other girl, also Sandra's age, was perhaps the daughter of Miriam, a black woman who came on Mondays to do the wash and on Tuesdays to iron. Sandra cherishes her memories of these friends and their adventures, but can't recall their names, although she's tried several times with an almost athletic effort. In order to discuss them, she assigned them the names Sibongi, Thembi, and little Gertie. She doesn't know why those names came to her, and isn't sure about what language she used to communicate with the girls. The three must have spoken some Afrikaans, she says, and she must have picked up some Swazi, but in any case they understood each other perfectly from the start.

Sometimes her friends walked up the hill from Driefontein in the morning with Nora, a slim, strong, affectionate woman perhaps in her early thirties when Sandra was a preschooler. Sometimes the girls showed up later. "Until they came, I spent time with Nora,"

Sandra says. "My mother was already in the shop. When Nora wasn't busy, she played hide-and-seek with me, or I would sit outside on her lap when she was drinking tea. When Nora was busy, I played with my doll."

Sandra and the girls might spend time in the kitchen grooming the doll, named Melinda, combing her long, yellow curls, bathing her, and mending her clothes. But they preferred to be outside. "My mother would always tell me, 'Mgqibelo! Wear a hat! Never go out in the sun without a hat!'" Her father, too, often reminded her to put on the big floppy bonnet, white with pink roses, that tied under her chin. "'Mgqibelo' was my mother's nickname for me; in Swazi it means Saturday, the day I was born." It's pronounced mmm-kee-BELL-o, with a little hum in front, to Sandra's ear a word as pretty as a dove's call. Abraham Laing didn't approve of it, nor did he approve of her playing with Thembi, Gertie, and Sibongi.

"My father was very strict," Sandra Laing says. That's the word she used most often to describe him in our early conversations. "He was strict with me, and with the workers." The Laings employed a helper in each store. In Brereton Park, Stefaan Zwane swept the floor, stocked the shelves, waited on customers, carried heavy boxes, loaded *bakkies* and donkey carts, chopped the wood that fired the shop's coal stove, and manned the two petrol pumps out front, where the dirt roads to Panbult and Piet Retief intersected. He also milked the cows, took them out to pasture in the morning, and fetched them in the late afternoon. Twice a month Stefaan helped Abraham pick up goods from the Panbult train station in the *bakkie*. A black watchman came after dinner and camped in front of the store until morning, sitting near a small fire. "When the watchman came with his bicycle, I would take it and ride it around," Sandra says. "I was friends to Stefaan and the watchman. My dad didn't like that."

Nora spoke Swazi and Afrikaans. Sannie spoke Swazi well, Sandra says, but her father was content to struggle with the few words necessary for maintaining *baaskap*, bosshood. Abraham rarely addressed Nora. "Papa just said 'Morning' to her," Sandra says.

"She was scared of my dad. She never spoke to him, but spoke to my mum. Leon was like my father with Nora and Miriam; he would greet them but not talk to them."

Abraham was strict with the customers, too. Sandra could tell her father didn't like the customers; he never laughed and chatted with them the way Sannie did, and he wouldn't let their hands touch his when he took their money. Their nickname for him in Swazi was Shesa, because when they came to the counter to pay he snapped, "*Shesa, shesa!*"—"Hurry, hurry!"—and tapped the counter impatiently to show them where to drop their coins. "My father didn't want my mum to talk to people in the shop. She mustn't make friends with them, just sell to them."

Most mornings, Abraham left for the Panbult shop before Sandra woke up. She'd eat breakfast with her mother and Leon when he was home from school. Nora fried up eggs and bacon and sometimes *boerewors*, farmer's sausage, on top of the big coal stove, and made toast in the oven. Sandra remembers the Laings having indoor plumbing and a telephone, but no gas or electricity. The lamps and refrigerator ran on kerosene, and the stove, fueled by kindling-lit coal, heated pipes that brought hot water to the bathroom. Nora, Miriam, and the girls took their breakfast on the back *stoep* or under a tree. They ate mealie pap—corn porridge, a staple of poor blacks—from a special set of cups, dishes, and silverware that only they used. Geese and chickens patrolled the yard for scraps. "The kitchen in Brereton Park was two rooms—a cooking room and a washing-dishes room," Sandra says. "The laundry Miriam did by hand outside in the yard or, if it was raining, in a covered place behind the kitchen." Occasionally Abraham came home for lunch at one o'clock, but often he stayed in Panbult all day.

Sandra enjoyed helping her mother in the store. Some mornings, after breakfast, Sandra and Sannie might cross the gravel drive, its edges muddy in the rain and powdery during dry spells, and open the shop together. By then, the watchman had put out his fire and headed home to Driefontein. Two big jacaranda trees near the shop drizzled pale purple petals on breezy spring days and provided shade year-round. Next to them, a pair of blue gums—eucalyptus trees—sent up a clean liniment smell. Even before the shop opened at eight, customers sat on the ground beneath the trees. Some had bounced up the track in *bakkies*, some came by bicycle or donkey cart, but most walked. The crowd swelled once a week when a white doctor from nearby Dirkiesdorp drove in to treat people in a room behind the shop.

In spring, Sandra would run to the slender, fragrant tree called yesterday-today-tomorrow, which grew just to the left of the shop's entrance, and wait for her mother to lift her into its sweetness. The tree produced flowers of three colors—white, pale lavender, and dark purple—with a piercing scent, delicious but a little sad, that seemed to jump up her nose and pinch her heart. The yesterday-today-tomorrow was her favorite flower then and still is, Sandra says.

Sometimes Sannie let her break off a branch and bring it inside. She'd put the wand of blossoms in a soft-drink bottle filled with water and set it on the counter that ran nearly the length of the shop to the left of the door. Sandra thought the yesterday-today-tomorrow mixed beautifully with the other glorious shop aromas: the knife-sharp stink of the plum-colored kerosene—called paraffin, pronounced with the emphasis on the "feen"—that Sannie or Stefaan pumped out of big tins; the perfumed sting of washing powder; the snap of masala and peri-peri, popular spice mixtures; the earthy breath released when Sannie opened a big jar of licorice pipes.

Sandra can conjure up the contents of that shop with greater ease than she can reassemble some of the most important events of her life. The Laings sold nearly everything a person needed, except fresh produce and meat: sugar, flour, salt, and "mealie-meal"—ground corn for making pap. Milk, juice, and soft drinks, called cooldrinks in South Africa, kept in the glass-fronted paraffin fridge; ice cream from the paraffin deep freeze. Biscuits, potato crisps, Lucky Star brand tinned fish, baked beans, and packets of *biltong*, pungent South African beef jerky. Face soap, pins and needles, spools of thread, rolls of cotton wool, buckets, basins, blankets, string. Cough mixture, blue jars of Vicks, and yellow-orange packages of

Lennon's old-fashioned remedies, like *Wonderkroonessens*, Wonder Crown Essence, for wind and indigestion. Pencils, pens, exercise books, and small toys—dolls, motorcars, kites. Clothing, too: shoes, socks, shirts, trousers, sweaters, dresses.

Sugar and mealie-meal came in fifty-kilo burlap sacks, Sandra remembers. "My mother used a metal scoop to fill brown paper bags that she put on a big hanging scale like a baby's cradle. I liked to read out the weight to her." When Sandra was older, she sometimes took customers' orders if the shop was crowded, and relayed them to her mother or Stefaan. She had a good memory then, trusty as pencil and paper.

When the shop was empty, Sandra and Sannie played games. "My mum loved to play with me Snakes and Ladders, or cards," Sandra says. "Sometimes Leon would play, too, if he was home. Leon helped in the shop on holidays. It was fun. Leon and I together might pack sugar, or when my mum was selling clothes and she pulled out what people wanted to see, then we straightened them and put them away. Leon was always nice. He would take a walk to look at the cows with me, and he taught me how to ride his bicycle. He was very patient." Sandra slipped on gravel when she was first learning to pedal and scraped her thigh so badly she couldn't wear panties, but she got right back on the bike. She was bold and happy then, she says, active and sharp-eyed. If Leon noticed that she looked different from him, he never said anything.

Helping her mother count cash at the end of the day was nice, but her favorite job was postmarking letters with an official rubber stamp and then helping Sannie toss them into a canvas postbag that Abraham would take to the train in Panbult the next morning.

Sandra remembers owning only one storybook, *Jack and Jill*, in English. Her parents knew English, but spoke to Sandra exclusively in Afrikaans. She doesn't recall their reading to her in any language. "It can be that they did," she says, "but I don't remember."

She and her friends liked looking at the pictures in *Jack and Jill*, which involved an interesting amount of falling and spilling. But they weren't ones to sit quietly for long; they were explorers, experimenters, run-and-shouters, sing-and-jumpers. They staged beetle races or poked at *shongololo*, centipedes, until the creatures curled into spirals, and then rolled them down the road like tiny hoops. They probed anthills with sticks and helped the little *goggas* struggle upward; they herded the ducks and chickens. When customers left Brereton Park in donkey carts, they'd hitch a ride until they could barely see the Laings' house in the distance, then jump out and run home. "We older girls did," Sandra says. "The little one was afraid of donkeys." Sandra recalls the foursome as just the right combination of shy and brave. Stefaan, the store helper, made them a swing out of a piece of wood suspended by thick rope from a tall tree branch, and they dared each other higher and higher. They were mad for climbing trees. The yesterday-today-tomorrow was far too fragile, but they'd scramble up the wattle and the willow. Unfortunately, they were much better at up than down, and nearly always had to shout for Stefaan or a customer to climb up and fetch them. The stranded girls clung to the backs of their rescuers, who, laughing and cursing, warned them not to do it again, knowing that the foursome would ignore them and repeat the process with undiminished delight.

Though the three girls came to play with Sandra in Brereton Park nearly every day, she wasn't allowed to visit them in Driefontein, a patchwork of small brick, cinder-block, and wooden houses with thriving vegetable gardens, along with less substantial shacks of cardboard and corrugated tin. Driefontein was notable as one of the few places in South Africa where a black person could own property during the years of apartheid. The land was originally purchased in 1912 by the Native Farmers Association of Africa Limited, a cooperative started by Pixley ka Isaka Seme, a black South African lawyer who that same year co-founded the South African Native National Congress, an association of activists that later became the anti-apartheid African National Congress (ANC), ultimately the political party of Nelson Mandela. Seme unsuccessfully fought the Natives Land Act of 1913, passed by a coalition government of Afrikaner and English colonists who'd joined forces to form the Union of South Africa in 1910. The law designated 87 percent of South African territory as whites-only areas, and prohibited black people from owning property there. The rest—13 percent of the land for more than 85 percent of the population—was reserved for blacks and coloureds. Most black South Africans lived then as subsistence farmers. Suddenly landless, the majority were forced to work for wages on white farms or in mines and factories. The law had created, quite deliberately, a migrant labor pool of men separated from their families, who might be moved to remote townships or barren rural areas set aside as "tribal homelands" or "native reserves," also known colloquially as Bantustans. But the people of Driefontein stayed put on land they owned, and would successfully stave off later government attempts to oust them.

Sandra and her friends often played in the rondavel, the round thatched hut next to the shop, built of concrete blocks instead of mud and sticks in the traditional African way, where Abraham stored bags of red corn for the cows. And the girls looked forward to the day, once a month, when a government clerk came to the shop to distribute pension checks to the old people of Driefontein. Elderly whites got theirs in the mail, but black pensioners, no matter how infirm, were required to pick up their checks—a fraction of the amount received by whites—in person. It may have been tough on the old ones, but Sandra, Thembi, Gertie, and Sibongi were delighted when the yard around the shop turned into a sort of bazaar. Vendors set out piles of clothing or pots and pans; they arranged inviting pyramids of mangoes, papayas, tangerines, and tomatoes, impressive towers of pineapples, mounds of cooked chicken. Sandra and the girls dashed from heap to heap, sometimes helping themselves to fruit, sugar cane, or *phuto*, dry corn meal that they mixed with *amasi*, sour milk, and ate with their hands.

Sandra only welcomed keeping still when she was with her grandfather. For part of the year Alfred Laing lived with the family in a guest rondavel on the forest side of the house. Sandra remembers him as a gentle, comforting man, but very old and often ill. He never mentioned her color, she says, and he called her *Sandrike*, little Sandra, an affectionate diminutive. No one else called her Sandrike. She and Oupa were very fond of each other and enjoyed spending long sessions sitting together on the back *stoep* of the house,

watching. They watched clouds change shape, or the progress of the
sun across the blue clockface of the sky. They watched the grass dance
in the wind and butterfly swarms stitch the air with gold. They
watched the circling of red hawks and the graceful flight of the birds
Oupa called *flapper*, with improbably long tails like the trains of ball
gowns. In spring, the fields around Brereton Park were thick with cos-
mos, in pink, white, purple, and chocolaty maroon. Sandra remembers small sounds in the stillness—the click of sun beetles, "hard
things that sing when it's shiny out," the light clatter of breeze-stirred
leaves, the squeaking of the pump when Stefaan filled the cows'
drinking trough.

Sometimes Oupa sat on the *stoep* while Sandra and the girls
played games nearby. One of their favorites, called *zingando* in Zulu
and Swazi, resembled the game of jacks, but was played with stones.
Sandra often ran into the shop for sweets. Black licorice pipes and
whips were her favorite. She also liked the jawbreakers everyone
called "niggerballs" (still popular in South Africa, but advertised in
print as "nickerballs"), which started out red or blue and turned various colors as you sucked on them, diminishing finally to tiny black
pebbles. The girls would remove the shrinking spheres from their
mouths every few minutes to check the size and hue. "I could take
as much sweets as I like," Sandra says, "but sometimes my mum
would say, '*Ag*, that's all, my God—you have sweets for Africa!' As
soon as she wasn't looking, I would put a few more pieces under
my shirt."

Back then, the thing that made Sandra happiest, she says, was
working in the garden beside her mother, pruning roses, gathering
pumpkins, or turning earth, glad as a bird, while Sannie bestowed soft
words of encouragement. Sannie also taught Sandra to sew neat
stitches by hand, to peel potatoes properly, and to cook good *boerekos*,
farm food—*bredies*, thick stews with beef or lamb, and *boerebeskuit*,
biscuits from a stiff dough. Nora often prepared the family's evening
meal before she went home at five, but sometimes Sandra helped her
mother make dinner. "I liked to cook yellow rice," Sandra says. "My
father always knew that I had cooked when we had yellow rice. And
I liked baking chocolate cake. My father also knew it was me who had

made the chocolate cake." Sannie demonstrated the right way to set the table and fill the lamps with paraffin. Sometimes when Stefaan milked the cows, Sannie would skim the cream from a bucket of milk, pour it into a bowl, and beat it into fresh butter, allowing Sandra to do some of the churning. Every Sunday, when the shop was closed, Sandra helped her mother bake bread, because Abraham refused to eat the packaged stuff they sold to customers.

Abraham generally said a speedy grace, something like "Lord, bless the food that we eat and let us never forget Thee." Four times a year the family went to church in Piet Retief for Communion. Twice a year, two of the church's twelve elders came by for a *huishesoek,* a home visit, sometimes with the *dominee,* the minister, himself. Every member of the Dutch Reformed Church in each district received such a visit, whether they went to church regularly or not. The elders inquired after the welfare of parishioners' bodies and souls and led the family in Bible reading and prayer. Abraham Laing made a point of being absent during these visits.

When he came home from work, Abraham was usually too tired to play with Sandra. But on Sundays, she says, they often walked out together to hang over the pasture fence and count the cows. Or they might hunt for *turksvy,* prickly pears, which they both loved. Peeled and chilled in the fridge, *turksvy* made a treat better than ice cream. To celebrate special occasions, such as Sandra's first day of school, Sannie made prickly-pear jam. Some of Sandra's happiest memories of her father involve the two of them out on a summer Sunday, cautiously gathering cactus fruit. "We had to be very careful," Sandra says. "They're nice, *turksvy,* but they grow on a tree full of stings."

On weekdays, before dinner, Abraham bathed and then read the newspaper. Sannie and Sandra washed up afterward and then joined Abraham in the sitting room. The only decoration Sandra can recall is the Laings' wedding photo, framed in silver and propped on the sideboard. Abraham returned to his reading or listened to news on a radio powered by fat batteries. After the news came music, and Sannie might work a bit of embroidery or do some bookkeeping while Sandra sewed doll clothes or drew on scraps of paper until her mother said it was bedtime. After she washed, her mother tucked her in and kissed her good night; sometimes her father, too. When Sandra lost a tooth, she put it in a shoe under her bed for the tooth mouse, who left a coin in its place. In this way, the seasons turned.

From her bedroom window, Sandra could see far beyond the family's garden and the windbreak of acacia trees to fields of mealies, wheat, and sunflowers, rolling pastures where sheep and cattle grazed, and an uptilted plain, green with pine plantations that ended at the foot of faraway rocky hills. In summer, Sandra watched storms approaching from miles away, the sky bruising dark blue and gray long before she heard the thunder. And the lightning! Like roots of fire. The South African highveld endures more annual lightning than most places on earth. A lightning strike could cost a forest, so firespotting towers dotted the logging roads. In dry winter, when the pastures turned brown, farmers burned the dead grass on purpose—so it would grow back a brighter green, her mother told her.

Once Sandra and the girls started a fire. They'd seen Leon, home on holiday, do something extremely intriguing. In a patch of brush between the store and the forest, he lit a big kitchen match, the kind that Nora used for the coal stove, and dropped it in dry grass. He watched it for a while, tending the flames with a stick, then stamped the fire out with his shoes. Sandra, who wasn't quite five, wanted to duplicate this fine spectacle. When Leon went back to school, Sandra and her friends snatched a box of matches from beside the stove, squatted behind the store, and ignited a parched bush, hoping to have the satisfaction of extinguishing it. "But when we tried to blow the fire out, we couldn't," Sandra says. "And then we ran away. The fire was so big! The grass and trees were burning. My mum saw flames going to the pine trees and shouted for Stefaan and the customers to help her." They threw basins and buckets of water and beat the burning brush with wet burlap bags until the fire died. For the rest of the day, the girls hid in the rondavel behind bags of red corn. Sandra was afraid her father would smack her. Instead, when Abraham came home and Sannie told him what had happened, he was calm. He asked Sandra to help him pour water on smoldering patches of grass so the wind couldn't rekindle the fire. "He said he wouldn't punish me because I'd only been copying Leon and I didn't know little girls shouldn't light fires."

In our early conversations in her tiny sitting room in Tsakane, or in the yard, on kitchen chairs placed under a peach tree on the small lawn bordered with roses and lilies of which she was justly proud, Sandra often talked about the past, happy moments and painful ones, in a voice drained of affect, even when she wept. She spoke as if she were narrating someone else's life. Because of her memory gaps and habitual reticence, the source of which I would come to understand, eliciting history sometimes took a lot of time and effort. We'd often loop back and examine the same anecdote from various angles.

But when she told the story of the fire, her voice acquired heft and dimension. She offered details without my having to draw her out, and she savored them; she held her head high, and she laughed out loud for the first time since we'd met, a delightful brook trickle of a chuckle. She seemed to revel in her naughtiness. "I had pluck then," Sandra said.

5

PRICKLY PEAR

BEFORE SHE WENT AWAY TO SCHOOL, SANDRA WAS AFRAID of only two things: her father's bad moods and snakes. One summer evening, Sannie leaned out over the garden before she closed Sandra's bedroom window and a snake spat venom at her, spraying white foam on her glasses before it slipped away. "After that," Sandra says, laughing, "I wouldn't wee in the tall grass like my friends because I was afraid a snake would bite my bottom." At Piet Retief Primary, Sandra added new fears to the list.

"I don't think school was so bad at first," Sandra says. Those years are a shadowed blur, though several key scenes illuminate the murk. Luckily, several of her former classmates and their parents have been able to fill in some of the blanks. Each, of course, filters the past through his or her beliefs, biases, and blind spots. Nevertheless, they agree on many of the details and the larger picture of what school, and Sandra, were like in the early 1960s. All remember a girl who arrived at Piet Retief Primary as an energetic, curious, eager-to-please little person, but who became unhappy and withdrawn.

For even the smallest children, boarding school life was highly regimented. Each morning at half past five a bell rang to wake the students, who ranged in age from six to thirteen. A teacher came around to make sure that everyone was out of bed and lined up to wash in the two communal lavatories, one on the girls' side and one on the boys', each equipped with five child-sized toilets, five little sinks, and two showers. The rooms were chilly in winter, and the children shivered as they dressed. At 6 A.M., the teacher returned for inspection, checking to see that everyone was in uniform and the beds were neatly made. Then all the children sat in the little wooden chairs beside their beds, and the older ones took turns reading out loud from the Bible.

Another bell called them to the *eetsaal,* the dining room, which they entered in neat lines. The children stood behind their chairs, boys and girls at separate tables, until the teacher in charge read a prayer or a Bible passage and rang the bell that meant they had permission to sit and eat a silent breakfast of porridge or rusks—dry, sweetened biscuits—with milk, coffee, or tea. Then they brushed their teeth, grabbed their book bags, and, at the sound of another bell, walked without talking to the school, about a mile away, in orderly double lines, separated by sex and arranged by grade.

A sweet-natured young woman named Miss Theron taught Sandra's pre-primary class. She began the school day, as did all the teachers, with yet another prayer. Afterward, the children might play with clay, practice writing numbers and letters, or sit in a circle while Miss Theron held a big book on her lap, each page showing a picture and the word that named it: dog, ball, flower. Once a week, the younger children gathered in the school's main hall and sat on little benches while a visiting music teacher played piano and led them in Afrikaans songs and the national anthem, *Die Stem van Suid-Afrika,* The Call of South Africa. "At thy will to live or perish, O South Africa, dear land," they sang in duckling voices.

During recess—break, they called it—girls and boys were separated again. The girls played hopscotch and skipped rope. In physical training class, Sandra remembers, she ran and jumped, played netball—volleyball—and tennis, threw the javelin and discus. She doesn't recall dancing with hoops, but her classmates do.

The children walked back to the hostel in lines for lunch, also eaten in silence, followed by study hall. Then came games on the grass—statues, hide-and-seek, or war, in which little squares of land were defended against invaders. In the late afternoon, except when it rained, the children all sat outside, overlooking the neighbor's cow pasture, and cleaned their shoes. "When we first arrived, to scare the little ones, they told us that at five o'clock a ghost walks there with a bell," says Emilia Marsili, Sandra's roommate for the four years she attended Piet Retief Primary and now an elementary school teacher in Barberton, about an hour's drive from Piet Retief. "Of course, it was the cows." Still, for a while, Emilia says, the newcomers shrieked every time they heard a cowbell, urging each other on to deliciously escalating panic.

Emilia reminded Sandra about the cows in January 2002, when the two were reunited for the first time in thirty-six years. Sandra and I met Emilia and her mother, Anna, in Barberton, a piney hill town known for its still-active gold mines and a prison notorious during the apartheid era for the mysterious and fatal accidents that befell opponents of the regime who were held there. Emilia, born the same year as Sandra, is married and has two children. Anna, in her eighties now, and her husband, Angelo, a former Catholic priest who became a farmer in Swaziland, have retired nearby.

Sandra found Anna vaguely familiar, but not her daughter, even after Emilia reminded Sandra that they'd been close friends for the four years they roomed together. "We often skipped rope," Emilia said. "Remember the skipping songs, Sandra? 'Two little black birds sitting on a wall, one called Peter, one called Paul?'" Sandra didn't, although she remembered playing badminton, maybe on the hostel lawn. Emilia was shocked at how little Sandra recalled from their school days. And she had her own little lapses. "I remember your parents driving up in that donkey cart," she said to Sandra. "*Ag*, man, what are you talking about?" her mother said. "It was a Volksie, right, Sandra?" I asked mother and daughter about the school's curriculum, the hostel routine, the girls' games, and the sorts of punishment meted out by teachers. Sandra had no questions of her own, and answered softly and briefly when the Marsilis asked about her life. She looked down at her plate of fried fish for most of the conversation, often laughing heartily at bits of school lore, although she didn't remember having experienced much of it.

In the hostel, dinner was preceded by a prayer and took place in silence. The children were required to eat every bit of food given to them and then take their dishes back to the kitchen. One of the kitchen ladies, all of whom were black, particularly liked the children from Swaziland, perhaps because they were fluent in her language, and she slipped them slices of bread if they came to the kitchen door between meals. After dinner the children studied, bathed, and returned to their rooms for *stilte tyd*, quiet time. "But it wasn't quiet, ours," Emilia said. "Each room had a prefect, a standard-five [seventh-grade] child, chosen for exemplary Christian behavior, who would lead us in Bible readings or songs, and maybe sometimes she'd do a Bible quiz. I don't think it was forced; it was natural. I still know my Bible from that time." The girls and boys knelt for the final prayer of the day just before lights-out at nine o'clock, the hour when the curfew siren sounded in Piet Retief warning black people that it was time for them to be off the streets. On warm nights the smell of sweet grass came through the open window, sometimes spiked with the dirty-sock stench of the paper mill on the Panbult road, depending on the wind. Saturday morning began with an hour's study hall, but then the day was free for sports and games. Older children could walk to the center of town, escorted by a teacher, to see a movie at the cinema or eat fish and chips. On Sunday mornings everyone paraded to the whitewashed Dutch colonial church near the school for services and religious instruction. There they learned that God saw everything they did and wasn't pleased with much of it, and that after the great flood dried up and the ark was unloaded, Noah cursed his son Ham for looking upon him drunk and naked; that's why Ham's dark-skinned descendants can never be anything but servants, *houtkappers en waterdraers*, wood choppers and water bearers. The seven schoolday prayers and Sunday services were supplemented by compulsory attendance at Wednesday-evening prayer meetings.

Most of the boarders in the hostel came, like Emilia, from nearby Swaziland, where their parents raised cattle or grew sugar cane, cotton, timber, or fruit. A few of the hostel children lived on outlying farms just far enough away from Piet Retief to rule out a daily commute. The boarders were allowed one weekend home each month in addition to four long school holidays.

Emilia says she and Sandra were often in the company of a group of girls from Swaziland—Annike, Feni, Marike, sometimes Emilia's big sister Anita. Elize Lötter, also from Swaziland, came later. "We were all friends," Emilia said, "the whole group. There was not one that sat outside and did nothing. Sandra was included in the group. The kids from Swaziland treated her fine. Maybe other kids were mean to her. I was too young to know. But I think Sandra was always part of the fun."

Sandra can't say, because she doesn't remember much fun. But she recalls with painful clarity that early in her first year at school, a group of girls began teasing her incessantly. She doesn't know the names of her chief tormentors—there were four of them, she believes, girls from outside Piet Retief, not from Swaziland—but she knows what they said. They called her Blackie and *Kroeskop,* Frizzhead. "What are you doing at this school?" they demanded to know on the playground. "*Jy's nie wit nie!*" "You're not white!" They said their parents had forbidden them to play with Sandra. Isabeau Dutoit Coetze, who still lives in Piet Retief, was three years ahead of Sandra in school. She remembers, though Sandra does not, that the children sometimes called her "Turksvy," prickly pear, probably because of her hair, Isabeau thinks, although in Afrikaans you call someone "Turksvy" when they're a thorn in your side. The children refused to use the water fountain after she'd drunk from it, Isabeau recalls. "They said, 'We don't want your germs,' and sent her to the back of the line." But Emilia doesn't remember this. "It was so long ago," she says.

Sandra complained about the taunting to Mr. Van Tonder, a standard-five teacher who'd become head of the hostel in 1961, the year before she arrived. "He just laughed at me, or said I must stay away from the other kids," Sandra says. Johannes Van Tonder and his quiet wife, a seamstress, lived in a small apartment in the hostel. They were childless until long after Sandra was expelled, when they had a son. Van Tonder was by all accounts a rather stiff and stern man, in his early forties when Sandra started school. He wore glasses with heavy black frames, and favored starched khaki safari shirts and trousers. On warm days, he switched to shorts and knee socks, into one of which he tucked a comb, a sartorial flourish then common among rural Afrikaner men. He always carried a stick, a classroom pointer that he tapped on desks and walls or thwacked against his shoe for emphasis. Too often, in the children's view, he used it to administer punishments, hitting malefactors across the knuckles or on their backsides. Generations of kids called him "Wollie," wooly, but not because of his hair, a smooth-enough brown pelt. None of the former pupils Sandra and I talked to knows the reason for the nickname, although a couple conjecture that it might have been because of a large, mesmerizing mole on his right cheek that seemed to sprout dark fur. The parents found him unfriendly—"bombastic," one says today, "rather militaristic"—but they approved of his commitment to discipline.

Emilia Marsili's older sister Anita remembers being impressed by the fact that on the morning walk to school, Van Tonder's shoes remained shiny no matter how dusty the road. A student a few years ahead of Sandra who returned to Piet Retief Primary years later as a teacher reports that among his colleagues, Van Tonder was notorious for being undemonstrative toward his family. This man once saw Van Tonder dropping his wife off at the train station; the couple, he says, shook hands goodbye.

Sometimes Sandra told Leon about being picked on. "He said I mustn't worry, I must just play with my friends." Leon was well-liked, his classmates report, and not just because he liberally dispensed the sweets he brought from his parents' store. He was a friendly, funny boy, nicknamed "Jood," Jew, because Abraham was a shopkeeper, an occupation often held by Jews in South Africa. In Piet Retief, however, shops were run by Afrikaners, like the Laings, or by Indians.

Anita Marsili says that on a class trip to Cape Town, Leon kept them in stitches. He sometimes played on the trampoline in Isabeau Coetze's yard, and her mother, a teacher at the high school, once coached him for a public-speaking competition. "Leon was also a very good athlete," Isabeau says. "But he had no self-esteem. After Sandra came to school, Jood began walking with his head down a lot of the time. I think he was just too shy to face the world. I mean, you can imagine it must be quite difficult. Okay, she's at home, that's all right. But now all of a sudden it's school, everybody's vicious. You know what schoolchildren are like; they start teasing and they can be nasty."

During the first long holiday of 1962, two months into the school year, Sandra, not yet six and a half, begged her parents to let her stay home. She knew she wasn't welcome at Piet Retief Primary. "I told my mum and dad that I didn't want to go back to school because children were teasing me and Mr. Van Tonder wasn't nice," Sandra says. When she repeated the names the children had called her, the blood left Abraham's face. "He shouted something like, 'You are a white child! You have the right to go to that school, and you're going.'" He told Sandra to ignore the children, and to go see Mr. Van Tonder when they teased her. Abraham wouldn't listen when she and Leon tried to explain that it wouldn't do any good.

Whenever Sandra complained to Van Tonder, he'd simply order her to stay away from the other children and ignore their remarks. He never punished her persecutors, or even told them to stop, she says. Several of Sandra's classmates and their parents agree today that Wollie Van Tonder didn't seem very fond of children in general, and actively disliked certain groups of them in particular.

Wollie vocally and vigorously disapproved, for example, of those students who took their lessons in English instead of Afrikaans, nearly a quarter of the school population. Was Afrikaans not good enough for them? he'd ask, tapping his stick against his shoe, and just who did they think they were? At break, he'd make the English-medium students stay on the far side of the courtyard, away from the others. He was still smarting over the Anglo-Boer War of 1899–1902, a struggle between the British and the Afrikaners for control of South Africa sparked by the discovery of gold and diamonds in the mid-nineteenth century. The war left the Boers vanquished, humiliated, enraged, and impoverished. British soldiers carried out a scorched-earth campaign, torching farms and orchards, slaughtering livestock, and packing women and children off to concentration camps—the first time the term entered the world lexicon—where 28,000 of them, mostly children, died of disease and starvation. So did nearly 14,000 of the 116,000 black and coloured servants imprisoned with the Afrikaners. More than a century later, a sense of victimization and the hatred of all things English remains florid among some contemporary Afrikaners, particularly in Piet Retief, which was burned to the ground during the war.

The playground at Sandra's school was ruled by a rigid hierarchy based on perceived loyalty to Afrikaner culture. Isabeau Coetze was best friends with Principal Schwartz's daughter. "We'd laugh and talk on the bus," Isabeau says, "but then we couldn't speak or be seen together at school, because I was an English-medium student."

Van Tonder liked the Afrikaans-speaking children from Swaziland even less than he liked the English speakers: the Marsili sisters and two other boarding students from Swaziland, Elize Lötter and Anco Steyn, best friends from the same farming village. "He said to us, 'What are you doing here, *kaffir boeties?*'" Elize remembers. "'Why don't you go back to your *kaffir* land?'" Kaffir, originally Arabic for infidel, is the equivalent of nigger in South Africa. He called the children *kaffir boeties*—literally, "*kaffir* brothers," colloquially, "nigger lovers"—because Swaziland had no apartheid laws. Van Tonder mocked and punished Elize for her loopy penmanship. "You're no artist, Lötter," he'd say before ordering her to bunch her fingertips so he could smack them with his stick. Corporal punishment was acceptable at school, and Mr. Van Tonder wasn't the only teacher who embraced the biblical admonition against rod sparing. "But we survived it," Emilia says cheerfully. "We survived Wollie, too. He didn't take nonsense from us little ones, especially not from us Swazi kids, but Wollie wasn't too bad. He looked after us." Her mother agrees. "I think he was a good man," Anna Marsili says. "He had the children's welfare at heart."

Van Tonder seemed to like Sandra least of all the children in the school. He didn't reprimand the girls who called her names, or punish them when they hid her pencils, pilfered her sweets, or stole money from a little wallet she kept in her cupboard. The girls denied their crimes, and Van Tonder sided with them.

After she came back from the first long holiday in April, Sandra says, she couldn't stop crying, even in class. "Why did my parents make me go back?" she wonders mildly, sighing. "Twice a week I cried so hard the teacher would call Leon to come to class. He'd try to cheer me up and tell me I musn't. I told him it was Van Tonder and the kids. The crying stopped, but not much. I was always unhappy. I couldn't go further with my schoolwork. I was behind a lot. I couldn't learn; I couldn't concentrate. I was too sad."

On school holidays, Sandra continued to play with her Swazi girlfriends, who went to a Driefontein school very different from well-equipped Piet Retief Primary. Soon after coming to power in 1948, the National Party introduced two divergent systems of schooling: Christian National Education (CNE) for white children and Bantu Education for black. One stated intention of CNE was to inculcate the Christian values of apartheid, including white supremacy. Bantu Education, on the other hand, was deliberately inferior, designed to prepare the black population for a life of menial labor and to prevent the creation of an educated class capable of an organized uprising. In a speech before the South African senate in June 1954, H. F. Verwoerd, later prime minister but then minister of Native Affairs, was brutally frank about the aims of Bantu Education: "What is the use of teaching the Bantu child mathematics, when he cannot use it in practice?

That is quite absurd. Education must train people in accordance
with their opportunities in life, according to the sphere in which
they live." On another occasion, Verwoerd announced, "If the native is being taught to expect that he will live his adult life under
a policy of equal rights, he is making a big mistake . . . There is no
place for him in the European community above certain forms of
labour." The Coloured Persons Education Act of 1963 and the
Indian Education Act of 1965 assured that these minorities also
received inadequate schooling. According to the South African Institute of Race Relations (SAIRR), founded fifty-seven years ago
as an anti-apartheid watchdog and research organization, in 1962,
the year Sandra started school, the government spent ten times
more on white students than on black.

Sandra's first year at school was Leon's last. His way of deal-
ing with her troubles, she says, was to stay as far away from her
as possible. He was kind when the teacher called him into class
to comfort his sister, or when Sandra sent a boy to tell him he
should meet her outside the study hall with some candy from the
supply stashed in his room. But he tried to make these contacts
short. "Leon was friendly, but we didn't talk," Sandra says. Isabeau
Coetze remembers, "To us as children, my mother used to say, 'Feel
sorry for Sandra, because she's the only one at that school that's
different.' And I really had a lot of sympathy with her. But I can
tell you I think I've got more sympathy with the eldest brother because he was going through his puberty at that stage, and everybody
was making jokes of him and teasing him about his sister. You know
how harsh children can be. They'd scorn him because he had a sister who was different. They'd ask, 'How can white parents have a
black daughter?' "

Leon sent for Sandra only once that first year, to tell her that
Oupa had gone to heaven and she wouldn't see him anymore. "I
was sad, because Oupa did love me a lot," Sandra says. "No more
playing games. And the only person who called me Sandrike was
gone. When I went home next, he was already buried. My parents didn't mention him, but Nora did. She said, 'Don't worry.

He's resting now.'" Sandra was especially glad to see Nora. "I didn't tell her anything ugly about school. I didn't want to think about it at home."

The harassment escalated. Sandra's shoes began to go missing from her cupboard, and she'd find them in the shower, waterlogged. When she retrieved them, the mean girls and a rotating cast of confederates screamed with laughter. "Look," one of the girls would shout. "Sandra wet herself and her shoes are full of wee!" The four ringleaders also laughed at Sandra when they all showered together. "They pointed at me and said, 'Look, she's dirty all over! Sandra, you must learn to wash better!'" She began changing clothes behind her cupboard door, and tried to press herself into a corner when she showered.

Confused, Sandra asked her mother why the girls said such things. "Don't worry about them," Sannie Laing told her. "They don't mean anything by it." Sandra was quite sure they did mean something, although she didn't know what. Sandra thinks the teasing in the shower may have triggered her first conscious awareness that she wasn't the same color as her parents and her brother—neither as light as they, nor as dark as her three Swazi playmates and Nora. But she still wasn't clear about what that difference meant. "That year I think I asked my mother, 'Why do I look more like my friends at Brereton Park than the kids at school? Why aren't there any white kids who look like me?' She only said, 'Ignore the children, don't worry, we love you.' I saw my hair and skin were different from the other kids'. I asked my mum and dad often why I look different. I asked, 'What does it mean that the kids call me black? Why do they say, "You look like my nanny's child"?' My parents only said I musn't listen, I must pay no attention." Sandra did her best to obey. Still, she felt a growing sense of being shameful and bad in some mysterious way.

When her first year at school ended, Sandra tried talking to her mother again about the teasing. Sannie continued to insist that nothing was wrong, but she sent off to Johannesburg for a bottle of hair straightener. It stank like stove cleaner and burned like battery acid. Patches of Sandra's hair fell out. "It made a big sore on my crown," she says. "My mother put medicine on it." Sandra had to wear a *doek*, a headscarf, like Nora's. The scabs didn't heal until just before school started again, and Sandra's hair grew back as curly as ever.

6

DANCING IN HER CHAIR

PLENTY OF TIMES, WHEN THE MEAN GIRLS CALLED HER Blackie and *Kroeskop*, Frizzhead, and said she looked like their nanny's child, Sandra punched them until she raised blue bruises on their arms. They didn't hit back, Sandra says; they'd just cry and run to Van Tonder, who punished Sandra, usually with a few strokes of his stick. "Once I was called to Van Tonder's office, and he hit me so hard on my bum that I couldn't sit at school the next day. Those girls laughed at me and said, 'Look, she's dancing in her chair.'" Sandra told her parents, she says, but they didn't know what to do.

At some point during Sandra's four years at Piet Retief Primary—she's not certain when—Van Tonder called the Laings in for a meeting about her behavior. "He sent a letter to my parents and they came to the school to talk about it. The girls' parents were also there. Me, the four kids, their parents, my parents, and Van Tonder. The parents of the kids said I must stop hitting; if I don't, I must go to another school where they teach people who can't live with other people. My father was very cross and said the kids must stop teasing me; it's not true the things they're talking. Then the parents of those girls said if I don't stop, they are going to make a case against the school. My father said to them they can go ahead, because it's their kids who are teasing me. The kids said I'm lying, not them. 'It's not true,' they all said. 'I didn't say those things to Sandra.'

"My father was very cross that day. But he believed what I said. My mum only said the kids must stop doing this and we must all be friends. I didn't say anything. Maybe I was too scared to talk. I remember that I started crying and left. After a while my mother came looking for me and found me sitting outside. She said I mustn't cry, everything would be all right. My father came, too, and we sat in the garden for a while, the three of us. He said that I must try to be friends with the children. I said, 'Those kids don't want to be friends. Their parents tell them what to say.' My parents again said everything will be all right. Then I walked with them to the car and they left.

"After I came back from saying goodbye to my parents, those four girls were standing in a corner laughing. Their parents were gone, too. The very next day, they started again: 'Here comes Blackie! She thinks that we will let her stay at this school. This is our school. We don't want to go to school with black people.' That day I just looked at them. But it wasn't long before I hit them again."

Sandra says that Van Tonder locked her in a dark linen closet after one of these retaliatory attacks. Emilia Marsili, Elize Lötter, and their mothers don't recall the incident, but none finds it out of character for Van Tonder, or beyond the scope of punishments regularly dispensed at South African boarding schools in the 1960s. "*Ja*, it's possible. I wouldn't put it by that Van Tonder," says Elize's mother, Rita Joubert. All four of her daughters attended Piet Retief Primary. And if Sandra's memory of the closet is a metaphor manufactured after the fact, meant to express her sense of feeling chastised, confined, and in the dark, it's an apt one.

Once someone hid Sandra's textbooks so she couldn't do her homework. "The next day in class the teacher gave me five hundred lines: 'I must do my homework every day.'" Sandra remembers very little else about schoolwork, except liking numbers. "I was crying all the time, and I couldn't concentrate or do my work, so I was two years in grade one." When she did move on to grade two, she was quick to grasp the concept of *tiens* and *einheids*, tens and units, and she was always good at sums, she says. But one day the teacher asked her an arithmetic question, and when she stood up to give the answer, no sound emerged from her mouth. The other children laughed and Sandra sat down in tears. After that, she was afraid to speak in class. She worried about where her voice had gone, and whether it would desert her again.

Her anxiety deepened when Leon came to tell her that their mother had been attacked by thieves in Brereton Park. "Stefaan was not at the shop; my mum was on her own. Three black men came in and hit her on the forehead with the flat part of an ax. She passed out, and they stole clothes, and money from the till, and her watch. When my mum came round, she called my dad, and he called the police. The three men were caught the same day."

By the time Elize Lötter met her, in 1965, Sandra was often anxious and silent, the kind of quiet, Elize felt, that's a scream turned inside out. Three years older than Sandra, Elize had transferred from a school in Swaziland, where her father owned a timber plantation that supplied wood for mine props. She was assigned to the same room as Sandra, Emilia, and six other girls. Elize and her friend, Anco, who lived in the boys' side of the hostel, thought then that Van Tonder had it in for Sandra, and as adults they remember far more of the particulars than she does. If Sandra attempted to explain why she was hitting the children who teased her, Elize says, Van Tonder yelled at her for being impudent; if she was silent, he'd yell at her for being in a *dwaal*, a daze. "I can remember she always used to wear a little Alice band in her hair, and she was quite tiny. Van Tonder used to shout at her a lot, and she would back away from him, terrified," Elize says. "I can see this little figure pressed against the wall; she would wet herself and the wee would run down her legs and the children laughed."

The worst thing that Van Tonder did, in Elize's estimation, was to chase away the few children who were happy to be Sandra's friends. "He would say to us, 'What are you doing with her? Just leave her alone! Stand aside!' So that children who were close to her were scared away. She was perceived by Wollie as a troublemaker and a rebel who would always do everything wrong. She was alone most of the time." Emilia Marsili doesn't remember any teasing, name calling, or pranks; she doesn't remember Van Tonder's shooing children away from Sandra or menacing her any more than he did the others. "I can only remember little pieces of that time, but she was always with us," Emilia insists. She recalls no special problems, and no talk about Sandra's skin color. "Only, when she was gone, nobody knew where she was. And they never explained to us."

As Sandra got older, she says, she rarely punched other girls, but she was still angry. Elize witnessed occasional outbursts of unfocused rage: "Sandra would shout and scream out of frustration." Rita Joubert, Elize's mother, says, "I remember seeing this very unhappy little girl. People talked about it, especially the parents who had kids in the hostel. They were a bit upset because Sandra, being unhappy, was naughty. Not naughty in an ugly way, but to draw attention to herself, because everybody just ignored her. And I would say the few times I saw her she was always crying. *Ja*, she was always crying." The man who ran the Piet Retief cinema in those years, now retired, said recently that he never met Sandra and doesn't know much about her—except that he recalls hearing in the early 1960s that she was "completely wild, like a little monkey brought in from the bush." Such tales, like the story of Sannie's alleged affair with the black shop assistant, circulated throughout the *dorp*. Elize remembers her mother telling her, long after she was out of school, about an incident involving Sandra that was discussed at a meeting of the School Committee, an advisory board of parents and teachers that included Van Tonder. Her mother wasn't at the meeting, Elize says, but other parents told her about it. "They said Sandra got angry one day and smeared her own feces all over the toilet seat in the girls' loo," Elize says. "I didn't know about it at the time. I don't know if it's true. I kept thinking, after I heard the story, what might have motivated her. I tried to put myself in her shoes, this little thing who's not accepted in the school environment. Maybe she was trying to say that her life was shit." Sandra doesn't remember this episode, and her response, when I told her what Elize had reported, was a short burst of laughter and a rueful shake of the head. She asked no questions and made no comments.

Elize says that from the time she became Sandra's roommate until Sandra was expelled a little over a year later, the younger girl cried herself to sleep regularly and wet the bed nearly every night. "We would quickly turn the mattress," Elize says, "myself and another girl, so that if one of the two teachers in charge of the girls' side came, she wouldn't discover it." There were humiliating days when the mattress had to be aired on the lawn. One teacher was a kind woman, also named Van Tonder but no relation to the head of the hostel, who often comforted Sandra by patting her head when she wept at night. Sandra became so anxious that she vomited almost every evening. Mr. Van Tonder was sure she was putting on an act to attract attention. Called to her room, he'd shake his head with exasperation, and tell Elize, "*Ag*, for God's sake, take her to sick bay." Sometimes, after an especially bad night, Sandra spent the next day in the infirmary. Elize, Emilia, and a few other girls envied her those holidays and wanted to stay out of school, too, so they mixed shoe polish and saltwater and drank it one night after dinner. The nurse was puzzled by the strange, short epidemic of nausea.

On free weekends, Elize says, Leon came over from the high school, two miles away, to pick up Sandra and escort her to the car, where Abraham waited, usually without Sannie and Adriaan. "You never saw the mother," Elize says. "You saw the dad." Leon was having a harder and harder time acknowledging a connection between him and Sandra, Elize says. "Leon would say his parents didn't really accept her and she wasn't really wanted, but they didn't know what to do. That Anco and I can remember—Leon sharing with us how difficult it was, and that they didn't really want to be with her. Was that his point of view, or his parents'? I don't know. Possibly what could have happened is that in the enclosure of the home, they would show her love and affection, but outside, how could they do it? She was perceived as not acceptable."

Elize and Anco remember Leon standing quietly at the hostel

door with his hands in his pockets, waiting for Sandra; then he'd sign her out and they'd walk to their father's car. Leon had stopped holding his sister's hand.

Sandra and Elize both insist today that as children they didn't understand why their classmates called Sandra names and Van Tonder seemed to hate her. "I remember in the evening Sandra would constantly want to know, '*Wat is dit met my*? What is it with me? Why am I being treated this way? What's wrong with me?'" Elize says. "She didn't understand, and I didn't understand, either. I've been doing a lot of soul-searching, and for me it never came up race; for Emilia or her sister Anita, either—I asked them recently. But, remember, our friends were black in Swaziland. I don't want to say we didn't notice color, because that would be racist, but it didn't matter," Elize says. "Playing with black or coloured children was okay where we came from, so we didn't know Sandra's troubles were because her skin is a different color, I promise you. We didn't put it together, even when we heard the other children say things like 'Two fair people can't have a dark child' or 'The mother slept with the gardener.' The kids talked out of their parents' mouths. At the time, we didn't understand what they meant." Elize was aware that black people were treated differently. Before she went to Piet Retief Primary, when she still attended a village school in Swaziland, she had gotten into trouble for standing up when a black school inspector entered the room, and for calling him sir. She tried to ask her mother why that was wrong, but was grumpily hushed.

Several studies by psychologists in both South Africa and the United States have shown that children become conscious of physical differences among the races in a rudimentary way around the age of three; by the age of six they're fully aware of these distinctions. In American children, this awareness doesn't generally solidify into an attitude toward race until the age of eleven or so. But research done during the apartheid era suggested that children in South Africa developed attitudes about the relative value of each race earlier than American children, since race there determined power, wealth, and opportunity more dramatically and immutably.

How is it possible that Sandra didn't connect her persecution to her skin color? I asked her that question several times during our first few long talks, and she consistently gave the same answer: Her father said she was white, and his word was law. "My father told me I was white. He thought of me as his white little girl. So I thought some white kids must look like me. That time, I knew what the signs that said *Net Blanke* [Whites Only] meant. I knew when I would go to town with my mum that places were white and nonwhite. And I knew that black people couldn't go in the white side. But my father said I was a white person, and I went to all the white places with my mum and dad."

When we'd known each other a few months, she supplemented her answers slightly. "I saw I look different," she said, "more like Nora and my [Swazi] friends, but I don't know what it means." And, "I think I knew about black and white at seven, but not what it meant." The only thing that really mattered to her was that her father told her she was white. She had been taught not to question him. What he said was more powerful than what she saw.

It's not surprising that Sandra lost faith in her own perceptions; adults regularly told her that what she observed plain as day wasn't really there. Van Tonder insisted the children weren't stealing her candy or otherwise tormenting her; her father declared that she was just like any other white child, and that the kids who said otherwise meant nothing by it. "Put it out of your mind," her parents often said when Sandra reported the cruel things her classmates did at school. "Don't listen to the children. Pay no attention." She took their injunctions literally. Without making a conscious decision to do so, Sandra gradually shut down her analytical and observational powers; the less she saw and pondered, the less she hurt. In her groundbreaking book *Trauma and Recovery*, Harvard University psychiatrist Judith Herman, MD, explains that children in crisis sometimes accept their parents' false pronouncements and misguided perceptions despite empirical evidence to the contrary, in order to keep from having to think of the people they most depend upon as foolish, powerless, dishonest, or cruel. To acknowledge that Sannie and Abraham were any of these things would leave Sandra feeling terrified and undefended in a confusing, often hostile world. To protect herself, Sandra relinquished her own shrewd assessment of the situation and retreated, as many traumatized children do, into a kind of numbness. Allowing herself to know what she knew was too dangerous.

Wollie Van Tonder retired from teaching in 1990; elderly and infirm, he has long refused to talk to the reporters who occasionally call him for a comment about Sandra. He seems to have spoken to the media only once, in a 1977 documentary called *The South African Experience: The Search for Sandra Laing*, made for British television and also aired in the United States. The filmmaker, Antony Thomas, who was raised in South Africa and moved to England in his late twenties, told Van Tonder and other residents of Piet Retief only that he was chronicling small-town life in the Transvaal. He didn't mention that it was in the context of tracing the life story of Sandra, then twenty-two. She didn't see the film, which led to Thomas's being barred from South Africa, until she was in her thirties.

In one scene, filmed eleven years after Sandra was expelled, a teacher at Piet Retief Primary leads children through a lesson in the differences between black and white people, a revealing example of Christian National Education in action. First she and the children discuss the fact that Africans have darker skin, flatter noses, and thicker lips than they do. "Where do black people work?" the teacher asks in Afrikaans. She holds up pictures of farmworkers cut from magazines and glued to a sheet of cardboard. "Planting mealies, and with animals. Now we come to the whites. There are many kinds of work whites do," the teacher says. She shows the children pictures of a teacher, a nurse, and a doctor.

Mr. Van Tonder appears in the film, first welcoming a new crop of six-year-olds to the hostel and then describing his job to Thomas, who is off-screen. "Parents give the children to us," Van Tonder says, smiling into the camera, "and they tell us, 'Here is my child; you know what to do with my child.' I think the main success we like to have in the hostel is to develop this child as a person which one day will be acceptable to the people of South Africa." Later, he notes, "It is our Christian duty to love everyone. I love the black man. If I didn't love him, I wouldn't help him. I will help him until he has reached our level."

When the camera stopped rolling, Van Tonder continued earnestly explaining his view of racial differences to Antony Thomas. "To the best of my knowledge, the exchange went something like this," Thomas recalls today. "'I don't hate the black man,' Van Tonder said. 'In fact, I love the black man, but I must learn to wait until he reaches the same level as what I am.'

'And how long do you think that will take, Meneer Van Tonder?' I asked. Pause. 'I would think about four thousand years.'"

7

SCANDAL-TONGUES

W AS IT TRUE, WHAT THE LITTLE *SKINDERTONGE*— "scandal-tongues"—said at school? Principal Schwartz suggested in his confidential letter that Sandra was the child of a white woman and a black man. Sannie and Abraham insisted she was not, and in the course of challenging Sandra's reclassification signed an affidavit swearing that they were her biological parents.

A 1967 article in the *Rand Daily Mail,* a now-defunct liberal English-language newspaper, described the Laings' fight against Sandra's reclassification: "Mrs. Laing said she was aware that gossip had suggested that Sandra was not her husband's child. This was completely false. Mr. and Mrs. Laing swear that Sandra is their child. 'That I know without doubt,' Mr. Laing [said]."

The people of Piet Retief didn't believe them. "They thought she had an affair with a black man, unfortunately, *ja,*" says Sandra's classmate Isabeau Coetze. "And that's why the child was the poor victim." Rita Joubert agrees. "The mother was the guilty one, they thought. She was totally an outcast in town. Nobody wanted to speak to her. They were more sympathetic against [sic] the father than against the mother." Although Rita lived in nearby Swaziland, she often popped over the border to shop in Piet Retief, and attended church there. "The town didn't mix with the Laings. Some condemned them, and some felt very sorry for the little girl, as we did. The whole family suffered. The boys suffered because they were teased about having a coloured sister, and the little coloured was in a terrible state because they didn't accept her at school. You could see she didn't fit in. It was a terrible thing, in the apartheid era, to put a poor little thing like that in a white school. Some parents took their kids out of that school and sent them to Ermelo [the nearest large town], because of Sandra." Sannie Laing had to stop going into town, Rita said. "People didn't say anything insulting to her face, but they didn't speak to her, or even greet her."

In the early 1960s, Rita had her own run-in with the moral vigilance of an Afrikaner community, and felt the sting of their disapproval, albeit for an infraction far less serious than alleged illicit sex across the color bar. "In our Swazi village," Elize says, "my mum taught a yoga class for the wives of well-off farmers. Then she got a visit from a group of church elders ordering her to stop, because yoga was unchristian!"

After the death of Elize's father in 1986, Rita remarried and moved back to South Africa, where she'd been raised. In 2002, Elize and I visited her in Parys, an Afrikaner town in the Free State province, a place so conservative that Rita has warned Elize never to bring any of her black friends when she visits, not even if she leaves them in the car, for fear of what the neighbors would think.

I asked Rita if she'd ever heard the story I'd been told that Sannie Laing had a secret, dark-skinned sister who'd been paid to leave town. "No, I never heard that," Rita says. "But the mother had a shop, and in the shop was an African man working for her, and we heard that he was the father of Sandra." The trouble with that rumor is that when Sandra was born, the Laings worked together in a different shop, the Balmoral Cash Store, about forty miles from Piet Retief, and employed a different helper. The family relocated to Brereton Park when Sandra was an infant. Some of Sandra's former classmates wonder today whether moving to such an isolated place might have been a way of dodging neighbors' rude remarks about the dark-skinned baby.

People hearing Sandra's story for the first time usually ask why she doesn't just have a DNA test. Such an assay didn't exist until

1975, and by that time Sandra and her parents were estranged; Sannie and Abraham have since died. The kind of paternity test available in 1966 couldn't have proven beyond doubt that Sandra was Abraham's child. The blood test was exclusionary only—that is, using blood type and the presence of certain enzymes, it could definitively rule out a man as a child's father, or include him as a possible father, but it could not pinpoint a single male parent. Abraham took a blood test the year after Sandra was expelled. He wasn't excluded as the father, and that seemed to satisfy him, according to Sandra's recollections and press reports at the time.

The question of Sandra's paternity could almost certainly be settled today by a sibling DNA test, which would show whether Sandra's brothers are half or full siblings, and thus whether Abraham is Sandra's father as well as theirs. But Sandra hasn't had contact with Adriaan since she was fifteen and he was five, and he's adamant about keeping it that way. She's recently begun reforging a relationship with her older brother Leon, over the telephone. The process is tentative and fraught, and Sandra feels that asking Leon to take a DNA test would be fatal to their fragile connection. She could submit to a DNA test herself, and no doubt some of the genetic markers indicating relatively recent African ancestry would show up; the results would be the same for many white South Africans. But the test wouldn't tell her whether or not Abraham Laing was her father.

Of course, white South Africans crossed the color line, before and after Sandra's birth, despite the fact that the Immorality Acts of 1927, 1936, and 1949 outlawed having sex with, or even kissing, a member of another race. These "discrepancies between hardline prescriptions and messier practice," as the historian Ann Stoler puts it, had been taking place since white people arrived on the continent. How else to account for the million and a half or so people designated *kleurling*, coloured, at the time Sandra started school?

During apartheid, the great majority of interracial sexual liaisons involved white men and the black and coloured women who served them and were by law subordinate. Often the sex was coerced, and always it involved an unequal distribution of power. The punishment for breaking the so-called Love Laws was unequal, too: In

1984, for example, in Potchefstroom, a white man was acquitted of sleeping with a coloured woman—yet she was sentenced to six months of hard labor for sleeping with him.

A very few white women had permanent, public relationships with black men. In 1953, Regina Brooks, a young woman from Orange Free State went all the way to South Africa's Supreme Court to get her race officially changed so she could marry the black policeman she loved. Certainly some white women had clandestine sexual relationships with nonwhite men. But Sandra doesn't think her mother was one of them.

For one thing, Sandra believes her mother wouldn't cheat on her father with anybody. "My father was boss, and my mother wouldn't do that," she says. The more I learned about the culture that shaped Sannie, and its obsession with the ideal of racial purity, the more I agreed with Sandra. Sannie was pleasant to her black customers and isolated from her white neighbors. But it's hard to imagine her resisting the indoctrination that began at birth and was reinforced constantly with unsubtle messages from family, church, school, and state, all reminding her that it was God's intention that black and white not mix except as master and servant, and that for a woman, sex with a member of another race was an unforgivable sin.

Sandra offers more concrete evidence: photographs of herself with her baby brother Adriaan, taken when Sandra was eleven or so, and Adriaan was about a year old. The children look startlingly alike, although there's more Abraham in the boy's face and more Sannie in Sandra's. Adriaan's baby hair is the same froth of tight curls, and his skin is darker than his parents' and elder brother's— but just enough lighter than Sandra's so that he escaped her fate and was accepted at Piet Retief Primary six years after her expulsion. (He kept his frizzy hair short, and though the kids nicknamed him "Brown Bread" for his dark complexion, they accepted him as a white child. A couple of Adriaan's classmates remember him as a good athlete, one of the gang, and a favorite of Mr. Van Tonder.) If both Sandra and Adriaan have a black father, that means Sannie Laing must have defied her conservative upbringing, taken huge risks, and been very careless in the early 1950s—and then, ten years later and fifty miles away, repeated the process, a highly implausible (but not, of course, impossible) scenario.

The most likely explanation for Sandra's skin color and hair texture is the one that the Laings consistently offered to government officials and the press, although they weren't clear on the details. From the earliest newspaper accounts until Sannie's 2000 interview in the London *Sunday Times*, the couple publicly attributed Sandra's looks to a trick of genetics. "If her appearance is due to some 'Coloured blood' in either of us, then it must be very far back among our forebears, and neither of us is aware of it," Abraham Laing told the Johannesburg *Sunday Times* in 1967. "If this is, in fact, so, does it make our family any different from so many others in South Africa?"

Not according to the research of South African geneticist J. A. Heese, published in the early 1970s. After close study of colonial marriage and birth records, Heese concluded that about 8 percent of the genes of any modern Afrikaner are non-white, a declaration that earned him death threats. More recent DNA studies of the Afrikaner community put the number slightly higher, at 11 percent, based on the presence of mutations and markers, including, for example, the gene for a particular form of hemoglobin known to have been introduced to South Africa in 1684 by a shipload of slaves brought from the west coast of Africa.

"The races have been mixing for so long in South Africa that a case like Sandra's, though uncommon, is not impossible," says Trefor Jenkins, MD, until 1998 the head of the Department of Human Genetics of the South African Institute of Medical Research at the University of the Witwatersrand in Johannesburg. I went to see him to learn more about the genetic mechanism that produced Sandra. A Welshman who came to southern Africa as a mine medical officer in 1960, Jenkins became interested in genetics when he treated children with sickle-cell anemia. He was part of the scientific team that discovered in the DNA of the !Kung San people of the Kalahari Desert the oldest genetic traces in modern humans, and he was involved in the Human Genome Project, a thirteen-year international quest to identify all of the approximately

25,000 human genes and determine the sequences of the 3 billion chemical base pairs that make up DNA. Jenkins is a lecturer in bioethics, and has long opposed the use of science to justify racism. To fully understand Sandra's situation, Jenkins said, I'd need a quick history lesson.

Indigenous South Africans and people of European ancestry have been swapping genes since 1652, when the Dutch East India Company established a station under the command of Jan van Riebeek to supply water and fresh food to ships sailing between the Netherlands and its commercial colonies in India and Indonesia. Within two years more colonists had arrived, most of them Dutch, to farm and raise cattle.

The land the whites claimed had been occupied for 15,000 years by the San, nomadic hunter-gatherers whom the white invaders called Bushmen, and for at least 2,000 years by the Khoikhoi, herders and farmers whom the white people called Hottentots. Anthropologists and historians refer to the two groups, small people with yellow-brown skin, as Khoisan. (The name is offensive to some, but nothing that has been proposed to take its place has been generally accepted.) The settlers had yet to encounter a third group, living in the center of the country that's now South Africa, which is twice the size of Texas. These farmers, herders, and makers of iron tools had moved south from central and western Africa beginning around the first century A.D. Taller, huskier, and darker than the Khoisan, they were labeled by white scientists Bantu, the name of the group of languages they spoke.

Five years after the first whites arrived, the East India Company released a group of workers from their contracts. These free burghers forced the Khoisan—at gunpoint—to work the land that had once been their hunting and grazing ground, but there was still a labor shortage. Van Riebeeck solved the problem by importing slaves from India, Indonesia, Madagascar, and Mozambique, and from East and Central Africa. The Dutch Reformed Church, to which most settlers nominally belonged, didn't condemn the slave trade, although it did forbid keeping Christians in bondage. As a result of this moral loophole, few slaves were baptized.

The company slave lodge served as a brothel with regular posted hours. Burghers and sailors on shore leave—the "Lords of Six Weeks," they were called—took their pleasure with slave women. According to company records, during the first twenty years of settlement, three-quarters of the children born to women of the slave lodge had white fathers. The children of free fathers and slave mothers were slaves. "But many of the female children became the mistresses and, in some case, the manumitted legal wives of burghers," writes Yale historian Leonard Thompson. "As a result of these relationships, the 'black' population of the colony became considerably lightened, and the 'white' population became somewhat darkened." A few European men married freed slave women, but extramarital liaisons were more common. On the inland frontier, where the number of white men far exceeded that of white women, European farmers had sexual relationships with slave and Khoisan women, and sometimes married the latter. Some of the children of those liaisons looked like and lived as whites (passing their mixed genes into the so-called white gene pool), but in general they weren't absorbed into the white community. Instead, they formed a large population of mixed-race Dutch speakers who came to be known as *kleurling,* coloured.

Jenkins gave me a quick refresher course in genetics. "The markers of race, skin color and hair texture," he explained, "are among those human characteristics determined not by a single gene, but polygenically—by several genes, possibly four or more; the exact number hasn't been determined." A few human traits, such as eye color, Jenkins reminded me, follow the simple rules of inheritance determined by the nineteenth-century monk Gregor Mendel, who discovered that in peas, the gene for smooth roundness is dominant over the gene for a wrinkly surface. In human beings, the gene that codes for brown eyes is dominant over the gene for blue eyes. You can't cross two wrinkly-pea plants and produce a smooth pea; two blue-eyed people can't produce a brown-eyed child.

"But skin color," Jenkins explained, "is a different matter from eye color and pea texture." Most genetically determined human characteristics—skin color, hair texture, eye shape, height, intelligence, metabolic rate—are the result of polygenic inheritance. If the several genes coding for these traits were governed by simple Mendelian inheritance, the world would be inhabited by the very tall and the very short, dunces and Einsteins, Laurels and Hardys, the obsidian-skinned and the marshmallow-white, with nothing in between. "Instead," Jenkins explains, "polygenic traits are expressed as a gradation of small differences, a continuous variation."

Teachers of introductory genetics classes often explain polygenic inheritance this way: Suppose that skin color is controlled by six genes, three from each parent. Assign capital letters, A, B, and C, to genes that signal the body to activate specialized skin cells that produce the pigment melanin. The more melanin produced, the darker the skin. Then assign lower-case letters, a, b, and c, to genes that tell the body to produce less melanin, resulting in lighter pigmentation. The more capital-letter genes a person has, the darker her skin. A person who receives three "dark" genes from each parent (AA, BB, CC) produces the maximum possible amount of melanin and has extremely dark skin. A person who receives all "light" genes (aa, bb, cc) produces the minimum amount of melanin and has very pale skin.

But the offspring of parents who each have a mixed array of genes could show a range of skin colors between very light and very dark. For example, a person with three capital-letter ("dark") genes and three lower-case ("light") genes (AaBbCc) has a medium amount of melanin and a skin color halfway between very dark and very light. If two people who each have that intermediate skin color had a child, she would inherit one of sixty-four possible gene combinations, resulting in seven possible skin colors.

Apply the textbook case to South Africa: If a white seventeenth-century Cape Town burgher had a son with a black woman, the boy would inherit three "light" genes and three "dark" genes. And if that boy later had a child with a mixed-race woman, this third-generation offspring might receive three "light" genes from each parent and look white, or he might receive three "dark" genes from each parent and look non-white. In that way two very white-looking people could have a child considerably darker than they, and two dark-skinned people could have a child much lighter. The genes responsible for maximum pigmentation could remain unexpressed for several generations, Jenkins says, until, by chance, two people, both coming from a long line of white-looking ancestors, each contribute enough melanin-producing genes to create a child darker than they.

In the spring of 2003, a South African magazine used the term "genetic throwback" to describe Sandra's appearance. Technically, that's incorrect; a throwback is the sudden appearance of a recessive genetic characteristic that's been passed on, generation to generation, but not expressed. (An example: A man and woman, each carrying one recessive gene for the inherited disease cystic fibrosis, and neither suffering from the disease themselves, each pass on a recessive gene to a child who then manifests the disease.) But the term *throwback* as popularly understood served as shorthand in the South African press for the mechanism that would explain Sandra, if she weren't the result of an illicit interracial relationship. Either possibility was horrifying to her Afrikaner community, though the "throwback" explanation less so.

Sandra sometimes wonders why there aren't more people like her, other dark-skinned children of light-skinned parents. They probably exist, but they've remained below the radar of the press. Some may have been just pale enough to escape public notice. Others may have lived with their white families among neighbors more inclined to overlook differences in appearance than were the people of Piet Retief. Dark-skinned children born to light-skinned parents in the coloured community, where a greater range of difference was tolerated, were more easily absorbed. When Sandra was in her twenties, she was introduced to a four-year-old boy named Corey whose white parents had placed their much-darker son in foster care with a coloured township family.

Another child like Sandra whose story did make the papers, in the 1980s, was a Cape Town boy known to the press only as Basil E. According to newspaper reports, he began life classified as white, like his parents and siblings, but was reclassified as coloured after the parents of schoolmates complained about his appearance. Unlike the Laings, Basil's parents didn't take his case to court, but complied with the recommendation of the Social Welfare Department that he be put up for adoption. He ended up living in a children's home in the Transvaal, where his biological parents visited him twice a year.

Did Sannie Laing have an affair with a black man? Or is Sandra's appearance the result of polygenic inheritance consistent with the social history of South Africa? The truth probably wouldn't have mattered to Sandra's classmates in Piet Retief, their parents, the School Committee, or Principal Schwartz. They didn't care how Sandra came by her color; they just wanted her gone.

8

Skin Complaint

ANDRA DIDN'T LEARN ABOUT THE LENGTHY AND aggressive campaign to remove her from school until thirty-seven years after it was set in motion. In 2001, under the provisions of South Africa's first Promotion of Access to Information Act, passed by a post-apartheid Parliament, she filled out a form requesting all government documents relating to her race classification. A friend drove to Pretoria, the nation's administrative capital, to photocopy the contents of the file on Sandra and the Laing family, more than seventy-five pages of government correspondence, memos, affidavits, and copies of official documents such as birth and marriage certificates. I had the contents translated from Afrikaans into English for my benefit.

The file also contained a pile of newspaper clippings about Sandra and her family, in English and Afrikaans. Not long after she was kicked out of school, reporters and photographers from South African papers began visiting Brereton Park regularly. So did television crews from overseas; television was banned in South Africa until 1976. "I don't know who told the papers about me," Sandra says, "but I think maybe my father." Abraham's letters to government officials at the time suggest that he thought press coverage would help win public sympathy for him and his wronged child. Certainly Principal Schwartz wouldn't have wanted the attention.

Sannie and Abraham spoke to journalists, but wouldn't let them interview Sandra. She was, however, photographed for the papers and filmed for foreign newscasts hugging her parents, chasing a goose, playing with Adriaan.

Documents in the file reveal that Sandra's arrival in Panbult with a police escort couldn't have been a complete surprise to Abraham Laing. More than a month earlier, the Department of the Interior had informed him of Sandra's reclassification and ordered him to remove her from school. He had, clearly, refused.

A memo in the file refers to two other letters supporting the complaint that Principal Schwartz sent to the Department of Education on Sandra's first day of school. One came from a representative of the National Party in Piet Retief and the other from a member of the Eastern Transvaal state legislature; both asked that the minister of the Interior, G. Du Preez, remove Sandra from the school. "The above-mentioned child," the legislator wrote, "according to a variety of people, will never pass for white and cannot be allowed to attend the school with white children." Both men noted that parents and pupils objected to Sandra's presence in school and suggested that she be reclassified as coloured.

They had the legal right to make such a suggestion; so did any other concerned South African citizen. The Population Registration Act of 1950 contained a provision that allowed for correcting classification "mistakes" made during the first official national reckoning of race under apartheid, the 1951 Census. The director of the Census, an official appointed by the minister of the Interior, was in charge of assigning race. If at any time he received information indicating that a person's race classification was incorrect, he could alter the classification, as long as he first notified the person or a legal guardian, in the case of a child, and offered a chance to contest the change.

The minister of the Interior replied by letter to Principal Schwartz and the two other men who wanted Sandra reclassified, noting that, according to the Population Registration Act, he couldn't respond to unofficial complaints. So in late 1962, the School Committee of Piet Retief Primary, which included Mr. Van Tonder, filed

an official affadavit with the director of the Census, urging that
Sandra be classified as coloured, not white. They paid a fee of R100,
(then about $140), to be forfeited if the reclassification they pro-
posed were rejected. By law, the director of the Census had to send
a copy of the affadavit to the party in question.

In response to the affadavit, the Department of Justice appointed a magistrate, a local judge, to hear the School Committee's
objections to Sandra. But in January 1963, before that hearing
could be held, the committee withdrew its official complaint. Principal Schwartz wrote to the Department of the Interior that he had
reason to believe the Laings were about to remove Sandra from the
school voluntarily.

According to a detailed summary of Sandra's case that appears
in her file, in late 1962 or early 1963 a member of the School Committee visited Abraham Laing at his shop in Panbult, told him about
the school's discomfort with his daughter's presence, and offered him
the chance to send her to a mixed-race boarding school for diplomats'
children in Pretoria. The man who made that visit, unnamed in the
report, was Willy Meyer, at the time a successful, politically active
cattle and cotton farmer in Swaziland. Born in Piet Retief and an
elder in its church, Meyer sent five children to Piet Retief Primary,
three daughters and two sons.

Sandra didn't know as a child about Meyer's offer to arrange
schooling for her in Pretoria. She first learned about it in 1998,
when the SABC news program *Special Assignment* filmed a segment
about her, a "Where is she now?" piece produced by Karien van der
Merwe, who also served as on-air interviewer for that show. Sandra and Karien, an Afrikaner her age who grew up in Durban and
attended a school much like Piet Retief Primary, became friends.

In November 2001, Karien, Sandra, and I drove in killing heat
to see Willy Meyer, now retired in Pongola, a sugar-cane growing area
in northern KwaZulu Natal province, sixty miles from Piet Retief.
Still formidable at eighty, Meyer was dressed in khaki shirt and
trousers, and held himself like a general. He'd been a bit under the
weather, he said, and needed a walking stick; nevertheless, he had
the commanding presence of a man used to giving orders. His wife

joined us in the cool, shuttered parlor, densely furnished with three overstuffed sofas, several heavy armchairs, and many low tables; she served us tea and cookies and then sat with us, occasionally filling in a name or detail. Meyer was interested in our quest to recover Sandra's history, and a cordial, almost courtly host, even when he launched into a spirited defense of apartheid.

Abraham Laing was "a stubborn bugger," Meyer recalled, a description that made Sandra smile. Meyer first saw Sandra when she was a preschooler and he was a church elder on a *huisbesoek*, the quarterly call paid to every family in the congregation. Abraham, as usual, wasn't home for that visit. Meyer said he remembered chatting and praying with Sannie Laing and Sandra's two brothers, although he could only have met Leon, since Adriaan wasn't born until Sandra was ten.

His first glimpse of Sandra took him aback, Meyer said. "She was the smallest thing. Friendly. Man, she was like all other little girls. Sandra was brought up like any other child; there was no difference. She spoke Afrikaans. But you noticed immediately her appearance, even when she was little. I was surprised.

"But you know, there are so many reasons for that. It happens in these things that three and four generations back, something went wrong." Meyer was familiar with the local gossip. "They actually blamed the mother. Now, I'm not going to say that is the case. It could have been the mother; it could have been anybody else. It didn't really worry me. As far as her parents were concerned, they accepted her as a white child . . . I don't think they ever discriminated against her. And Laing clearly believed she was his child."

The Laings didn't come to church, Meyer said. "They were just on the books. And when Sandra came in the picture, people just sort of tried to ignore her. *Ja*, the Laings stayed to themselves."

At this point in the conversation, Sandra, who had been listening with downcast eyes as she sipped her tea, began to weep. Karien suggested that the two of them leave to wander Meyer's extensive gardens.

"When Sandra went to school," Meyer continued, "she was classified as white. It was the apartheid era. I don't want to blame

apartheid, because it was a very good thing," he said. "The policy was
then that every group of people must maintain their own culture and
their own place of living. We didn't approve of integration. They accepted that in America, and I think America is very, very sorry. You
must either be a proud Zulu, or a proud Xhosa, or a proud Swazi, or
if you're in the coloured community, be proud of your community. I
had a lot to do with the coloured community in Swaziland, trying to
uplift them. But every culture is different, and you can't mix them.
Unfortunately, the outside world regarded Africa as for the African,
not for the Europeans." The term "the outside world," meaning any
place not South Africa, also shows up in government memos about
Sandra.

In 1961, just before the Meyer children entered Piet Retief Primary, a law was passed in Swaziland, then a British protectorate,
ending school segregation. "Swaziland schools were thrown open
for everybody," Meyer said, "and I objected to it. I said, man, that's
not right. You must have your Afrikaner schools separate and your
Swazi schools separate, because you've got different cultures. In
America they tried integrating schools, and people started marry-
ing each other. That's the thing I never believed in. If a European
marries a black woman, what is the offspring? It's neither here nor
there. The black people don't accept him and the white people don't
accept him. He's got no nation, he's got no country of his own. And
I believe the good Lord doesn't want that. When you get these in-
termarriages, it's not love—it's sex. It's sex behind it."

"So I, in Swaziland, then organized very hard to try and separate the children. I was chairman of the agricultural union and served
on various different bodies. But we couldn't change the policy of the
British government; they said no, it's all open."

Meyer consulted an official in South Africa's Department of Education in Pretoria. "I said, 'For goodness sake, all these Europeans
in Swaziland, accommodate them in your schools.'" The official
agreed to allow white children from Swaziland to attend schools in
South Africa, then waffled and said there was no room. "I had a personal contact in Pretoria," Meyer continued. "I went to him and said,
man, this is the situation, and that's not acceptable to me. He sent

me back to the same department, but to a higher authority, who said, 'No, you're quite right, Mr. Meyer, we've got to accommodate these children, because they are the future of this country.' He gave instructions to the Piet Retief headmaster that they must accept the white children from Swaziland in the school."

But then something quite unexpected happened to thwart Meyer's plan for saving his children and their white classmates from integration. "Sandra came to school. And people said to me, 'You told us our children musn't go to integrated schools, but there you've got integration.'" Meyer was in a funny spot. He'd convinced his friends and neighbors in Swaziland to incur the inconvenience and expense of shipping their kids off to boarding school in order to avoid dark-skinned children like Sandra, but there she was.

"I went to see the headmaster. He said, 'Man, I have a big problem.' That was little Sandra. 'My staff is objecting to it, everybody outside is objecting to it, what can we do?' I said, 'Man, can I try and help you?' and he said yes. I first went to Sandra's father at Panbult. I said, 'Man, this is the situation. Her brothers [sic] are suffering a lot. Can't we put her into a private school?' He said, 'Mr. Meyer, I haven't got the money.' I said, 'I'll try and organize it for you.' Laing was so pleased. I went back to my contact in Pretoria, explained it to him, and he was very sympathetic. And my contact—you can say it was Albert Hertzog, he's dead now—he called another guy, and there it was decided that she'd be transferred to one of these interracial schools in Pretoria, and the government would pay all the cost. Hertzog, he's the guy who helped me a lot, even in Swaziland. We had no cooperation from the South African government because Swaziland was a British government."

Albert Hertzog, son of former prime minister and Boer War hero General J. B. M. Hertzog, served as South Africa's minister of Posts and Telegraphs from 1958 to 1968. Hertzog was a hardliner who broke with the National Party because he found its interpretation of apartheid too liberal; in 1969 he helped launch the ultraconservative Herstige Nasionale—Refounded National—Party. He's most famous for his vehement opposition to the introduction of television into South Africa on the grounds that it would lead to

"the downfall of civilizations." Hertzog was too reactionary even
for Prime Minister John Vorster, a Nazi sympathizer interned during World War II for leading a group that opposed South Africa's
entering the war on the side of the Allies. He dropped Hertzog from
the cabinet in 1968, and television arrived in 1976. That Hertzog
played a minor part in Sandra's destiny was a surprise.

"Eventually," Meyer said, "it was decided that Sandra could
go to a mixed school in Pretoria where all these foreigners are—am-
bassadors' children, you know. A very high-quality school, and all
her boarding and lodging would be paid; her father wouldn't have
to pay. So I was very pleased." But Meyer encountered an obstacle
the next time he visited Abraham Laing. "Man, I tell you, Laing was
a difficult guy," Meyer said. "I had his full cooperation, but when
I came back to the shop, he says to me, 'Hey, out you go. I want
nothing to do with this, this is politics.' I said, 'Man, it's not politics; your child's future is on this. It's for the sake of her and her
brothers.' He said, 'Nothing doing.' I was desperate. I had everything arranged, and her father wouldn't cooperate. When he threw
me out of the store, I was fed up. I thought, 'I can't do anything
for him now.' I was trying to help that family, her and her brothers. The mother was cooperative. No problems with the mother."
Meyer refused to conjecture about whether or not Sannie and Abraham got along. "That I can't tell you. I wasn't so deep involved in
their house."

What caused Abraham to balk? A later letter from Principal
Schwartz, reprinted below, suggests that the Pretoria school arrangement depended on Abraham Laing's accepting a coloured classification for Sandra. That would certainly be a deal killer. But Meyer
insisted, in a follow-up call, that Sandra needn't have been classified
coloured in order to attend the mixed-race school he'd found for her.

Principal Schwartz had been delighted and relieved by the
plan to send Sandra to school in Pretoria. "He was very shocked
when he found out that Laing wouldn't allow it," Meyer said.
"What worried me was the future of this child. Things might have
gone wrong in the family background three or four generations
back, so I'm not going to blame anybody. But I blame her father

for the situation Sandra is in. If he would have allowed her to go to that school—it was a very high-standard school—she would have got mixed up with other nations, she would have had a very good education, and the government would have paid for it. I won't say the South African government itself, but the contacts I had would have paid for it.

"What happened to Sandra wasn't a personal attack. I went out of my way to help her. I felt sorry for her. That's why I went to all the trouble. You know, it takes me time to see people and beg people, and try to maneuver things. You can imagine; the boys—Jood is the one I remember—they always teased him: 'Oh, your sister's a bastard.' It's not right, and for her, too. They were degraded completely because of her color."

Sandra and Karien returned from the garden, we chatted briefly about the plants and the weather, and Willy warmly shook hands with all of us before we left. When I related the parts of the conversation they'd missed, what bothered Sandra most was that Abraham Laing had insisted on keeping her at Piet Retief Primary long after he knew she wasn't wanted.

Once Abraham Laing turned down the scholarship offer, Willy Meyer, Principal Schwartz, and the rest of the School Committee launched Plan B. They arranged for another official objection to be lodged, not by the school this time, but by a state bureaucrat who wrote that he was filing an affadavit in his private capacity as a concerned citizen who believed that Sandra should rightfully be designated coloured, not white. But the minister of the Interior declined yet again to review Sandra's reclassification, on the grounds that the affidavit didn't qualify as official.

In July 1964, according to the case summary in Sandra's file, Abraham Laing wrote to the minister of the Interior asking for a definition of "white," a request that suggests he'd received copies of the School Committee's objections to his daughter's race classification. The response from the Department of the Interior contains a definition of whiteness taken straight from the text of the Population Registration Act of 1950. It sounds like an Abbott and Costello routine: "A White is any person who in appearance obviously is or who is generally accepted as a white person, other than a person who, although in appearance obviously a white person, is generally accepted as a Coloured person." Trefor Jenkins, the retired University of the Witwatersrand geneticist, says, "When I would read the definition out loud to my students, they would burst into peals of laughter." A "Coloured" person, the law continues, is "any person who is not a member of the White group or the Black group." While an individual's descent might be taken into account, the Population Registration Act stated, more weight would be given to "appearance and general acceptance." That can't have cheered Abraham Laing.

A year later, in August 1965, when Sandra was a few months shy of her tenth birthday, the minister of the Interior again was asked to reconsider her classification as white, this time by the director of Education, most likely at the request, yet again, of the Piet Retief School Committee. The minister of the Interior instructed Principal Schwartz to submit a full report. In that document, dated September 30, 1965, Schwartz repeated his contention that Sandra spoke very little Afrikaans; in order to communicate with her, he wrote, he had to "ask the secretary of the school, who can speak Zulu, to act as an interpreter." He also notes that her appearance "is definitely that of a person with mixed blood between a white person and a Bantu." The report continues, translated from Afrikaans:

Adjustment to School

. . . From the beginning of her stay at the hostel, she showed signs of possible psychological deviation. She often wet her bed at night and even during the day she seemed to have little control over her bowel movements. Sometimes she defecated in her pants.

Other signs that indicate she has psychological deviations include:

She is a tattletale (often tells stories about other children).

She accuses other pupils of having stolen sweets or
money from her without any substantial evidence
even after a full investigation.
She also takes the blame on herself for other pupils'
wrong doing.
Her behaviour clearly indicates that she tries to get sympathy from the teacher.
It seems as if she is emotionally frustrated and deeply
unhappy as a person.

She has also complained several times to the Senior
Duty Teacher that the other pupils tease and make fun of
her. For example, she came and cried, "Sir, the children say
I am a *kaffir*."
She is often very aggressive and bullies other pupils.

Acceptance:
. . . At the moment there are only two smaller children in the
hostel who are willing to play with her. These two girls are
also among the less intelligent pupils.
Most of the pupils still refuse vehemently to play with
her, associate with her, or accept her.
At inter-hostel school functions, most of the children avoid
her. All the boys, especially, avoid her without exception . . .
It is for this reason that, when she was enrolled in this
school on 30 January 1962, I wrote the letter to the Inspector
of Education in Ermelo [the district headquarters]. In the
letter I gave an anthropological description of the child's
appearance.

Other information of note:
Several parents who have children enrolled in this school and
hostel have protested to me personally. They do not want this
pupil to be allowed to attend the school or stay in the hostel.
Some of the parents have refused to have their child sleep
in the same room in the hostel as the child. Some of the

parents still refuse, even now, that their children be placed in the same room with her.

Some of the parents even threatened to remove their children from the hostel and this school.

Members of the public at large have also made comments about this child's appearance and have mentioned their disapproval about her being allowed to attend a school and stay in a hostel that are both intended for white children only.

Personally, I feel it would be best for her if she were to be placed in a community where she would feel accepted and to which she would be able to adapt and therefore be a happier person . . .

Dutifully Yours,

J. P. Schwartz, Principal

When Sandra and I met for lunch with Anna and Emilia Marsili, I showed them a copy of the 1966 report that Principal Schwartz sent to the Department of the Interior. They were astonished by much of it. I asked what they remembered about Principal Schwartz. "He was okay," Anna Marsili said. "He had a broad nose and close-set eyes, and his nickname with the children and the parents was the Baboon. Once I went there to complain about something, and he said, 'I may look like a baboon, but I'm not a baboon.'" Emilia perused the report. "Hah! Ma, listen: 'The only children willing to play with her are also among the less-intelligent pupils.' Oh, my goodness! Now they're saying I'm stupid!" She laughed. "What would they say if they learned I'm now teaching the children of South Africa?"

Anna shook her head. "So Schwartz was a monkey after all!"

Emilia went over Schwartz's letter point by point, refuting its assertions: But of course Sandra spoke Afrikaans, it was her mother tongue. Well, if she was incontinent, perhaps Van Tonder was scaring the piss out of her. She told tales and took on blame both? She had it covered, then. Deeply unhappy? Who wouldn't be?

"'She accused other children of stealing sweets and money from her.'" Emilia read. "Maybe that was right, Sandra—maybe we did steal your sweets! And look, it says she had to cry in the hostel because she wanted to be with her brother. They could have said my brother had to cry because he wanted to be with his sister! I can believe that kids called her names; that happens today in schools, too."

The women were surprised that Schwartz called Sandra "psychologically deviant." Emilia said, "No doubt she was upset, but it all has to do with interpretation, not so? I will tell you that the hostel kids, the ones from Swaziland, didn't give her trouble. Our friends back home were black kids, and when we came to school and there was another one, so what? It was natural. But it can be that the others gave her trouble." She handed back the photocopy of the letter. "*Ag,* no wonder Sandra blocked everything bad."

According to Sandra's file, when the minister of the Interior received this second letter from Schwartz requesting Sandra's removal, he decided to send someone from his staff to have a look at her. She had no idea she was being inspected, and neither did her parents. On November 25, 1965, the day before Sandra's tenth birthday, David B. Naude Cloete, an administrative official, filed a report saying that Sandra was "obviously and at first glance a non-white and would never be accepted as white."

Two days later—this isn't in the summary—Leon, who was seventeen, came over from the high school to tell Sandra that they had a new baby brother. He walked her to the hospital in Piet Retief, where Sannie cradled a tiny, slightly paler copy of Sandra, with the same tight curls and honeyed skin. The infant Adriaan grabbed his sister's finger in his fist and wouldn't let go. "I don't remember anything else, except I felt happy," Sandra says.

After Cloete made his report, the minister of the Interior decided at last to launch an official review of Sandra's racial classification, according to the case summary:

A letter went out on 2 December 1965 to the child's father, saying that information had been placed before [the minister] which indicated that his register was incorrect because it was clear that the child was in appearance not white, and that he was contemplating altering his register accordingly. He stated further

that if the father wished to make any representations he should
indicate the place and time, and added that this could be done
either in the Magistrate's Court at Piet Retief, or at Ermelo, or
even at the office of the department in Pretoria . . .

[The father] replied on December 7, not submitting any
reasons [that Sandra should not be reclassified] but requesting
a preliminary deposit for his pending legal costs. On December
13, he was again asked to submit his reasons. Four days later,
he wrote and said that he needed the assistance of an advisor.
On January 4 [1966], he wrote that he was planning to submit
reasons and that he was making the necessary arrangements
with his advisors.

The next section of the summary matches Sandra's recollection of
a trip to Pretoria with her father around that time. The drive was
memorable because Abraham allowed Sandra to eat ice cream in the
Volksie, having encountered a force even stronger than his fear of
stained seat covers. They'd stopped for lunch at a restaurant in Ermelo, a town halfway between Brereton Park and Pretoria. "The
owner came over and said my father could finish his food," Sandra
says, "but I would have to wait outside because this was a place only
for whites. My father said, 'This is my daughter!' but the man
didn't listen." Abraham Laing wondered loudly as they left how decent people could be treated this way. He ran into a snack shop and
bought Sandra a vanilla ice-cream cone to eat on the road.

Sandra remembers the interrupted lunch and the ice cream,
but not the more significant event later that day. "The father, together with the child," the summary continues, "came to the offices
of the deputy minister on the 14th January, 1966. The father entered the deputy minister's office first, and alone. He stated that
the child's appearance was due to some skin complaint and that he
was about to consult a skin specialist in that regard." Sandra was
called in from a waiting room. "The deputy minister spoke to the
child and had a good look at her whilst so doing. He then asked the
child to leave. The father thereupon requested the minister to leave
the classification as it was. The minister states that there is no doubt

that the child's appearance is such that she is not white and would not be accepted anywhere as white."

The deputy minister referred the matter to the under minister in charge of the population register. "Full facts were placed before the latter, and he decided that the only thing that could be done was to alter the classification." On February 2, 1966, the department informed Abraham Laing by letter that his daughter's race had been officially changed from white to coloured.

Two weeks later, Abraham finally submitted his formal objection to Sandra's reclassification: She was the white child of white parents, he said, officially declared White on her birth certificate, and raised white. Therefore, her reclassification was illegal, illogical, and ludicrous. The Ministry of the Interior notified Abraham that some time in the near future, he could bring his objections before the Transvaal's Race Classification Appeal Board. Made up of three or more citizens appointed by the Department of the Census and presided over by an active or retired judge, the appeal boards—one for each of the four states then comprising the Union of South Africa—decided disputed race classifications.

Principal Schwartz and the School Committee didn't want to wait for the near future. They wanted Sandra gone immediately. When her father refused to come get her, they had her delivered to him.

9

AN AFFRONT
AGAINST NATURE

BRAHAM LAING WASN'T SO DIFFERENT FROM WILLY
Meyer and the other protesting parents. He
wouldn't have wanted his daughter going to school
with a non-white child, either. "My father thought
black people are not the same as white people," Sandra says. And
to Abraham, anyone not officially white was black, despite the
fine taxonomic distinctions of apartheid. "Their job is to work for
white people. He thought black people aren't as smart as white
people, and don't have the same feelings. If the government said
I was black, he'd have to think about me that way. And people
would think his wife had an affair with a black man. That was a
bad thing. A very bad thing."

Maybe the worst. One of the founding texts of apartheid ide-
ology, *Race and Race Mixing*, written by geneticist Gerrie Eloff in 1941,
couldn't be clearer on the subject.

> The preservation of the pure race tradition of the *Boerevolk* must
> be protected at all costs in all possible ways as a holy pledge
> entrusted to us by our ancestors as part of God's plan with our
> People. Any movement, school, or individual who sins against
> this must be dealt with as a racial criminal by the effective
> authorities.

If Abraham had to think of his daughter as black, then he would have to think of himself as the most disgraced of cuckolds and Sannie as a criminal sinner.

Sannie was nine and Abraham thirteen in 1929, when Boer War hero J. B. M. Hertzog was elected prime minister by promising that his National Party would save Afrikaners from the *Swart Gevaar,* the Black Peril. The term ostensibly described a threat to white employment by black workers, but was "frequently expressed in terms of the defilement of white women by black men," writes Saul Dubow in *Scientific Racism,* an invaluable guide to parsing the texts and subtexts, including terror of racial pollution, that informed the Piet Retiefer's attitude toward Sandra. The very terms that Principal Schwartz used to describe Sandra in his letters—aggressive, emotionally frustrated, dishonest, psychologically deviant—echo the pseudoscientific pronouncements about race that fueled the National Party's Black Peril campaign, an episode of politically driven public hysteria that can only be understood—as is so often the case when it comes to unraveling the source of Sandra's troubles—by going back even further in history.

An unprecedented surge of exploration in the fourteenth and fifteenth centuries brought Europeans face-to-face for the first time with people whose appearance, customs, and beliefs were unsettlingly different, and whose lands—in Africa, the Far East, and the New World—were tantalizingly rich in resources. Acquiring these riches, and the labor to exploit them, required conquering, perhaps even enslaving, the inhabitants. Such ill-use of fellow human beings was clearly immoral and unchristian. The way around that problem was to declare the vanquished not quite human. Most, but not all, Europeans regarded non-Christian people with eyes, skin, and hair different from theirs as childlike and simpleminded at best, and at worst stupid, soulless, sinister, and sexually depraved. "Africa and the Americas had become a fantastic magic lantern of the mind onto which Europe projected its forbidden sexual desires and fears," writes Anne McClintock, an English professor at the University of Wisconsin, in her enlightening and entertaining book *Imperial Leather: Race, Gender, and Sexuality in the Colonial Contest*.

Dutch settlers arrived in Cape Town ready to be disgusted and fascinated by Africans, though few had seen any. Their preconceptions were shaped by the reports of earlier visitors, like this one in a popular seventeenth-century travel book by a physician with the Dutch East India Company. He wrote of the Cape's indigenous Khoisan inhabitants, "They yet show so little of humanity that truly they more resemble the unreasonable beasts than man . . . Miserable folk, how lamentable is your pitiful condition! And Oh Christians, how blessed is ours!"

Such attitudes were systematized in the eighteenth century, when European scholars began categorizing humankind into groups ranked according to physical, intellectual, and moral attributes. They reserved the top spot for themselves—a handy way to justify the subordinate position of colonized people.

In 1735, Carl von Linné, a Swedish biologist who'd already classified the world's plants and animals according to their appearance, offered a taxonomic scheme for humans. He divided them—by skin color and temperament—into African Man ("cunning, slow, phlegmatic, careless and ruled by caprice"), Asiatic Man ("stern, haughty, avaricious and ruled by opinion"), American Man ("tenacious, contented, choleric and ruled by habit"), and the best of the lot, European Man ("lively, light, inventive and ruled by custom"). A few years later, the German naturalist Johann-Friedrich Blumenbach posited three races: Caucasian (Europeans, whom he theorized originated in the Caucasus Mountains), Mongolian (Asian), and Ethiopian (African); later he added American and Malayan. Blumenbach believed that the Caucasian race was the first to emerge, and that the others represented various degrees of subsequent degeneration.

With the creation of races came the creation of racism, says Roger Sanjek, professor of anthropology at Queens College, New York. Before then, he writes in his introduction to the comprehensive anthology *Race*, "certainly people fought and conquered and even enslaved each other, and divided themselves into hierarchies—but not based on unchangeable physical differences." Greeks felt their civ-

ilization was the most admirable—Aristotle called northern Europeans politically disorganized, and Asians lazy—but skin color
wasn't linked to dominance or to slavery. "In earlier slave social
orders, the same physical types might, as fortunes changed, be either slaves or slaveholders."

By the mid-1700s, most whites in the Cape Colony had been
born in South Africa. They called themselves *Afrikaners*—Africans—
to distinguish themselves from newly arrived immigrants born in
Europe. The Dutch East India Company went bankrupt in 1795,
but the system of race relations it established, built on white supremacy, slavery, and segregation, continued. The Afrikaners, afraid
of being overwhelmed by the much larger slave and indigenous population, and believing that their survival depended on ruling with
an iron hand, enacted a body of laws that foreshadowed the policies of apartheid.

When the British took the Cape from the Dutch in 1806, the
Afrikaners fiercely resented the influx of English-speaking settlers,
and the imposition of their laws, culture, and language on the Boers.
In fact, the concept of apartheid was originally popularized to describe the need to keep Afrikaner and English cultures separated.
The Afrikaners especially hated being treated as inferiors. They
were spared from seeing the irony of their position by their belief
that the people to whom they'd done precisely the same thing
weren't people at all.

The last straw for the Boers was the British abolition of slavery
in 1834. Two years later, the first of several bands of fed-up *voortrekkers*,
pioneers, headed northeast into South Africa's interior, one of them
led by Piet Retief, a failed businessman fleeing debt perhaps as
ardently as he sought freedom. Eventually, thirty thousand people
would make the so-called Great Trek; some of Sandra's Roux ancestors were probably among them. Piet Retief's niece, Anna Steenkamp,
later explained what motivated the *voortrekkers* in an essay that appeared in the September 1876 issue of *The Cape Monthly Magazine:*

> It is not so much [the slaves'] freedom that drove us to
> such lengths, as their being placed on an equal footing with

Christians, contrary to the laws of God and the natural
distinction of race and religion, so that it was intolerable
for any decent Christian to bow down beneath such a yoke;
wherefore we rather withdrew in order thus to preserve our
doctrines in purity.

The presence of the several thousand coloured servants who
accompanied them testified to the fact that the bastions of purity
were regularly penetrated.

Much of the new territory claimed by the voortrekkers appeared
to be uninhabited, a fact that led to the Afrikaner myth of the empty
land—the insistence that black and white arrived at the same time.
In reality, the area had been cleared of its tribal inhabitants during a
decade-long period of Zulu conquest. The Zulus challenged the Boer
intruders, and Piet Retief lost his life, but the voortrekkers prevailed
after a decisive encounter with the Zulus in 1838. In the early 20th
century, this victory of the outnumbered but better armed Boers at
the Battle of Blood River would be celebrated by Afrikaner nationalists as a sign that God meant the *volk*, the Boer people, to rule South
Africa. Five years after the battle, however, the British claimed the
land won from the Zulus, and granted the Afrikaners vast tracts of
land farther into the heartland. This area became the independent
territories known as the Boer republics—the Orange Free State and
the Transvaal—the charters of which bluntly stated that equality between black and white would not be tolerated.

The British left the Boers to themselves for the next thirty
years or so, until diamonds and gold were discovered in the Transvaal. The British annexed the diamond fields in 1871, and then
took over the whole gold-rich Transvaal. The Boers fought back in
two conflicts they call the Wars of Independence, one from 1880
to 1881, and the other, what the rest of the world called the Boer
War, from 1899 to 1902. The British army was so efficient at burning farms and slaughtering livestock that after the war, many de-
feated Boers, humiliated and landless, had no way to make a living.
They flocked to the cities, where they competed for factory and
mine jobs with the black people they'd always dominated. To add

insult to injury, Lord Alfred Milner, the British high commissioner, insisted that school lessons be taught in English, a policy bitterly resented by the Boers.

Yet victors and the vanquished ultimately joined forces when the British government realized that it needed to forge an alliance with fellow whites in order to retain control of South Africa's black majority; blacks outnumbered whites by nearly seven to one. The two British colonies, Cape Colony and Natal, and the two Boer republics joined to become the Union of South Africa in 1910. The Afrikaners wouldn't sign off on the deal unless the British accepted racial segregation as national policy.

The constitution of the Union of South Africa gave greater weight to votes cast in rural areas, where Afrikaners were still in the majority, so their political power increased. Though Afrikaners accounted for only about 12 percent of the white population, they were able, for example, to pressure the government into a form of affirmative action called job reservation, the setting aside of certain skilled-labor positions for whites only. British and Boer together passed the Land Act, preventing blacks from owning property and banishing them to distant homelands when their labor was no longer required in white areas.

But the Afrikaners didn't own the factories, or the mines, or the banks. Poor whites, almost all of them Afrikaners, competed for resources with poor blacks—but there were opportunities to become allies, as well. Some poor blacks and poor whites began to live harmoniously in inner-city slums. One of the reasons the British came up with the idea of removing urban blacks to remote townships outside the city limits was their fear that the two groups, finding common cause in their struggles, might join forces to demand political power. So the potential for integration and unity fizzled, and just as their frontier ancestors had more than two hundred years before, most Boers in the early twentieth century feared both engulfment by the black majority and cultural obliteration by the British. They saw themselves, in fact, as the most oppressed group in South Africa.

To boost and consolidate their political power, Afrikaner leaders had founded the National Party after their defeat in the Boer

War. And in 1918, they formed an influential secret society called the Broederbond, the Brotherhood, to promote Afrikaner interests in politics, education, religion, and finance. Religious and political leaders whipped the Afrikaners into a frenzy of Boer nationalism based on hatred of British capitalists, the notion of the Boers as a chosen people, and the ideal of racial purity. National Party politicians made speeches warning of "vigorous" and "virile" masses of Africans flooding the cities. "Fear of racial mixing spoke directly to white anxieties about their vulnerability," writes Saul Dubow. In the 1960s, J. B. M. Hertzog's son Albert, Willy Meyer's ally, used his father's "Black Peril" imagery in a speech to Parliament arguing that television should not be introduced in South Africa. He warned that it would incite in blacks not just a passion for equality, but even more dangerous desires.

> It is afternoon and the Bantu houseboy is in the living room cleaning the carpet. Someone has left the television set on. The houseboy looks up at the screen, sees a chorus line of white girls in scanty costumes. Suddenly, seized by lust, he runs upstairs and rapes the madam.

To pump up their rhetoric, leaders of the National Party turned to two newly emerging "scientific" theories. One was Social Darwinism, the idea that social categories, classes, and hierarchies—with whites on top—were the result of natural laws based on innate differences among the races of man. It was a specious and distorted application of Charles Darwin's theories of natural selection, and a neat rationale for imperialism and racism: The oppressed are oppressed because nature means them to be. Another new discipline useful to the National Party was eugenics, a term coined in 1883 by Francis Galton, a cousin of Darwin, to describe a body of practical strategies for selective breeding to produce better human beings, a program that took as a given the superiority of the white race.

"Hysteria about the consequences of race mixture was to a considerable extent supported by eugenic theory [which suggested] that the offspring of racial 'crossing' suffered physical and moral de-generation," Dubow says.

The coloured population, concentrated in the Cape province, evoked ambivalence in the Afrikaners. The two groups shared a language, and although some coloured people were Muslims, most belonged to the Dutch Reformed Church—a separate branch cre-ated so that white and coloured wouldn't have to worship together. The coloured community served as a buffer group, granted just enough privilege by the government to keep it from aligning polit-ically with the black majority. Coloured people were subject to forced relocations and received inferior educations, they didn't have to carry passes, weren't barred from as many jobs as blacks were, and until the early twentieth century, could vote in the Cape province, though only for white representatives. "Brown Afrikan-ers," they were called, when it suited the white minority. But the existence of a coloured population gave the lie to the manufac-tured myth of race purity, which is impossible genetically; in life, only hybrids exist.

"Race scientists" of the early twentieth century expended a great deal of energy proving that the products of race mixing were deviant and dangerous. This notion was popularized in the 1920s by the South African husband-and-wife team of Harold B. Fan-tham, a zoologist, and Annie Porter, a parasitologist. They believed that coloured people, as a "hybrid race," were naturally unstable and less intelligent than whites, and claimed their research proved that racial mixture led to physical abnormalities ranging from weak lungs and other malformed organs to vanity, sexual promiscuity, devi-ousness, violent outbursts of temper, and criminality.

That Principal Schwartz subscribed to the views of Fantham and Porter is suggested by the wording of his letters about Sandra to the Department of Education. Schwartz and the members of the School Committee were also likely to have been familiar with the novels of Sarah Gertrude Millin, extremely popular in South Africa—especially *God's Stepchildren*, a melodramatic and overtly racist 1924 saga about the descendants of a white missionary and a Khoisan woman. In it, tragedies caused by the "curse" of mixed blood befall generation after generation until one family member realizes that to end the curse, he must atone for his ancestors' sin of racial mixing by exiling himself to live among people of color in order to protect white society from his tainted bloodline. "The coloured race," Millin wrote, "is nothing but an untidiness on God's earth—a mixture of degenerate brown peoples, rotten with sickness, an affront against Nature." In an insightful essay on her work, "Blood, Taint, Flaw, Degeneration: The Novels of Sarah Gertrude Millin," Nobel laureate J. M. Coetzee writes that to Millin, "the flaw in the blood of the half-caste . . . destroys the peace of the community by revisiting its repressed sins upon it . . . Mixed blood is a harbinger of doom."

Most of the parents of Sandra's classmates were raised on such literature. To them, Sandra symbolized curse and contagion; of course their children couldn't share a room with her. Principal Schwartz and Willy Meyer certainly seem to have thought that way, and those parents who disagreed didn't feel strongly enough to oppose them.

The sin of race mixing was much on the mind of Prime Minister Daniel François Malan, winner of the 1948 election that made apartheid the official policy of South Africa, a quarter century after Hertzog's Black Peril campaign. An ordained minister of the Dutch Reformed Church, Malan immediately urged Parliament to pass the first Immorality Act forbidding any sexual contact between members of different races. It was only one of hundreds of statutes meant to keep black and white separate, ranging from the apparatus of so-called grand apartheid, such as the laws preventing blacks from entering white areas except as laborers, to the petty—those forbidding blacks from photographing whites, for example. But the "Immo Act" was notable for addressing directly the Afrikaner fear of racial impurity—and indirectly, perhaps, their anxiety about the legitimacy of their claims to domination. Between 1950 and 1980, more than eleven thousand five hundred people were convicted under these so-called Love Laws. Most of them were white men and black or coloured women charged with transgressions ranging from a fleeting embrace to marriage. Court records show that lawyers debated the difference between a platonic and a romantic kiss.

The book considered to be a how-to manual for apartheid, *A Home for Posterity*, was written in 1945 by Geoffrey Cronje, a professor of sociology at Pretoria University. Cronje was part of a group of Afrikaner leaders, including future Prime Minister Hendrik Verwoerd, called the architect of apartheid, who attended German universities. There they became infatuated with the same philosophies of romantic nationalism that caught the imagination of Adolph Hitler. Apartheid was necessary, Cronje wrote, because "the evidence is that the European is capable of higher intellectual achievement than the Negro." He offered scientific "proof" that "miscegenation led to racial decline." His book is dedicated to his wife and "all other Afrikaner mothers, because they are the protectors of the purity of the blood of the Boer nation." The popular ideal of the *volksmoeder,* the mother of the nation, made a woman's purity synonymous with the triumphant survival of the *volk*.

The idea that Sannie Laing had failed to maintain the purity of the *volk* was too painful and humiliating for Abraham to entertain; her straying would make him not just a cuckold, but also a traitor to his race, a criminal, as Gerrie Eloff said in *Race and Race Mixing*. For an Afrikaner man like Abraham, the possibility of a nonwhite branch somewhere near the root of the family tree was unpleasant but bearable. That his daughter should be officially coloured was impossible. That his wife had consorted with a black man was unthinkable.

Not all apartheid supporters were Afrikaners, obviously. The National Party came to power in 1948 by a margin of only eight parliamentary seats. Apartheid could never have risen, or lasted, without the complicity of whites who weren't Afrikaners, the allegedly more liberal British (the bulk of the alleging is done by English-speaking white South Africans). And not all Afrikaners, of course, approved of National Party policies. Anti-apartheid activists included heroes such as the jailed lawyer Bram Fischer, Beyers Naudé, a minister of the Dutch Reformed Church who quit first the Broederbund and then the church after he began to ques-

tion the morality of apartheid policies, and hundreds of anonymous dissident Afrikaners who joined forces with the African National Congress to fight racial discrimination. But Principal
Schwartz was not one of those people, nor was Abraham Laing.
His fight was to keep his daughter white, not to end the human
rights abuses, the inequalities of apartheid, and the suffering of
the oppressed majority.

Abraham refused to believe that his wife had betrayed him, but
he did think his party and his *volk* had. Imagine Abraham Laing's
confusion when Sandra was reclassified: He grew up believing that
the policies of his government represented the will of God. Suddenly,
the government, acting for God, wanted something that was terrible for his family. An article in the *Rand Daily Mail* in March 1967,
a year after Sandra was expelled from school and from the white
race, records Abraham's anguish: "Mr. Laing said that because of
what had been done to his child, he felt he could no longer vote for
the Nationalist Party. 'It is too tragic to countenance, this power possessed by the authorities which can suddenly change a little girl's
happiness into misery.'"

10

PIGMENTOCRACY

BUT SANDRA WASN'T MISERABLE. ON THE DAY SHE LEFT school, her stomach unknotted for the first time in four years. She couldn't wait to change out of her uniform and shed her shoes. "I didn't know what was happening," she says. "I was glad to be out of school, but I wondered why I was gone. I just went into my room and unpacked my suitcase, and then I went to the garden." She thinks maybe she checked on the pumpkins she and her mother had planted, loosening the earth with a garden fork as Sannie had taught her so they could breathe better. Her head filled with questions: Where would she go to school now? Was a charge being laid against her? What had she done wrong? Why hadn't her parents let her leave school sooner? What in heaven's name was wrong with her? Then she heeded the parental injunction to pay no attention, let the mind fog absorb her anxiety, and bent to her digging.

In Sandra's government file is an undated clipping from the London *Daily Telegraph*—most likely from 1966—that represents the sort of coverage Abraham probably hoped for when he alerted the press to his family's problem.

[Sandra Laing] was recently expelled from an all-white boarding school after the parents of some of her school friends had complained to the school board that she was not white. The Interior

Ministry investigated and, presumably because of Sandra's appearance, changed her racial classification to coloured.

Sandra's parents are both classified as white. Both have "white" identity cards. But [Mr. Laing] must now take Sandra's case to the Appeal Board. As Mr. Laing says, "If there is coloured blood somewhere in the background that we did not know about, then this could happen to a great many South Africans." But whether or not there might have been such blood in Mr. Laing's ancestry, the law has made it possible for one group of persons to "inform" on his daughter and has forced him to the iniquitous position of having to appear before the Appeal Board to protect his child.

In 1966, the key legal criteria for officially determining the race of a South African were appearance and general acceptance. Abraham knew his daughter would have a hard time with both. The Race Classification Appeal Board would call witnesses, most likely Mr. Schwartz, Mr. Van Tonder, and the parents of Sandra's classmates, who would attest to a notable lack of acceptance in the community. Officials might ask about Sandra's friends and associates, but they couldn't consider association without simultaneously considering appearance—not since a 1962 amendment to the Population Registration Act prompted by the odd case of Mr. David Song. A Chinese merchant, Song had presented to the Durban Appeal Board an affidavit signed by 350 white neighbors and colleagues who swore they accepted him as white. The board granted a classification change from coloured (subcategory: other Asian) to white. The switch horrified the minister of the Interior, who lobbied for closing loopholes in the law with an amendment.

Before witnesses testified, members of the board would carefully evaluate Sandra's appearance, using a battery of pseudoscientific tests. After assessing the breadth and flatness of her nose and perhaps measuring the size of her nostrils and the height of her cheekbones, the board might call in a barber to analyze her hair's texture and spirality. She could be given the "pencil test": a board member would place a pencil in her hair, and she'd be asked to bend forward. If her hair was straight enough that the pencil slid through she'd be declared white; if not, coloured. Some citizen-experts insisted the test was the way to tell coloured from black people. The board might also consult a chart showing gradations of skin color.

Sandra would, at least, be spared the "scrotum test"—which involved calculating the paleness of the testicular sac—and the "blue bum" test, which applied only to infants; officials looked for a small patch of pigment on the sacrum, seen most commonly in newborns of Indian descent, that later disappears.

Other tests used to decide whether someone was black or coloured included checking the fingernails (black people were sup-posed to have pinker cuticles than white or coloured people), squeez-ing earlobes (blacks' were said to be softer), and peering at eyelids (because those of black people were believed to contrast more starkly with facial skin than those of white or coloured people). San-dra could be asked questions about daily life meant to reveal the truth about her race. The board often asked people appearing be-fore them what they ate for breakfast; those who answered mealie pap—cornmeal porridge—were clearly black. Did the appellant sleep on a high bed (considered to be the custom of coloured peo-ple) or a low bed (thought to be preferred by black people)? Did he play soccer (thought of as a black sport) or rugby (believed to be a coloured pastime)? In Cape Town, in the early 1960s, a man hoping to change his classification from Native to Coloured got his way because he came to his hearing wearing a waiter's uniform, and board members considered waiting tables to be a coloured job. Sometimes the presiding magistrate suddenly pinched people in or-der to hear what language they used when they cried out in pain.

Sandra and Abraham would be entitled to bring a lawyer with them when they appeared before the board, but the hearing wouldn't be conducted like a regular court case. In matters of race classification, the burden of proof rested on the person whose race was in question, no matter who had questioned it—even if it were someone with a score to settle or an overactive imagination. That was the case with Johannes Botha, a white mail carrier visited twice at his Durban home in 1960 by a coloured man who was selling him a used car. Neighbors worried that the man might be a relative and that Botha could be passing for white, so they reported the family to the Group Areas Board, the body that enforced residential segregation. Investigators came to his home and quizzed his wife thoroughly. Botha's race classification ultimately remained intact, but not before he'd been scared three shades whiter. The *New York Times* quoted his shocked response at the time. Like Abraham Laing, he was having doubts about his party. "I thought apartheid was right," Botha said. "But this hit us like a blooming bomb. It struck me: This can happen to anyone."

Records show that while appeal boards were sometimes approached by whites requesting a race change in order to marry a person in another group, or by coloured people who wished to be designated black in order to continue doing business in the black community, the majority of cases involved coloured people "trying for white," or black people hoping to be reclassified as coloured. Is it surprising that someone would want to leave an oppressed group for a more privileged one? In 1970, four years after Sandra's classification was changed, white miners earned twenty-one times a black miner's wages.

The average waiting period between applying for a classification change—or having one sprung on you—and appearing before an appeal board was fourteen months, and often the process took longer. During that time, applicants did whatever they could to bolster their cases. Geneticist Trefor Jenkins says he was often consulted by frantic families seeking genetic proof of race for a reclassification hearing. "I called myself a fairy godmother," Jenkins remembers. "I would say, 'What race would you like to be?' I could always find some genetic marker to do the trick. But I don't think a board ever accepted my testimony."

An appeal-board decision could be fought in court, though few appellants could afford the legal fees. Those who went to trial found that the courts sometimes disagreed with the appeal board—further evidence of the highly subjective nature of race classification. According to the 1967 annual report of the South African Institute of

Race Relations (SAIRR), which includes a summary of Sandra's case, a woman in Cape Town who was considered by the appeal board to be "obviously non-white in looks" was later found by a judge to be obviously white. "There was similar disagreement over the appearance of a man who was sunburned from working in the open . . . [He] won an appeal against his classification as a Coloured when a judge decided that he was 'A White of the Mediterranean type.'"

When neither the courts nor the appeal boards could reach a clear decision about appearance, then a person's associations were scrutinized: "A man who looks White, and is readily accepted by the community as being White, for example, could be refused registration as such if many years previously he attended a Coloured school," the 1967 SAIRR report notes, "or if a large proportion of his friends were Coloured, or if he had not rejected and forsaken all family members who were not classified as White." The Supreme Court, the report says, "refused to apply this last test, stating that it was an unwarranted extension of the [Population Registration] Act, and insupportable on humanitarian grounds."

Members of the Race Classification Appeal Board included retired judges, but most were civil servants appointed by the Department of the Census and given no special training. The decisions they handed down disrupted families, and sometimes destroyed them. The SAIRR reported the case of twin boys, one of whom was classified native and the other coloured. And in 1974, newspapers carried the story of Raymond Du Proft, a white man, who fell in love with Diane Bassick, a light-skinned coloured woman. Unable to marry legally, they lived as husband and wife in a white neighborhood and home-schooled their five children, who couldn't attend the local white school because they were all classified as coloured. Attendance at a coloured school would have been used as proof that they were non-white. Diane and the children applied several times to be reclassified as whites, and were refused. When the oldest son, Graham, born the same year as Sandra, was nineteen, he and his pregnant Afrikaner girlfriend wanted to marry, but his coloured classification prevented a legal union. Distraught, the young man killed himself by jumping in front of a train. A few weeks after his death, the Appeal Board reclassified his surviving siblings as white.

The fate of these families is even more poignant and maddening when one considers the biological impossibility of sorting people in the way attempted by apartheid legislation. Appearing before South Africa's senate in 1967, the minister of the Interior testified that between July 1950, when the Population Registration Act went into effect, and the end of 1966, the year of Sandra's reclassification, his department was forced to investigate "a number of cases" because there was "a measure of doubt about a person's race." Quite a large number of cases, government records show: 48,000 whites, 179,000 coloureds, 26,500 Africans, 14,000 Malays (coloured people of Indonesian descent), 27 Indians, and 14 Chinese defied classification.

The large number of doubts and exceptions highlights the arbitrariness of race classification. For example, Chinese people were considered coloured, but because Japan was a valued trading partner, Japanese were classified as "Honorary White." So were visiting African Americans, who were allowed into hotels and restaurants that barred black Africans. A child like Sandra could be white one day and coloured the next. If the definition of the races could be this flexible and the boundaries between them so permeable, in the most rigidly segregated of societies, then what does race mean?

Not much, most scientists say. Obviously, people look different from one another, and fairly often you can guess the location of someone's ancestral starting line from her appearance. But the external features that tell us someone has African or Andean or Scandinavian roots—skin color, hair texture, eye shape, body type—are superficial adaptations to geography and climate. People living near the equator need dark skin to protect them from the sun's potentially lethal ultraviolet rays; people living in northern latitudes require skin unblocked by pigment so they can soak up enough of the sun's weaker light to trigger the cellular manufacture of the vitamin D they need for survival. Those most likely to thrive in the thin, frigid air of the Andes are compact people with big chests that can accommodate capacious, hardworking lungs. And so forth, the world over.

"Simply stated, there is no line in nature between a 'white' and a 'black' race," says Roger Sanjek. "Small local populations vary slightly from each other as one proceeds east to west from East Asia to Western Europe, or north to south from Scandinavia to the Congo basin." All human beings are hybrids. "Marble cake, crazy quilt, and tutti-frutti are all better metaphors of human physical variability than is the x number of races of humankind."

Even if the concept of race is a biological fiction, however, the social consequences of racial division remain painful facts.

A few years after Sandra was kicked out of school, another South African girl caused a stir because of her skin color. When doctors removed Jane-Anne Pepler's diseased adrenal gland, her fair hair and skin turned dark brown. In 1970, Jane-Anne's mother told the press, "All this is particularly embarrassing for us because we are a purely Afrikaner family and strong Nationalists. We believe in white supremacy. Some of her school friends have ostracized her completely, just as though she were a real nonwhite."

11

LESSONS AT HOME

TO SPARE SANDRA THE HUMILIATION OF BEING PARADED and poked like livestock—and perhaps because he feared that his appeal would be rejected—Abraham Laing decided to skip the Race Classification Appeal Board hearing and go directly to the Supreme Court of South Africa, Transvaal Provincial Division. His legal argument would hinge on procedural technicalities having to do with the way the minister of the Interior had been informed about Sandra's case. The court date was set for nearly a year away. In the meantime, so that his daughter could keep up with her studies, Abraham sent for a postal correspondence course covering mathematics, science, history, and geography. Sandra did homework every day while Abraham tended the Panbult shop, and they reviewed her lessons at the kitchen table in the evening.

"My father and I were close during the time I was at home," she says. "I knew he was making a case, but I still thought it was about hitting the children at school." Because of that she sometimes felt a bit guilty and worried, but on the whole, life was pleasing and easy in a way it hadn't been in a long time. Sandra doesn't remember her parents being particularly anxious the first few weeks she was home. "But maybe they didn't want me to see." Much later she would learn that while she was out of school, the Laings were plagued by anonymous phone calls and letters that called Sandra a bastard and her mother a whore.

Abraham wanted Sandra to spend her days either studying or helping Sannie in the shop—no running about with Thembi, Sibongi, and Gertie. "But my mother let me play with them," Sandra says. They climbed trees, and didn't need rescuing anymore; they held long tournaments of *zingando*, the stone-throwing game. Sometimes they'd wrestle with Bruno, the huge mastiff her father had acquired as a guard dog. Adriaan tried to toddle after them wherever they went. He looked more and more like Sandra, except that her skin was the color of milk tea, and his a bit lighter, like oatmeal with a trace of honey. I once asked Sandra how she'd describe her skin color. "Just brown," she said. Then: "Maybe brown like brown sugar." At the time, I briefly considered the fact that I've never been asked to scavenge for adjectives to describe my skin color, and probably never would be.

Often Sandra would hoist her little brother onto her hip and take him wherever she and her friends were going. Adriaan stayed home with Nora, though, when the girls ventured farther away toward Driefontein. They liked wading in a little nearby *spruit*, a creek. Nora packed a picnic basket and one of the girls carried it on her head, the way their mothers did. Sandra tried to copy them, even though she knew Abraham wouldn't like it. She never acquired the glorious balance of Thembi, Sibongi, and Gertie.

One day they went down to the *spruit* at lunchtime and spent hours building a little village of sand and sticks. "I forgot to go back for my lessons," Sandra says, "and my father came looking for me. I heard him calling my name and shouting '*Nu kom datlich!*' Come here instantly!" He spotted his daughter and came crashing down the riverbank. Thembi, Gertie, and Sibongi ran off home. Sandra tried to dance away from Abraham, but he grabbed her, scissored his legs around her, and spanked her. Then he marched her up the hill. It's the only time she remembers him hitting her. "He was angry that I was late. And he didn't want me to go far from home. And maybe," she added, "he didn't want me to have black friends because it could hurt my case."

During the time Sandra was at home, Abraham occasionally took her with him on short trips to pick up goods for the shop from wholesale warehouses. She remembers accompanying him to a whites-only cinema in Ermelo, the town where she'd been asked to leave a restaurant. But no one protested when she sat next to him to watch *Wir My Leid,* Hear My Song, a movie about a crippled boy. Once, on the way to Barberton in a thick mist, another car hit them near the little resort town of Badplaas, which had a natural hot spring. It took almost a week to get the car fixed, and they stayed at a hotel with a big pool. Sandra had a wonderful time, except that her father nagged her constantly about wearing a hat. "I see now he didn't want my skin to get darker in the sun."

Six months after Sandra was expelled, in September 1966, Prime Minister H. F. Verwoerd was assassinated, stabbed by a parliamentary messenger as he sat in the House of Assembly. His attacker, Demitrios Tsafendas, was motivated more by madness than politics; though he was reported to have been obsessed by his mixed-race status, he told authorities that his tapeworm had instructed him to commit the crime. Classmates of Sandra's who remained at Piet Retief Primary report that the children were saucer-eyed at the sight of their teachers weeping over the assassination. Mr. Van Tonder, who kept a photograph of Verwoerd in his office, was devastated.

Sandra remembers nothing of Verwoerd's death, or her parents' reaction to it. The events and figures of the larger world rarely penetrated her daily life, partly because she was a ten-year-old in an isolated rural area, and partly because she was a ten-year-old who protected herself from pain by noticing as little as possible. Still, the policies forged in that unnoticed realm had directly affected her, and would do so again.

Two troubling episodes marred the relatively peaceful months after her expulsion. One occurred during a visit from her maternal grandfather after his wife's death, in 1967, and not long before his own demise later that year. Ouma and Oupa Roux had stayed with the Laings fairly often, rotating among the homes of his three daughters. Oupa Roux wasn't as nice as Sandra's other grandfather, the one who'd watched the sky with her, but he was "all right." One day, though, he was cross with her and called her a *meid*, a *kaffir* girl. When Sandra was growing up, Afrikaners sometimes playfully called their children *kaffir* and *meid* (essentially, nigger and nigger girl) as affectionate nicknames; some still do. But there was nothing playful about Oupa Roux's exasperated tone. Sandra, eleven then, was shocked and ran to tell her mother. It was the first time anyone in the family had suggested out loud that she wasn't just like them. Sannie was furious. She asked her father what Sandra could possibly have done to earn such an insult. "He didn't answer," Sandra says. "He went to the guest room and shut the door. Later I heard him tell my mother he was sorry, he'd just been grumpy and wouldn't do it again. He left the next day to go stay with my aunt." Several months after she first told me that story, Sandra recalled why her grandfather was angry with her: She had hidden his pipe in the cushions of the sofa because she didn't like his teasing. "He always played by putting his pipe against me, and I always screamed and told my mum, 'Oupa's burning me!' But I wasn't really upset. It didn't burn so; he was just playing. My mum would say stop. Maybe she knew it was a game. I don't think he meant to hurt me. It was a game. That's all I remember."

The other incident, far more disturbing, occurred one evening at dinner, when Adriaan was already tucked into his crib and Leon was away at school. "I don't know what happened between my mum and my dad," Sandra recalls, "but we were all sitting at the table eating when my mum stood up and went to the bedroom. When she came out, she walked through the kitchen hiding something under her clothes." Sandra could tell from the shape that it was one of the pistols her father kept for protection in the shops and in the house. Sannie ran out the back door, and Abraham went after her. Sandra was terrified that her mother was going to shoot herself, or him. She could hear their voices outside, low and hard, but she couldn't tell what they were saying. Then Sannie came back in and didn't say anything, just shut herself in the bedroom. "My father stayed a long time outside walking around." Eventually, a frightened Sandra put herself to bed. "I thought, why does she want to do it? Is it because I did something wrong? Because I'm not in school? I still thought it was about hitting the kids. I didn't know it was about my color." The next morning, Sandra says, everything was fine. "Nobody said anything. I didn't think about it. I was busy with friends. I didn't worry that she might try it again." Is it possible, I asked her, that she was worried but hid the worry from herself? "It can be," Sandra said, and changed the subject.

Neither parent ever spoke of that night again, except to a reporter from the *Rand Daily Mail* in 1967 shortly before the Supreme Court handed down a decision in Sandra's case. 'COLOURED' SANDRA MAY GET REPRIEVE, the headline reads. "In March last year, Sandra was classified as a Coloured. It has been a year of 'sheer hell,' Mr. Abraham Laing, owner of two trading stores, told me. He said that his wife had spoken of suicide and of 'taking Sandra with her.'" Sandra says she didn't know about the "taking Sandra with her" part until she saw the news clipping from her government file, in 2001. "I don't know if she would have done it," she says. "I don't think so. I don't think she would have hurt me."

The article in the *Rand Daily Mail* went on:

> "If Sandra's classification is not changed then my husband and I will have to send her overseas [Mrs. Laing said.] She cannot live in South Africa as a Coloured, yet part of a White family.
>
> "Sandra has been brought up as a White. She considers herself White. She is darker than we are, but in every way she has always been a White person.
>
> "Even if it takes every cent of our savings and all we possess to let her live overseas, we will gladly sacrifice everything to make our child happy again."
>
> . . . "If Sandra remains 'Coloured,' does it mean she will have to be registered as a servant in order to live with us?" [Mr. Laing] added. "Or must she move away into a location? Will we be breaking the law if we take Sandra into a tearoom or a cinema, or take her on a train journey with us? And who would Sandra be allowed to marry?"

The clipping was sent to the Department of the Interior by Abraham Laing himself. He and his wife had received it anonymously in the mail from a concerned citizen who'd scrawled across the top of the newspaper photograph of Sannie and Sandra, "*Sy het n kaffir geslaap— nee geen wit man se kind.*" She slept with a *kaffir*—no white man's child.

On May 2, 1967, Justice Oscar Galgut issued a ten-page decision in *A. Laing v. The Secretary of the Department of the Interior*, much of it a review of the facts in the case. Under the law, he concluded, he could do nothing but endorse the actions of the Ministry of the Interior regarding Sandra's classification.

The Laings had lost. Sandra was to remain coloured.

Reporters rushed to Brereton Park. Newspapers all over the world carried the story, and the minister of the Interior got letters like this one, from the East London office of the Progressive Party of South Africa, the only anti-apartheid political party represented in Parliament at the time.

> Sir:
>
> We wish to record our protest at the inhuman classification of the Laing daughter from Piet Retief and appeal to you for the sake of all our consciences, to let this matter drop. How can you allow this innocent child to suffer?
>
> We trust your conscience is worried too and that you will not let down South Africa.

Another came from a Presbyterian minister in Pretoria:

> Dear Sir:
>
> I do not know all the rules and regulations with regard to Race Classification. However, I feel there must be something wrong when the child of a white father and white mother, daughter of Mr. and Mrs. Abraham Laing has been classified Coloured, because of a skin ailment [as reported in some press accounts]. I do hope you will be able to interfere in this matter without delay so that this family does not need to suffer any further.

The file contains several letters from concerned South Africans deploring the fact that Sandra had been denied the privileges of a white child, but none suggests that the system of bestowing benefits according to skin color should be abolished. While citizens express shock at the prospect of a white family's being torn apart, there is no mention of the millions of black families shattered by a migrant labor system that allowed black Africans but not their spouses or children to enter white urban areas in order to work and gave them only a few weeks' home leave a year. Perhaps those letters didn't make it into the file.

The Laings heard from people in England, France, the Netherlands, New Zealand, the United States, Iran, and Israel who'd read about Sandra in the newspaper and wanted to adopt her. Abraham and Sannie told reporters they would never give up their child. "My father read me some of the letters," Sandra says. "I didn't know what it was about. I asked why they wrote. He said they want me to go and stay with them; he didn't say why. I asked him, where is Holland? He said very far away. I said I don't want to go. He said he won't let me go there. I don't think he would have sent me. But maybe if I stayed coloured—I don't know."

The Department of Home Affairs—the new name for the Ministry of the Interior, as of 1967, sometimes translated from the Afrikaans as Department of Internal Affairs—was worried about all this publicity. "[We] need to give answers to people overseas who are asking how and why something like this can be done to a child in South Africa," one memo in Sandra's file says. "Foreigners who are well-meaning and are trying to refute the ill-meaning propaganda on South Africa are asking these questions." So in July 1967, the minister of Home Affairs wrote and signed a memo summarizing Sandra's case in order to help the Department of Information explain it to "well-meaning foreigners" and others. "I would like to add," the memo concludes, "that the actions of the Department in this case were not aimed at discriminating against the child in particular, as the outside world would like to portray it. It was, however, stipulated by the Law that the Department had to act on such representations [as made by the school principal and other complainants]. Similar actions will therefore have to be taken should it come to the Department's attention that there are any other persons who have been incorrectly classified. G. du Preez, Minister of Home Affairs."

In the Supreme Court decision, Justice Galgut had held out hope of an alternate route to what the Laings saw as the only happy ending. During the time Sandra's case was being considered by the court, Parliament had passed an amendment to the Population Registration Act that gave more weight to descent than acceptance in determining race. "The definition of 'White person' in Section 1 of the act has now been altered," Justice Galgut wrote. "I have not seen the new definition, but if it reads as I understand it does, then it seems that the Minister may be able to classify the child as White. If so, I can only hope that he will give the case his full consideration."

A memo from an unnamed official in the Ministry of Home Affairs, dated June 22, 1967, notes that Abraham would once again be invited to present his objections to Sandra's reclassification before a local appeal board. At that hearing, the memo suggests, the State Attorney should ask whether Abraham would be willing to subject himself and his daughter to a blood test. ". . . it is very unlikely that Mr. Laing would agree to such a test," the official writes. "It could then be argued that his refusal points to the fact that he does indeed have doubts as to whether he is the real father of the child." But Abraham did agree to blood tests. He submitted the results, along with an affidavit swearing that Sandra was his child, to the Minister of Home Affairs, and asked that Sandra be reclassified white based on the new legislation declaring descent to be paramount in determining race. Just in case, he and his lawyer began preparing arguments for an appeal board.

12

"DECLARE THE THING A BASTARD"

AND THEN SANDRA WAS WHITE AGAIN. ON JULY 25, 1967, the minister of Home Affairs sent the Laings a letter announcing that their daughter's reclassification had been reversed. Newspaper accounts of the ruling say the Laings wept with relief, though Sandra doesn't remember tears. She assumes Sannie wrote Leon the good news. He had left home—Sandra thinks it was immediately after high-school graduation, but she isn't sure—and gone to work in South West Africa, now the country of Namibia.

While publicity about Sandra's case may have contributed in a small way to the passage of the amendment that made her white— her name came up in parliamentary debate—the legislators were probably motivated by more pressing political considerations. In 1966, five months after Sandra was expelled from school, a law went into effect making it compulsory for all South Africans over the age of sixteen, regardless of color, to carry identity cards indicating their race. No one could work or attend school without one. Since 1951, many people on the racial borderline, most of them coloured and thus not required to carry a passbook, had dodged classification altogether, preferring to risk flying under the official radar. The passage of the new I.D. card law forced them to submit to classification, and as a result, the number of appeals against classification decisions had suddenly increased dramatically. This meant that

Sandra happened to make news at a time when the Ministry of the Interior and its regional Race Classification Appeal Boards were flooded with cases. The year that Sandra's classification was changed from white to coloured, the minister of the Interior received 268 objections to proposed race changes, nearly double the number of the previous year, some involving more than one person in a family. In 1967, eighty-eight appeals were waiting to be heard by the Transvaal board that would have handled Sandra's case. All together, there were still nearly 150,000 "borderline cases" to be settled, according to the SAIRR. The minister of the Interior was anxious to close any legal loopholes allowing people to be classified white when it was clear to him that they shouldn't be. The Population Registration Act Amendment of 1962, prompted by the case of Mr. Song, had made the law less porous; the 1967 amendment was designed to seal it tight.

Helen Suzman was a member of Parliament for thirty years, most of them as a representative of the liberal Progressive Party, and a fierce opponent of apartheid, for thirteen years the only one in the legislature. In her lively memoir *No Uncertain Terms*, she writes, "As I told the House, the basic reason for the introduction of the amending bill was the exasperation of the then Minister of Interior, P. M. K. le Roux, over the numerous successful appeals against existing classifications. Furthermore, even under the existing restrictive definitions, there were several court decisions which upheld appeals by aggrieved persons."

Seeking support for the amendment before the House of Assembly in September 1966, Minister le Roux said, "I cannot accept that there will be borderline cases for all time. If that is so, then the position is in reality so complicated that this legislation is not workable." The SAIRR had been saying the same thing for years. Its 1951 annual report declared, "The Population Registration Act has created at least as many problems as it has solved. Nature cannot be trifled with so easily. There are dark-looking people who have been classified as White, and light-skinned people who have become officially non-White. As a means of keeping the White community White, the Act must inevitably fail."

Nonetheless, the minister told Parliament his aim was "to close the gate so that we cannot continue indefinitely creating new borderline cases as rapidly as we already deal with existing cases." An amendment was necessary because, he said, in spite of previous legislation, there had been "a gradual, but nevertheless to my mind dangerous, integration of whites and non-whites." The proposed law stated: "A person shall be classified as White if his natural parents have both been so classified." In the absence of proof that both parents were officially white, the person's "habits, education and speech and deportment in general shall be taken into account."

Parliamentary records show spirited opposition to the amendment. On March 17, 1967, Sir de Villiers Graaf of the United Party, which included both liberal and conservative members, "maintained that Census forms and birth certificates did not provide adequate proof of race," the SAIRR reported. "Enumerators at the 1951 Census [on which all race classification was based] often filled in forms for people concerned, making their own judgments as to race, and these people possibly signed the forms in ignorance of the information given on them." There were a number of cases, he noted, of people entering a child's race as "mixed" on birth certificates merely to indicate, for example, a mixture of French and German parentage.

"Sir de Villiers Graaf asked where the sudden danger to the White group was that had caused the Minister to decide to close off the human studbook he had tried to create. He was endeavouring to classify the unclassifiable. The United Party considered that because of South Africa's history, the lines between the various racial groups must be elastic and impermanent."

In retrospect, one bizarre implication of declaring descent to be the key factor in determining race was that, genetically, nearly every Afrikaner could have been considered a mixed-race person. "If there had been a DNA test instead of the pencil test back then," a member of the African National Congress told me, "no Afrikaner family could have called itself white."

The bill passed, despite Sir de Villiers Graaf's arguments, and so Sandra was catapulted across the color line yet again. Reporters returned to Brereton Park after the re-reclassification. The following story, translated from the original Afrikaans, appeared on July 30, 1967, in the newspaper *Die Beeld*:

SANDRA WHITE AGAIN AFTER LONG BATTLE

Eleven-year-old Sandra Laing of the Eastern Transvaal, who seventeen months ago was declared a non-white, has now been reclassified as a white. But she will not be returning to the school from which the police removed her. . .

"The inspector advised me not to send her back to the same school. My wife and I have considered this matter and decided that it would be in Sandra's best interest if she went to a new school," said Mr. Laing. . .

"Our battle of more than seventeen months cost us, according to my estimation, about R1500, but I was prepared to go much further than that. Now I am glad that all that lies behind us and we are going to do our best to try and forget everything," said Mr. Laing.

However, he and his wife do not believe that the problems concerning Sandra's appearance are completely behind them. "There will always be people who will make the world difficult for her, but we pray that her education will be able to continue without interference from scandal-tongues."

After Die Beeld brought this family's problems to light, worldwide reaction followed. Television and radiomen, as well as representatives from overseas newspapers, descended upon the Laing's home and kept them busy for days.

"At one stage we were very disappointed in the government. It was so bad that we didn't even go vote in the last election, although we are fierce Nationalists," said Mr. Laing.

"Now we realize that it is human to make mistakes. It stands to reason that we are still bitter about everything that happened. All this hardship was unnecessary. But we are now grateful and want to leave the matter there," Mr. Laing said.

The English-language press weighed in, too. From the *Rand Daily Mail*:

> "These laws of the land are above a child's head," Mr. Laing
> told me this week. "A little girl does not understand why,
> because she is so dark, parents object to her mixing with their
> children at school. How could she understand, having been
> brought up quite naturally as a White child in a White family,
> why she was suddenly and unexpectedly classified as belonging
> to a different racial group?"
>   Mr. and Mrs. Laing are determined now to put the past
> behind them. "We must now live for the future," Mrs. Laing
> says. "The Department of the Interior has now declared
> Sandra White. This we accept as the final decision. Our
> immediate aim is to get her back into school again. She has
> been without playmates for too long now. The future must
> take care of itself. We have faith and we have hope. Our
> child's happiness is our only concern, and no matter what
> it costs us and no matter where we have to send her, we
> will gladly do anything to let the little girl live a normal
> life again."

After reading the above story, one of the clippings in her file, Sandra sighed. "I think my mum and dad did try their best to let me be happy," she said. A single detail, she felt, required refutation. "They said I had no playmates. But I did. Maybe my father didn't want the people to know I was friends with black kids." Perhaps he was worried that if the law were to be amended again and he was once more called upon to fight a reclassification, black friends might count against her.

Sandra's official reinstatement into the white race prompted someone to send the Ministry of the Interior another newspaper clipping with an anonymous note scrawled above her photo: *"Foeitog, dit is mos 'n kaffertjie."* Shame, it is a little kaffir. Another batch of indignant letters arrived, but to this group, Sandra symbolized something quite different. One example will do. The following handwritten letter was received on August 9, 1967:

> I cannot find the words to express my dismay, disbelief, and disappointment, anger and sorrow. I cannot understand how it could be possible for your Department to have made such a scandalous classification. I can only pity my race, my nation (the Afrikaner Volk) and my country. Because such a deed constitutes treason against everything the white man stands for. It is treason against the history of our forefathers. It is treason against the current generation of white Afrikaners. It is treason against the future of the white man in South Africa. Neither you nor your department has the right to equate the blood of a raceless person with the Blood of a White Man. IT IS NOT TOO LATE. Do a reclassification and declare the thing a "Bastard."
>
> I am not going to mention my name. It is not necessary. I am simply a white man who wants to keep his race pure.

By law, Piet Retief Primary had to take Sandra back. But the Transvaal Education Department told Abraham Laing that his daughter wouldn't be accepted as a boarder in the hostel, and offered to pay Sandra's boarding fees if Abraham would find another school for her. He refused at first, to the dismay of his wife and daughter, but then agreed to have her reassigned to a school designated by the Transvaal Education Department, in the village of Sheepmore, about thirty miles northwest of Piet Retief.

But then, in September 1967, the parents of the other fifty-three white students at the Sheepmore School threatened to boycott if Sandra was admitted. "I have my orders," the principal of the school, Louis Dreyer, told United Press International. "Even if it means that every child goes, I will have to accept Sandra." Abraham Laing wouldn't send her. "If the parents feel this way about Sandra," he's quoted as saying in the UPI dispatch, "what

humiliation and misery will face my little girl at that school?"
Abraham launched a search for a private institution that would
take Sandra.

Sandra didn't know about the uproar in Sheepmore, just that
her father was searching for a private school. Nine declined to admit her. "White schools, afraid of the attendant publicity and the
chance that Sandra may be subjected to humiliation by race-con-
scious children, have turned her away," the *Cape Times* reported. "To
safeguard Sandra against the innocently cruel remarks of playmates,
Mrs. Laing decided to enroll her in a convent." Catholic schools,
exempt from the strictures of Christian National Education, were
traditionally more liberal than public or Dutch Reformed Church
schools. But not quite liberal enough. "Yesterday," the *Cape Times*
piece continued, "a broken-hearted Mr. Laing said in an interview,
'Our latest attempts to have Sandra admitted to an East Rand convent failed.'"

> The mother superior of the convent told a reporter that while
> she felt very sorry for Sandra, she thought it would be unwise
> to accept her as a student."We have Chinese and White pupils
> at the convent and do not want to discriminate. If I could have
> had it my way I would have admitted the girl, but we depend
> on public goodwill, and as I see it we would only have trouble
> if we admitted her . . . There was a lot of publicity over the
> case and there would surely be repercussions if the child were
> allowed to go to school here. We have to consider the feelings
> of our parents and children."

The unnamed "*Cape Times* correspondent" who wrote the article is
sympathetic. "The desire of Sandra's parents, Mr. and Mrs. Abraham Laing, that she should grow up in the love and security any
other White child normally enjoys, is being threatened by fresh obstacles." The article seems to imply that love and security are not
normally enjoyed by non-white children. The correspondent makes
no comment on that matter.

Sandra's difficulties in finding a school came to the attention of the antiapartheid women's organization Black Sash, which issued the following statement in November 1967:

> The tragedy of Sandra Laing is the tragedy of South Africa. The direct chain reaction of cause and effect which is set off by viewing people as members of groups and not as human beings has, as its end result, the destruction of the life of a child, condoned by those who give this iniquity the consent of their silence.
>
> Those parents who have refused to allow their children to attend the same school as Sandra are the product of the sickness of our society.
>
> From the point of view of the Government it is difficult to understand why it does not have the courage of its convictions. In addition to a Law dealing with Race Classification it also has on its statute books a Law which makes education and school attendance compulsory for whites.
>
> Sandra Laing has been classified as white. She must attend school. The children at the schools where she has sought entry must also attend school. It seems that the Minister of Education has a duty to ensure that Sandra attends school and that the parents of other children are restrained from withdrawing their children from school. The Government cannot have its cake and eat it.
>
> The Government has taken more power into its own hands than is either normal or desirable in a democratic society, yet it abrogates its responsibility towards individuals who become victims of the state machine, nor will it exercise its authority against those of its supporters who have succumbed too well to its ideology. Sandra Laing is not unique. There are other unfortunate children like her. The Race Classification Laws are breeding grounds for tragedies and potential tragedies.

In December 1967, a month before Sandra went back to school, the South African weekly magazine *News/Check* updated her story. "This is an ugly case," concludes the unattributed piece.

By classifying and then twice reclassifying the child, the government has succeeded in declassifying her altogether, in turning her into a raceless individual, stripped of any social identity. The SABC Current Affairs [radio] programme, commenting recently on the Sandra Laing case, said sanctimoniously, "It is not in keeping with the policy or the Southafrican [sic] character to cause unnecessary pain to anyone." The truth is that not only has the pride of the Laing [family] been damaged by reclassification, but the good faith of the Southafrican government as well.

This brief commentary, ostensibly sympathetic to Sandra, reveals some deeply held beliefs of the era—that to be without a race classification is to be without identity, that being robbed of whiteness strikes a lethal blow to pride, and that while causing unnecessary pain may not have been government policy, causing necessary pain was something else again.

13

MEMORY IN TRANSIT

INALLY, A CONVENT SCHOOL RUN BY IRISH NUNS AGREED to admit Sandra. She was to enter St. Dominic's Academy in Newcastle, Natal province, in January 1968. Classes were taught in English, so Sandra would have to learn the language quickly. She started lessons at the kitchen table with her father, she thinks, and practiced in the shop with her mother. She remembers for certain that during the time she was out of school Abraham showed her how to play "the game with little dolls on a board—chess," and taught her to drive as soon as she grew tall enough to reach the pedals on the Volksie. She loved driving, though shifting was tough and Abraham got impatient if Sandra did something wrong, like releasing the clutch too quickly. "He bought me a typewriter, too, that came with a book," Sandra recalls. "He said I could work in an office someday, and learning to type would help me." Sandra practiced with pleasure. When she imagined a future life as a grown-up lady—a rare exercise—she pictured herself driving and typing.

One winter afternoon, after we'd known each other about seven months, Sandra and I were revisiting territory we'd already covered, talking about the time she prepared for a return to school after the government told her parents she was once more a white child. We were spending a few days at a hotel in Rosebank, an upscale, leafy northern suburb of Johannesburg, on a working holiday that involved taping more of her recollections, going to the movies—something she'd never done as an adult—eating lots of chicken with peri-peri sauce at Nando's, a fast-food chain Sandra loved, and generally giving her a break from running a busy and sometimes tense household. "I remember we went to buy a school uniform in Johannesburg. A blue blazer. I was glad to get a school uniform again. Both Mum and Dad came, also Adriaan. My mum and dad were very happy. We went to lunch in a restaurant. I don't remember any problem. I was happy that time after I got kicked out of school," she said. "We had a blood test, and the doctors told my father I am his child. So he started being nicer to me. He started to love me again."

I knew about the paternity test. But what did "He started to love me again" mean? "When had he stopped?" I asked. Sandra had, up to that point, painted a rather Edenic picture of life in Brereton Park before she started school, and, later, during school holidays. Her parents, she said many times, generally got along well, despite occasional arguments—the incident with the gun was notable—and her father's intermittent crankiness.

Over time, a consistent portrait of Abraham Laing had emerged. "He was very strict, but he loved me very much," Sandra said. He was angry sometimes, but he loved me. He was all right; he loved me a lot. He was more serious than my mum, but he often hugged me. Although Sandra seemed to have been more attached to her sunnier mother, she recalled comradely times with a pa who was very much the Boer patriarch, as I heard that archetype described by many Afrikaners: autocratic, hardworking, opinionated, inflexible, devoted to the protection of his family and its reputation; loving and concerned in his own blunt, stiff-necked, hidebound, undemonstrative way.

But that day, as we snacked on wine gums in the hotel room, waiting for her favorite soapie, *The Bold and the Beautiful*, to come on, Sandra gave the first sign that she had begun to remember, or felt ready to reveal, more disturbing aspects of home life. "My mom was easier and happier when my father wasn't there," she began. "When my father came home at night, she was afraid of him. She didn't treat me bad when he was there; she did hold me and hug me; she was just scared to play with me. She always said to me that I musn't do something wrong."

Sandra spoke with little affect. "Often, before I was kicked out of school, my father shouted at my mother, asking her if I was really his daughter," she said. "He'd say to her, 'Is she mine? Is she mine?' She never answered. He was angry. She was very still, and sometimes she cries." These quarrels, she said, happened maybe once a week, and afterward Abraham would send Sandra to her room. "I would look at him and he'd tell me to go away. Some weekends he was in a good mood. Other times he shouted at me, and he doesn't want me around him. Sometimes weekends when I was home I would stay in my room the whole day and just go out when I go to the toilet or to eat something." Exiled to her bedroom, she would lie on the rose-printed bedspread, look up at the framed picture of potted pink roses that hung over her bed, and try to puzzle out what she had done wrong.

Her parents quarreled in their bedroom, she said, and she overheard. She never heard her father apologize to her mother after these fights. She didn't remember whether her parents fought when Leon was home from school.

"I didn't know why my father said, 'She's not my child.' I wondered why. But I didn't think it was because I was darker. I never asked my mom why he said that. I was scared to ask. I thought I would make my mum angry or sad. I knew it was about me, but not why he thought I wasn't his."

A few hours later, Sandra said the arguments hadn't happened on her weekends home from school, but earlier in her life, before she went away, "in the evenings when he comes from the shop and reads the newspaper in the sitting room." But I thought the fights were in the bedroom, I said. "When he came home he'd have a bath and put on clean clothes. That's when they fought in the bedroom. In the morning or the evening I hear them talking in the bedroom. I'm in my room, or going to the kitchen. I asked my mum why he said those things, but she didn't answer me." I wondered about the shift from "I was scared to ask" to "She didn't answer." Sandra said she asked a few times.

The next morning, when we took up the subject again, Sandra criticized Abraham Laing directly, something she'd never done before. "My father was mean to me when I was little," she said. "I was staying out of his way. I felt always sad when my father and mother were fighting. I was angry and hurt that my father didn't love me. He was only pleased with Leon. I asked myself, 'Why can't he play with me?' When he went someplace, he always went with Leon."

By afternoon, she was backpedaling. "My father didn't always treat me bad and Leon better," she wanted me to know. "After the quarrels he was mean, but by the next day he was all right again. I did worry about it sometimes, because I always wanted to go with him wherever he goes, to town or to the shop, but when he was angry I was afraid to go. I just wanted to be with him, talking to him. He was not mean all the time. When he was in a nice mood, we looked for prickly pears, or he picked me up and sat me on the wall of the *stoep*, or we went to look at the cows. On Saturday afternoons, Stefaan wasn't there to help people with petrol, and my father came home from the shop in Panbult at one o'clock. He pumped petrol. I helped him, just keeping him company. I don't remember him saying anything nice, but I still had fun. Sometimes he was mean and sometimes he was nice.

"I was a little afraid of him. After a quarrel with my mother, he didn't want me in his sight, or he yelled. But when he recovered from a quarrel, then he would invite me for a walk. I was playing outside, or with my doll, and he'd call me. I was just happy he was in a good mood. After the quarrels, by the next day, my father wasn't mad anymore, and my mother wasn't sad, but I was still worried."

Sannie confided in Nora, the black housekeeper, about the fights with Abraham, Sandra says. "But my mother didn't want me to hear. They talked in Zulu, but I knew enough to understand them." Sandra often refers to Swazi and Zulu interchangeably; the languages are so similar that until a written form of Swazi was standardized after independence, in 1968, students in Swaziland used textbooks written in Zulu. "My mother doesn't know what to do because my father says I'm not his child. Nora knew that my mother wouldn't be involved with another man. I heard her say so. She said my mother must just tell him I am his child. She and Nora sat and had tea in the morning before she goes to the shop. Nora would make the tea and then they'd sit together. My mother had no white friends. She was very close to Nora."

It wasn't so unusual in apartheid South Africa for a white woman to confide in a black maid about marital troubles. They were together in the house, two women against the world of men. The relationship between employer and domestic helper could involve intimacy of a sort, but it rested on a hideously unequal distribution of power.

"I never asked Nora about these fights. Nora was like a mother to me, and I loved her. When I was little, Nora put me on her back with a blanket while she worked." That's the way a black mother carries her child, tied behind her with a blanket around the waist.

Not only did it take Sandra more than half a year of conversations before she announced that Nora was like a mother to her; it also took her that long to remember Nora's name. Until shortly before the conversation about her father not loving her, Sandra had been unable to retrieve the name, and referred to her nanny as Rose. Even now, she sometimes isn't positive that "Nora" is right, either.

"Nora was always nice to me, always helped me when things were bad. I think she saw that my father didn't treat me right. My father called me 'she'—most of the times when he talks about me he says 'she'—he didn't want to say my name, he just said 'she.' "

Being called "she" seemed to feel especially hurtful to Sandra. Her neutral tone acquired acid and edge when she talked about it; the memory unsettled her. But again, she soon worried about having been unfair to her father, and later that evening, she insisted on mitigating her earlier report. "When he was angry I knew he still loved me," she said. "I did wonder sometimes, but I knew he loved me. I only felt sometimes that he favored Leon. Only sometimes I was hurt and angry because I thought he didn't love me." She paused. "I was excited to go to school and away from him," she said.

"I was sad to leave my mum. But I thought it would be all right at school because he wasn't there."

Sandra can't call anyone in to confirm her account of Abraham's rages, her parents' quarrels, her banishment from sight. Even in the absence of corroboration, however, I believe it's useful to consider what the additions and emendations, the recalling and recanting, might mean. These newly remembered (or newly reported—or, it is possible, newly created) episodes introduced the possibility that Sandra arrived at school bearing a burden of guilt for an unnamed crime, already insecure about her place in the family, often anxious about a difference in her that she couldn't name, and hoping for respite from her father's unpredictable outbursts. According to this revised recollection, by the time she was seven, she was confused about the reactions she engendered in others, and had developed the art of not asking questions; exile and expulsion may already have become patterns in her life. She knew, even before classmates teased her and she aroused Mr. Van Tonder's puzzling disgust, that something about her was shameful enough to make her father periodically lash out at her mother and send Sandra to her room.

I was intrigued by these new memories, but concerned. My duty, I felt, was to arrive at a definitive version of Sandra's story. How would I know when we got there? What did these shifts mean? For guidance, I e-mailed Steve Karakashian, an American psychotherapist who works with the Institute for Healing of Memories, an organization based in Cape Town that helps people cope with the emotional aftermath of apartheid. "In general," he wrote, "we all have our toolbox of defense mechanisms that help us cope with threats, external and internal. These vary depending on the circumstances of the moment, so it is not surprising that we tell different versions of events at different times reflecting our different defenses. The more charged the event, the more likely this is to be true." Something Eudora Welty wrote in *One Writer's Beginnings* also proved helpful in approaching Sandra's shifting recollection. "The memory is a living thing," she said. "It, too, is in transit."

Before our brief hotel holiday ended, Sandra remembered

something else. After she was kicked out of school, she said, more and more often she took her midday meal with Nora and Miriam the laundress and her three little Swazi friends, sitting outside under a tree or on the back porch instead of eating with her family. "I think it was easier for me to talk to black people than to white people. Maybe I was testing did I belong with them."

14

THE WRONGED AND
SUFFERING PARTY

S ANDRA WAS TWELVE WHEN SHE LEFT FOR ST. DOMINIC'S. Two-year-old Adriaan cried and clung to her legs when she set out with both parents for Newcastle. Nora held him as they drove off. "He didn't want me to go," Sandra says. She was happy to be back in school, but worried that once her parents left her with a new crowd of white children, history would repeat itself. She half expected Wollie, or one of the girls who'd tormented her, to jump out from a corner. And she felt shy because she didn't know much English. Luckily, almost all the girls at St. Dominic's spoke Afrikaans, too.

Despite the correspondence course she'd worked on with her father, Sandra had fallen behind in the nearly two years she was away from school. So instead of entering standard five (seventh grade), she was placed in a standard-three (fifth-grade) class. She felt like a slow giant, and tried to make herself invisible. "At chapel in the morning I always went to sit in the very back, where no one could see me, and every day Sister Mary brought me to the front, until I went to the front on my own."

A couple of girls teased her about being so quiet, but Sister told them to hush and stop being unkind, and they did. "At first I was always sitting alone. I was scared to talk. But they made friends with me and never teased me about my skin." Gradually, she relaxed. The nuns were nice, and so were the girls she lived with. In the dorm room, a curtain surrounded each bed, and a nun slept in a cubicle in the corner. The girls weren't allowed to go outside the convent gates, but everything they needed was inside—swimming, hockey, tennis, netball, a bell tower, pretty grounds to stroll. Sandra remembers two special friends her age, both white, of course. One was from the town of Standerton, where her parents owned a soft-drink factory, and the other was from Zambia. She can't remember their names, but she remembers happy times. "After class, we danced to records in a big room. Those who knew taught the others." They listened to Elvis Presley, and to Jim Reeves' hit "When Two Worlds Collide," a song about star-crossed lovers. "What were the dances we learned? Was one a waltz? Whatever they were, I can't do them anymore."

The newspapers covered Sandra's adjustment to her new school. The *Cape Times* reported in early 1968:

> Yesterday her parents received their first letter from their over-joyed daughter. "She is radiantly happy," Mr. Laing said. "She said that she likes her friends and asked us to send her some sweets. There is no discrimination against her," he said.

The nuns gave Sandra extra tutoring in English, and her friends helped, too. She caught on fast to the basics. But instead of praising herself for quickly picking up a third language, she was slightly embarrassed that she wasn't as fluent as the other girls. Sandra was still so withdrawn, during class and after, that she could see the sisters were concerned about her. She didn't wet the bed or vomit anymore, but she was sometimes anxious and confused. "I was still worried—maybe something will happen again there. I was very slow in school. I don't remember if I passed that year. I couldn't concentrate. Maybe I couldn't concentrate because I was thinking the same thing would happen as it did in Piet Retief." She did well at sports, though; she was goalkeeper on the field hockey team, and she played tennis. Her father was pleased with her progress, and that made Sandra happy.

"I still could talk more easily to black people than white,"

Sandra says. "I always talked in Zulu with Samuel, the driver at the school. He told me jokes and talked about his family. I could speak more easily and felt more comfortable with them." She couldn't say, then or now, why she felt more comfortable. "It just felt right to be with them."

Sandra turned thirteen at St. Dominic's and soon after got her first menstrual period, an event for which no one had prepared her. She thought she was sick or had hurt herself. Sister Mary explained what was happening in her body and why, although she was rather sketchy about how babies are made. Sandra's parents never told her about sex, Sandra says, although she'd seen cattle go at it and had a vague idea of what was happening. Her school friends filled in some of the details, to storms of giggles. But Nora was the one who told her what was what, on the next school holiday.

When she was home from St. Dominic's, Sandra almost always worked in the shop with her mother instead of playing with her three black friends from Driefontein. They didn't come up the hill as often to see her. She liked chatting with the customers, especially Petrus Zwane, a friendly, easy-going Swazi produce vendor in his twenties from Driefontein. He ran a little *spaza* shop, a minimarket, from his home. In Swazi and Zulu, *spaza* means "dummy," as in fake. Blacks weren't legally allowed to own stores but *spaza* shops (also called tuck shops, from British slang for "food"), stocked with cigarettes, tea, milk, bread, mealie meal, and other staples, flourished in an informal township economy that also included illegal bars, called *shebeens*.

With Sannie Laing's permission, Petrus had begun selling fruits and vegetables from his *bakkie* to the crowd that waited once a week outside the doctor's office behind the shop, and setting up a stall once a month on pension-check day. Sometimes he'd come to the shop on a bicycle that he leaned against the *stoep*. To tease him, Sandra would jump on it and ride it up and down the dirt track, as she'd done with the night watchman's bike when she was a little girl. Petrus would chase her, pretending to be furious but letting her elude him. Then she'd tell him she was stealing his bicycle for real, and pedal into the part of the yard where Bruno, the mastiff, was tied up. Petrus was afraid of Bruno and wouldn't follow Sandra. He'd stand at the edge of the yard trying to sweet-talk her into giving the bicycle back. She found it unfailingly hilarious to confound a grown-up in this way.

She looked forward to her chats with Petrus, always in Swazi, exchanging light banter that felt like batting balloons back and forth. "Everyone liked Petrus Zwane, even my father," Sandra says. Of course, her father didn't know that as time passed, Sandra spent more and more of her school holidays flirting with Petrus in the shop, she on one side of the counter, he on the other. But Sannie saw. "My mum said to him, 'What are you doing there with my daughter?' And Petrus said, 'I'm just talking, madam.'" Every silly thing Sandra said seemed to interest or amuse Petrus Zwane. Sometimes he came as early as nine o'clock in the morning and hung around all day. Sandra wondered what was happening to his vegetable business. Sannie worried about Abraham's catching him hanging around. "Every day at four thirty, my mother said to him, 'You'd better go now.'"

Sandra knew that Petrus had a wife and three children in Driefontein; his wife sometimes came to the shop. Still, Sandra daydreamed about him in class and scribbled his name in her exercise book. "I wrote 'SL loves PZ' in a heart," she says. "I just started liking him and then I started loving him." By the time she turned fourteen, Sandra burned with a schoolgirl crush.

Her father, meanwhile, was pursuing justice. Abraham wanted recompense for his pain, and he'd begun sending off letters even before Sandra left for her new school. On August 7, 1967, he wrote to the minister of Home Affairs:

> I wish to draw your attention to our great humiliation, loss of respect, psychological suffering, financial loss, and, in the case of my daughter, additional educational loss. This was all due to your Department's actions. I hereby wish to request from you a reasonable offer of compensation.
>
> Yours truly,
> A. Laing

The minister replied that the Population Registration Act didn't provide for the type of compensation Abraham requested. Abraham tried again.

> 16 September 1967
>
> Dear Sir:
>   I would inform you that it seems as though there is no law against providing compensation in this regard. I would therefore appreciate it if you would make me a reasonable offer.

Abraham sent a "third reminder" in October, then wrote again in February 1968, after Sandra entered St. Dominic's:

> Your Department seems to deliberately ignore my letter of 16 September 1967 and the several reminders thereafter. I therefore feel the need to let you know that your refusal to compensate me under the guise that the Population Registration Act does not make provision for such compensation, cannot be accepted under any circumstances.

A handwritten note at the bottom of this letter reads, "Please advise him that there is nothing to add to our letter of 24/8/67. The case regarding his application for compensation is considered closed." Abraham then tried the deputy minister:

> Honourable Minister Martins:
> Re: Compensation, Susanna Magrietha Laing
>
> My financial costs were R2000.00. The whole affair was very humiliating to us. We also suffered a great deal of emotional pain and felt extremely degraded. It caused my daughter to lose years of schooling to such an extent that she now feels inferior because of it.

This is not about the lawfulness of the Government's actions or about the fact that the officials had to act and did so in good faith. The fact is that the government made use of unofficial documentation (equal to that of scandalous tongues) submitted by uninformed extremists. On top of that, the Government did not approach the child's parents in this regard or inform the child's parents of its actions prior to the whole tragic affair. All the fuss could have been avoided if the Government had taken the necessary precautions.

What is done cannot be undone. It was not and cannot now be stopped. I, however, am the wronged and suffering party. Because of this I therefore ask you to please obtain reasonable compensation for me.

It could be argued that I would get more than enough compensation from selling the television, film and story rights. But, keeping in mind the extensive repercussions that would unleash, I would like to think of this course of action as a last resort.

Thank you.
A. Laing.

Despite Abraham's threat to sell Sandra's story to the movies, the government refused once again to pay him for his troubles, and he seems to have dropped the matter.

Sandra knew nothing of her father's futile quest for restitution. She was focused on the delight of learning that Petrus was jealous of Stefaan, the helper in the shop, because he and Sandra were such good, old friends. "There were other black men who liked me, too," she says. "A taxi driver who came around the shop, and a man who helped out with chores sometimes." Petrus said to Sandra that he could tell Stefaan wanted her. It was a lovely surprise, and rather mysterious, this being wanted, as thrilling to Sandra as setting the brush fire had been long ago. "I felt happy and lucky that men liked me," she says.

15

COURTING DISASTER

I KNOW MY FATHER WANTED ME TO MARRY A WHITE MAN someday," Sandra says. "There was a boy, I can't remember his name, but he came to our petrol pump with his motorbike and stopped by on Sundays sometimes to talk with my father. Sometimes he'd stay for supper. He was from Dirkiesdorp or Amsterdam, just out of school. I heard my father tell this boy that he could take me out to a cinema or tea shop. He tried to talk to me, this boy, but I didn't like him and just answered yes or no to his questions. He saw that I didn't want to be with him and didn't ask me out. I just didn't like white boys. I couldn't."

Instead, during visits home from school, Sandra nurtured her crush on Petrus Zwane. "He told me he wants to see me alone some time, away from the shop and my mother." Nora lived close to Petrus in Driefontein, and they knew each other well. Through her, Petrus arranged their first rendezvous, asking that Sandra meet him in the pine forest behind the house. "I said he must not come with the *bakkie*, but walk from Driefontein in the trees. Nora always tells me what time he's going to be in our place where we meet. It was just a place where we were always sitting, green grass between trees, pine and blue gum that smells like Vicks. He comes just behind the garage where my father's car is. I would sneak out of the house and Nora would tell my mother I was down at the river or walking in the fields." The girls, her old friends from Driefontein who visited her less often now, knew she flirted with Petrus in the store. "But they didn't know we saw each other."

Nothing happened in the beginning, Sandra says; she was shy and quiet. She just wanted to be with Petrus, chatting and laughing under the pine trees. She liked him very much, this sweet-talking, good-looking man. "Sometimes he gave me his jacket to sit on; then he started bringing an empty mealie sack to spread on the pine needles. The talk was about how we missed each other, how he thinks a lot about me and he wishes he could see me every day, how I mustn't let my father and mother know we're seeing each other."

Petrus teased her, relayed township gossip, asked questions about school. "And he said often that he was scared of my father, that if my father caught him talking to me in the trees, Pa would kill him. Petrus always said white people don't like black people. He told me about a time he was stopped by the traffic police and beaten with a chain for no reason. He still had the scar." Did Petrus think of her as white or black? "Petrus didn't say anything about my color," Sandra said the first time I asked her. "I think he saw me as black." But a few weeks later, she said, "Maybe he did see me as white, but because I was friendly with black people he wasn't scared of me. I think he saw me as white." Whichever the case, one day under the trees, Petrus kissed her, and her heart fizzed. Not long after that, they made love for the first time. Sandra was fourteen and Petrus twenty-four. Sandra told Karien van der Merwe, in Afrikaans, "He brought it up first. We were kissing and he said we must make love. I was scared I'd get pregnant. Nora said I musn't sleep with him, I will get pregnant. But I felt I just wanted to. We talked about it. He said he didn't want to force me. I said I was afraid, but I wanted to. Petrus was very careful not to hurt me. I liked it. It wasn't painful and I didn't bleed. He made me feel happy and good inside. I didn't climax the first time, but it was a nice feeling. Later I did climax. He was first and best.

"Afterward, I didn't feel guilty, but I felt shy. I couldn't look at Petrus, but he lifted my chin with his hands and told me to look in his eyes, that everything was okay. The second time we did it I said I'm scared of being pregnant. He said we must try not to be, your father will kill us. After that we met each other at least once a week and we did sleep together, but I didn't use anything and he didn't use anything. It was just luck that I didn't fall pregnant.

"I was always very careful so my mother wouldn't find out. After, I took a bath and washed my clothes." The lovers didn't discuss the fact that Petrus had a family, she says; he didn't say he was unhappy with his wife, or that he was going to leave her, and Sandra didn't ask any questions.

The romance might have run its course, with the same shifting ratio of damage to delight as any extramarital affair—especially one involving an older man and an inexperienced girl in the transports of first love—if Petrus's wife hadn't intervened. Before breakfast on a June morning in 1970, at the start of a long school holiday, Sandra looked out a window of the Laings' house and saw Lisa Zwane, Petrus's wife, sitting outside of the shop waiting for Sannie Laing to open up. Sandra didn't think Lisa knew anything about her affair with Petrus. "Lisa was under the big tree. I went outside, and Lisa called me over and told me, in Swazi, that she wanted to show me a photograph she'd found in Petrus's jacket pocket. It was me, in my school uniform. I told her it was my snap and I'd given it to Petrus. I told her the truth. I wasn't even scared. I don't know where my pluck came from. I told her that Petrus was my boyfriend. I just felt she won't hit me because she's scared of my father and mother.

"My mum came out of the kitchen door and called to me. She asked what was I doing. I said, 'That's Petrus Zwane's wife, and she was asking me something.' My mum said, 'Tell her it's not eight o'clock yet.' Ma thought she was asking about the shop. Lisa said she was going to tell my mother. I said you musn't tell. She said she has to tell because Petrus doesn't worry about her first anymore. I didn't think about taking him away from her; I just thought I'm glad I've got a boyfriend and I love him. I went back into the house. I was worried."

Lisa Zwane waited for Sannie to unlock the shop, followed her inside, and told her that she'd found Sandra's picture in Petrus's jacket. "I know this," Sandra says, "because Stefaan told Nora, and

Nora told me. My mother asked Lisa for the picture back but she wouldn't give it. Then Lisa told my mother that she was going to Panbult to tell my father. My mother asked her not to, but I think Lisa was too angry, and afraid Petrus was going to leave her. Ma begged her not to, but she went anyway. She took a taxi—a car, an old Valiant that someone used as a taxi—to Panbult to tell Pa about the picture.

"My mum left Stefaan in the shop and came to talk to me. She asked me if it was true about Petrus. I was silent. She said I must tell her. I told her that Petrus and I were meeting and talking, but not that we're making love. I was scared, and so was my mother. She said that if my father found out he would kill me."

16

CROSSING THE BORDER

HEN ABRAHAM GOT HOME THAT NIGHT, HE TRIED to slap Sandra as soon as he walked in the front door. "But my mother stepped between us," Sandra says. "He was shouting. Oh, he was mad. Pa said, 'Where did Petrus get your picture?' I said I gave it to him. He asked why did I give it to him. I said because he's my boyfriend. Then again he wanted to hit me, and Ma stopped him.

"He shouted, 'Why a black man? Why do you always mix with black people?' I didn't answer him. He said, 'Are you sleeping with the *kaffir*?' I said no, we're just talking. He said again, 'Why a black man? White people don't get involved with black people.' I didn't answer him. He said, 'I try to get you in a good school and give you a good education and now you're busy with *kaffirs*!'" Sandra swore to her father over and over that all she did was talk to Petrus; everyone liked talking to Petrus.

"He said I must go to my room. He never spoke to me again that night. I didn't come out. My mother brought dinner and came to say good night. She didn't talk to me about what happened. My father left early the next morning. Leon already wasn't living at home, and Adriaan was four."

Lisa Zwane had confronted Abraham on a Friday. On Sunday, Petrus Zwane drove his car up to the gas pump in front of Brereton Park General Dealers. "He didn't know that his wife had gone to my father. My mother was in the kitchen. My father saw Petrus through the window, grabbed his gun, and ran out the door. I screamed for Ma and we ran after him. He pointed a pistol at Petrus and said, 'I know what you're up to with my daughter, and I'm going to kill you!' Ma grabbed the gun from Pa. Petrus stood there frozen. My mother told Petrus that he must go and never come back."

But he still came to the store during the day, while Abraham was at the other shop in Panbult, and, Sandra insists, Sannie let him stay. "At four thirty, she'd remind him to leave. She didn't chase him away. Sometimes I wonder why. I don't know. Maybe she thought that if she chased him away, I'd run away. So she let him come, as a way of keeping me around. My father was the boss, but I think when he wasn't there she did her own things. Petrus said that when I was in Newcastle at school, my mother always told him when I was coming home, what day she was going to fetch me."

Lisa Zwane was so angry at Petrus that she moved back to her parents' house, leaving her children in the care of Petrus's parents, Jenny and Amon Zwane, who lived outside the town of Carolina, about an hour's drive from Piet Retief. Sandra thinks Lisa left the children because Petrus had paid *lobola,* a traditional dowry, when he married her, and according to Swazi custom, that gave him the right to keep their children with him or his family.

Abraham Laing barely spoke to Sandra for the whole six-week school holiday; he tried to avoid her. "I was heartsore," she says. "Heartsore" is a word Sandra uses often, in English and in Afrikaans. *Hartseer.* The more *hartseer* she felt, the more Petrus seemed like medicine. "My mother never stopped speaking to me. She didn't seem angry with me. She just said that my father must never find me and Petrus together." Sandra kept meeting Petrus secretly in the woods, even after Abraham threatened him with a pistol. Later, Sannie Laing would deny to the press that she knew anything about Sandra and Petrus's rendezvous.

In July 1970, Sannie took Sandra back to school, where she remained until December. Her parents visited on a couple of Sundays, but her father barely spoke to her. "He didn't show he was angry," she says, "but it wasn't like a dad must speak to his child. He was speaking to me like he doesn't like me anymore. He was cold. He didn't seem interested in me. He never hugged or kissed me."

Sandra wrote to Petrus from school. "My mother must have known I was writing to him, since she took care of the post, but she never said anything about it. I begged Petrus to come see me." He finally drove all the way to Newcastle and sent word to Sandra through one of the black gardeners that he was parked outside the gate. But Sandra was taking part in an all-day sports tournament and couldn't slip out unnoticed. Petrus drove home without seeing her.

Both of the Laings came to fetch Sandra in December for the Christmas holiday. Her father behaved as if she were invisible, she says. "To Adriaan I was still his big sister; he was overjoyed when I came home." By the time she returned to school in January 1971 to start standard six, eighth grade, Sandra believed that her father no longer loved her, which she found especially painful after the warm interlude of affection and approval while he was fighting her reclassification. Abraham came to St. Dominic's to take Sandra home for the Easter holiday of 1971. In Brereton Park, his escalating coldness, she says, was so distressing to her that she made up her mind to run off with Petrus.

"I didn't want to stay at home, because my father didn't love me anymore and I wanted to be with Petrus. I thought about it just a short time. I said, 'Petrus, we must leave.' He was scared at first; he said no, because my father might kill him. I told him we'd go while my father was at his shop, and I would get the money we needed. I ask him has he got family in Swaziland, and he did. We talked about passports. I didn't have a passport. He said he'd pay someone to walk with me across the border.

"My father had a wooden cash box that he took to work every morning and brought home at night under his arm. He kept the box unlocked in the dining room sideboard, behind little doors. Inside was paper money wrapped in cardboard with elastics around it." Sandra sneaked some cash out of the box and gave Petrus enough to buy a suitcase, some clothes, toiletries, and gas for the drive to Mbabane, the capital of Swaziland.

The morning they ran away, Sandra waited until Abraham left for his shop and Sannie for hers, then packed a few things in the new suitcase she'd hidden under her bed. She thought briefly about bringing her doll Melinda but decided not to. "I said goodbye to Adriaan, because he was with me in the house. I felt sad to leave him because he loved me very much. I didn't tell him I'm going for good. It was sad to leave my mum, but that time I was just thinking of Petrus. I didn't think about school. I didn't think what our life would be."

Petrus was waiting for Sandra in his *bakkie* and they took off. They saw a blue Volkswagen like Abraham's coming toward them, and Petrus nearly fainted. "I told him my father couldn't have found out so soon. A different white man was driving." The pair reached the town of Oshoek, at the Swazi border, in less than an hour. They couldn't drive through the checkpoint because Sandra had no passport or identity card; she wasn't sixteen yet, so it wasn't required. Petrus paid a man to walk her over the border away from the guarded crossing. They climbed a high chain-link fence, and then the man led her up and down rocky *koppies*—little flat-topped hills—through a forest and across streams. The fancy new sandals that Petrus had bought Sandra for their escape were ruined.

She met up with Petrus on a deserted road, and they drove to his uncle's house in a black neighborhood on the outskirts of hilly Mbabane, which seemed more like a country town than a capital. Sandra telephoned her mother from a public booth to tell her she was all right. "She said that Nora had seen me go." Nora wasn't in on the plan, but she'd spotted Sandra through the window, carrying a suitcase and heading toward the trees that fronted the dirt road, and she'd alerted Sannie. "Ma had called Pa to tell him I was gone. He wanted to send the police after me to bring me back, but Ma talked him out of it. She told me that she said to him, 'Let her go. Maybe she'll be happier there.' I told her I would be." Sandra and her mother were both crying when they hung up. "I think she did understand," Sandra says. "Maybe she thought I'd be happier because she saw I was happier with Nora and my friends."

Sandra believes that when Sannie stopped Abraham from sending the police to bring her back, she had no motive beyond keeping Sandra safe and happy. The thought certainly occurred to me that while Abraham believed retrieving Sandra would forestall shame, Sannie may have felt that their public ordeal would end only if Sandra went away. Sandra's exile might have been a big relief for her. Sandra thinks that's impossible.

Many times I asked Sandra why she left, and many times she gave versions of the same answer; there was no point in living at home if her father didn't love her. Later, she added a variation: "I was angry at my dad because he didn't want me to see Petrus, because he wanted to shoot him. I was angry because he didn't love me any more. I wasn't angry at my mother.

"I just wanted to be with Petrus," she says. When she left with Petrus, she hadn't imagined the future, and she had no plans. "I never thought about what our life would be like. I knew black people had a harder life than white people, but I didn't care. I just wanted to be with Petrus." In our very first conversation, in the crowded parlor of her township house, I'd asked her in what ways she's like her father and her mother. "Maybe I'm just like my mom—I like to work in the house and the garden," she answered. "We both like kids a lot. And I've got my mother's nose. You can say my father was stubborn. I am stubborn, too. I think so, yes." She'd smiled then. "Maybe if I want something, I want it. And I don't like somebody to say no."

I think Sandra's motivations were multiple; most people's are. And I think they weren't necessarily conscious; most people's aren't. Perhaps Sandra ran off with a black man to get back at her father, because she knew it was the thing that would pain him most deeply. Two shrink friends, one South African and the other American, both psychoanalysts, used nearly the same language to describe Sandra's actions when I told them her story in detail. The South African was familiar with her case from media reports. Eloping with a black man, they said, was a big "fuck you" to her father. He was especially impressed by her gumption. "She rejects the rejectors," he said. "The only analogy I can think of is of a gay person's 'coming out' to a hostile, homophobic world. We must congratulate her—her will to survive is strong."

Maybe leaving was the only way Sandra could get Abraham to

see what she was beginning to understand—that because of her appearance, she would never fit in the white world no matter how many battles her father fought on her behalf. Perhaps her departure was an unconscious act of solidarity with Sannie, a reenactment of the sexual crime Sandra overheard her father accuse her mother of committing. Perhaps it was the only declaration of independence she was equipped to make, an eruptive, irreparable, colossal, attention-getting act of self-definition. In her book *The Powers of the Weak*, Elizabeth Janeway writes, "The power to disbelieve, the first power of the weak, begins here, with the refusal to accept the definition of one's self that is put forward by the powerful." Was Sandra's running away a liberating act of refusal?

Or did she believe that her very survival was at stake? When Sandra was at school, so many people wanted her gone. Her parents seemed bent on erasing her in a different way, insisting that she deny what she felt and saw. Did Sandra feel threatened, on a barely conscious level, with emotional, maybe even physical, annihilation? Petrus's ardent attention must have been especially affirming, and a life with him may have seemed a safe haven.

It may have been that Sandra was simply a teenager brainless with love, making a dopey and impulsive decision. She was especially unskilled at judging consequences. Ordinary laws of cause and effect had been off-kilter in Sandra's life; punishments didn't fit crimes, asking questions brought unanticipated results, her interpretation of events was consistently contradicted by the most important people in her life. If more in her experience had been as sensible and predictable as arithmetic, perhaps she would have made a different choice.

Perhaps she felt . . . it may have been—these are things that you say when you're writing about someone who's dead or a subject who refuses to go on the record, and Sandra is alive and cooperative as I make these conjectures. But her own motivations are mysterious to her, or too frightening to plumb. Of course they were complex and barely conscious. How could she avoid a big dose of ambivalence, growing up on the racial borderlines of a rigidly stratified society? But she can't, or won't, analyze the alloy of emotions that drove her off, though I ask twenty different ways. And she's adamant about Sannie's having no thought but her daughter's welfare when she let Sandra go. A message from Steve Karakashian from the Institute for Healing of Memories once again helped me find perspective. "All children need to feel loved and safe," he said. "So this means many of us as children see certainty where there is very little and feel love in circumstances that don't seem very loving. This is how we try to reassure ourselves."

Sandra and Petrus spent their first week in Mbabane with his aunt and uncle. "It was a part of town with black people," Sandra says. "The uncle worked for the city helping to keep the drinking water clean, and he and his wife were kind to us." Then Petrus rented them a room down the street. He earned money the same way he had in Driefontein, buying fruit and vegetables from farmers in the countryside and selling them in the city. Sandra liked to go with him, jouncing past fields of sugarcane or grapefruit groves while boxes of produce slid and rattled in the bed of the *bakkie*. She was happy to be away from South Africa, she says. The couple had worries, but they laughed often and held each other close each night. She relaxed into the simple, pleasant rhythms of life in Mbabane, wondering occasionally what her family was doing, and whether Adriaan missed her. Years later, she learned that her parents never told her brothers exactly what had happened, just that their sister had gone away.

After a month, Sandra telephoned her mother a second time. Sannie wept to hear her daughter's voice. "She told me my father was angry I lived with a black man, after he'd worked so hard to keep me safe. He said that if he got hold of me he would first shoot me dead and then shoot himself dead. It scared me when my mum told me that. I think she was afraid of my father. I think that was the reason she told my father not to send the police. If I ever came back, she didn't want my father to do something like that."

A newcomer to South Africa soon notices a revealing quirk of Afrikaner speech—the ubiquity of the phrase *Ag, shame!* The *ag* is a gutteral Teutonic *ach*, the *shame* as it's pronounced in English.

Though the phrase literally means "ah, shame," it's used a hundred times a day in common conversation to mean a number of things: how cute, how sweet, my goodness, oh, dear! oh, no! and, of course, what a shame. It can be an expression of sympathy, empathy, approval, or disapproval. Another version of the interjection, the one Sandra says her mother favored, is *Siestog!* It means "Shame! What a pity!" A useful catchall, a barely conscious throwaway. But it is perhaps no accident that the word *shame* is so often in the air when Afrikaners speak.

The journalist and poet Antjie Krog argues persuasively that the apartheid-era Afrikaner community was what anthropologists call a shame culture, a term coined in the early 1950s by the historian E. R. Doods, who divided the world into shame cultures and guilt cultures. In *Country of My Skull,* her richly reported book about covering South Africa's Truth and Reconciliation Commission, Krog quotes a colleague who tells her, "'The usual catchy definitions are things like: People feel guilt when they fail themselves, shame when they fail their group. Guilt is linked to violation; shame is linked to failure. Shame requires an audience. Guilt does not. And shame is more overwhelming and isolating than guilt is . . . The basis of shame is honor. Honor functions when the image a person has of himself is indistinguishable from that presented to him by other people . . . Honor became [apartheid champion Hendrik] Verwoerd's driving force. To protect the honor of the Afrikaner, anything was permissible.'"

This drive to protect honor, coupled with the prevalence of gun ownership in South Africa (I saw "no guns allowed" signs in English, Afrikaans, and Zulu at a public hospital, a casino, and a movie theater in the East Rand) contributes to the national phenomenon of family murders—a man kills his wife, his children, and himself. They're usually committed by a man who thinks he's lost control of his home and failed as a patriarch, and so feels shamed in the eyes of the community. According to the Centre for the Study of Violence and Reconciliation in Johannesburg and Cape Town, 90 percent of family murders involve Afrikaner families. Statistics aren't kept consistently, but between 1986 and

1988, for example, 223 family murders were reported to police. The Afrikaner patriarch depends on his sense of authority for his sense of self; if one crumbles, so does the other. As the end of apartheid approached, in the late 1980s and early 1990s, the number of family murders rose, perhaps in response to feared loss of authority on a grander scale. Some experts consider family murders to be a sort of multiple suicide, since the patriarch regards the family as an extension of himself. Karien van der Merwe worked on a 2002 TV documentary about family murders, and she notes that the latest twist is an unprecedented appearance of the phenomenon in the coloured community, and among black policemen.

Would Abraham have committed murder? When he made the threat in 1971, he felt publicly humiliated and no longer in control of his family. He saw himself as having fought and sacrificed to keep his daughter white; now she was heartlessly throwing that hard-won whiteness away. News of her running off with a black man would get out, eventually; she was as good as announcing to the world that her mother was a whore, he a cuckold, and both of them race traitors. Sandra would learn later that her father felt she was flouting civilized values, shaming him unbearably, and betraying him in the most painful way possible.

Sandra believes Abraham might have made good on his threat to kill her and himself; she'd seen him point his pistol at Petrus. But she can't say for certain, since she never saw her father again.

17

In the Chokey

WHILE SANDRA AND PETRUS LIVED IN MBABANE, every two weeks or so he visited his children across the border near Carolina, a couple of hours away by car. Sometimes he saw his wife, Lisa. On one trip, Lisa told him she hadn't given up on their marriage. Petrus reported to Sandra that Lisa wanted him to bring her to live in Mbabane, too. "She said, 'Who's going to look after me?' He must look after her, also," Sandra explains. "She wanted him to support her." Petrus moved Lisa into another rented room in Mbabane. Sandra never saw her. "And soon she got angry because she thought he didn't spend enough time with her, and she went back to South Africa."

Not long after Lisa left, Sandra and Petrus were awakened just before sunrise by a mighty banging on their door. Petrus jumped from sleep and stumbled to open it. Two black policemen stood there. "Are you Petrus Zwane?" one said. Petrus answered that he was. "Where is the Boer child you stole?" they said.

"I didn't steal anybody," Petrus said. The policemen walked to the bed and trained their flashlights on Sandra. "*This* is the white girl you stole?" one said, and they started laughing. Sandra insisted to them that Petrus didn't steal her, but the officers said the couple had to go with them to the police station. "I was a little frightened, because I didn't have papers, but not too worried," Sandra says. "In Swaziland, it wasn't against the law for a white woman and a black man to be together, the way it was in South Africa." She added that most people who saw her without her parents assumed, as had the policemen, that she was coloured, not white.

Petrus was jailed in Mbabane as an illegal immigrant; Sandra was charged with entering Swaziland without an I.D. or passport and immediately sent back to South Africa. The Swazi police phoned the South African police to come get her at the border. She was driven to Badplaas, the town where she'd once stayed a week with her father waiting for their car to be fixed. There she spent a few days in a small, smelly holding cell with a bucket for a toilet and a metal shelf for a bed. She never cried, she says, because she was certain Petrus would come fetch her. Another of Petrus's uncles, who worked at the hotel where Sandra and her father had stayed, came to visit and brought her fish and chips. Sandra thought that was especially kind, since he'd never met her before. This fish-and-chips uncle told her that Petrus's wife was the one who'd informed on them to the Swazi police.

Then Sandra was transferred to the jail in Carolina, the district capital, where she was held for two months or so in a big cell with white metal bars and crumbling concrete walls covered in chipped white paint. The cell had a skylight but no windows. "We were many women in the same cell, usually more than six. Each day new ones would be taken in and others would leave," she recalls. "We slept on thin mattresses on the floor, and each morning we would roll them up and put them in one corner of the cell. The women were all older than me, and very nice to me." Sandra hadn't yet turned sixteen.

"There was a few toilets, and we kept them clean. They gave us toilet paper, and they gave us blue soap that I used to wash my clothes. We wore our own clothes. We women had to do the washing for the prison, and at the same time we would wash our own clothing. In the center of the jail was a quad. We did the washing there. We usually ate there, mostly *tinkhobe,* boiled corn, and we sat chatting there in the sun. When it rained we would go to our cell— we could move in and out to our cell when we wanted to at all times."

Sandra appeared before a magistrate, a local judge who handled child welfare issues, among other matters. He told her that Petrus was locked up and she would never see him again, so she might as well go back home. In fact, the magistrate said, unless she went home to her parents, she would spend the rest of her life in jail. "I thought he was just trying to scare me," Sandra says, "and I told him I refused and I was going to wait for my boyfriend to fetch me. The policeman in the magistrate's room laughed when I said that, because I was so young." The magistrate sent her back to her cell.

Petrus was released after serving a month in an Mbabane jail; he visited Sandra the day he got out, and every day after that. "A policeman would open the front door of the jail and let visitors stand in the entrance," Sandra says. "The visits would be about thirty minutes, and we always stood talking to each other. A policeman would be with us all the time, and anything that anyone gave me, food or clothes, was checked first."

"Petrus said I mustn't worry, the police wouldn't keep me locked up forever—they were just scaring me because they want me to go back home." He told Sandra that while she was in jail, he'd sent word to his mother Jenny Zwane that she must visit Sannie Laing in her shop and tell her that Sandra was in jail. Jenny was frightened that Abraham Laing might show up while she was there; Petrus's stories scared her. But she took a taxi to Brereton Park. Sannie already knew about Sandra's arrest, because the police had sent the Laings a telegram. "My mother wanted to see me, but my father said I could stay locked up." Abraham had forbidden her from going to Carolina to visit their daughter, and she didn't think she could slip away without his knowing it. "She gave Jenny some money and some clothing and asked her to look after me while I was in jail."

After a second month had passed, Sandra appeared before the magistrate again, with Petrus in attendance. Once more she refused to go back to her parents. This time the magistrate told Petrus to take her home.

If Abraham and Sannie had come to Carolina to take her back to Brereton Park, I asked Sandra, would she have chosen to go with them instead of with Petrus? She can't say for certain. "I think my father let them put me in prison to scare me," she said. "He wanted me to come home." This in spite of Jenny's report that Abraham wouldn't let Sannie visit their daughter, and Sandra's own belief that Sannie let her elope to save her from Abraham's violence. "But I was happier with Petrus. We loved each other and I wanted to be with him. So I chose to be with him rather than to go home. I thought about it sometimes that I might have hurt my parents. But in the end I still wanted to be with Petrus. My mother did feel very hurt, but she understood that I wanted to be with Petrus and that is why she told my father to leave me alone the day I ran away, to let me be. I don't think she rejected me. She was just scared of my father because he was very angry. I was scared, too. We were scared that he would do something to me because he was so very angry. Maybe I was too scared of my dad to go back with him." The conversation continued to chase its tail, with Sandra testing the idea of a loving father against the idea of a murderous one.

18

STRONGER INSIDE

THE DAY SHE WAS RELEASED FROM JAIL, SANDRA CALLED her mother from a pay phone. "I told her I'm out and I'm staying with Petrus's parents. She just said I must look after myself." Then Petrus took Sandra home to his parents' *kraal*, family compound, in Dorsbult, a black township between Carolina and Badplaas.

She immediately liked the Zwanes, especially Jenny, who had a kind, worried face. Jenny patted Sandra's arm as if the girl were a little cake. Amon Zwane was a tenant farmer. In exchange for labor, the white owner of a large farm allowed the family to cultivate a few acres, a sweet and fertile piece of land with a small field of mealies, a large vegetable garden, fruit trees, and a pasture for several horses and cows. Pa Zwane had two wives, according to the Swazi custom. Jenny was the senior wife; his "small wife"—the junior spouse—was called Little Gogo, Little Grandmother, and lived in the same *kraal*. "Pa Zwane went back and forth," Sandra says, "a week on this side, a week on that side." Jenny was in her fifties when Sandra met her, but she seemed older. "Little Gogo was far younger. She had two small children. They were good friends, her and Jenny, and they still are." Petrus, Jenny's only child, was devoted to his parents, and had warm relations with everyone in the family compound.

The Zwane *kraal* consisted of a main brick house with a tin roof and three rooms; everyone used it during the day for cooking, eating, and socializing, and at night Jenny, Amon, and Petrus's four children slept there. Four rondavels made of saplings and mud, with conical thatched roofs, served as bedrooms for Little Gogo and her two children, Sandra and Petrus, and Lisa, when she visited. The fourth was used for guests, and male friends and relatives often gathered there to drink homemade beer. The *kraal* had no electricity. The family burned paraffin lamps, cooked on a coal stove, and carried water from a nearby river.

Amon and Jenny met when he was a young man working on the white man's farm and she was a teenager on her way to fetch water. After they married, she worked in the farm kitchen. Petrus grew up in Dorsbult and went to the native school until seventh grade. Pa Zwane had more cattle, horses, and chickens than his neighbors, and he was much better off than the migrant laborers who went to Johannesburg, *eGoli,* the city of gold, to work in the mines and factories and only returned to their families in Dorsbult for a month out of the year. The Zwanes were able to stay together despite a national migrant labor system that separated husbands and wives and gutted the tradition of the extended family *kraal.*

Sandra liked Petrus's children and spent hours each day playing with them, especially the baby and only girl, Stiena, whom she tied to her back with a blanket and carried the way Nora had carried her. Boy was ten—just five years younger than Sandra—Kiki eight, Joki six, and Stiena seven or eight months old. She was a newborn when Sandra and Petrus ran away. Sandra was surprised to learn that Petrus also had an "outside son," Lucas, born to a woman in Carolina on the very same day that Lisa gave birth to Boy. Sandra had landed herself an amusing and attractive man, but not a faithful one, as she well knew, being the other other woman. At the time, though, she had no doubts about his devotion to her.

Petrus's wife Lisa came often to see the children, staying a week or two and then returning to her parents' house. "At first I was afraid of her, but then we became good friends," Sandra says. Lisa saw how much Sandra loved the children, and ultimately she didn't hold Petrus's wandering eye and traveling heart against her. Lisa was about

Petrus's age, around twenty-five. She joked a lot, she yelled a lot, she said just what she thought, and she drank a bit. When she drank, she quarreled with Petrus, but never with Sandra, the children, or Jenny, whom she respected. Lisa was, Sandra believes, fair-minded, though hotheaded.

Sandra became, in essence, a Swazi "small wife," although she didn't marry Petrus, either civilly or in the traditional Swazi way, with her father paying a bride price. "Maybe we never got married because I didn't have an I.D. that time," Sandra says. "Or maybe he didn't ask me." A civil marriage would have been illegal, in any case; in the eyes of the government, Sandra was white and Petrus was black, and the Prohibition of Mixed Marriages Act of 1949 prevented their union. They were already breaking the Immorality Acts and the Group Areas Act by living together. Sandra didn't know about these specific laws. "I just knew white people and black people couldn't be involved," she says. Luckily for her, the government was far more worried about black people lingering in white neighborhoods without the correct pass than they were about white girls with brown skin living in black townships. For a good long while, no officials bothered with Sandra.

Before Sandra left the Laing home, Sannie had begun teaching her the duties of an Afrikaner wife, by instruction and example. "She taught me sewing, cooking, cleaning, and washing if you didn't have help, and to respect your husband—that you must respect each other." Now her unofficial mother-in-law, Jenny Zwane, showed her what a Swazi wife must know. Sewing, cooking, cleaning, washing, and respecting your husband were certainly part of it. Sandra also learned to chop wood, fetch water, scrub the floor, and make mealie pap and wheat with sour milk. She learned how to heat baby Stiena's bottle on the coal stove, change her diaper, and wash it in a tin basin—all the things that Nora had done for Sandra at home. Jenny teased her about her early efforts: "She said, 'We'll all starve if you fetch one twig of stove wood at a time and pump one cup of water!' But she said she didn't mind because now I was her child and she liked having children in the house.'" Sandra felt that Jenny accepted her, approved of her, and had no wish to change her.

Jenny taught Sandra how to make beer from a packaged mealie-meal mixture that she bought in a shop. "You pour it in a basin, add hot water, and wait a few days for it to turn into beer," Sandra explains. "Some people add more yeast and sugar to the mix, but Jenny didn't. Her beer was a nice brown beer that Petrus and his father liked best." The secret was in knowing just when to take it out of the basin.

From her mother-in-law Sandra also learned Swazi social customs like lowering her eyes when she spoke to her elders, the opposite of the forthright gaze that had been encouraged at school. When Sandra menstruated, Jenny tried to show her how to use rags cut from soft, worn pillowcases instead of paper pads. "The women held them just by tucking them between their legs; they didn't wear panties. But I never got it right."

Sandra was happy with Jenny, working, talking, and looking after the children. She settled into a comfortable routine. "I woke up around six in the morning. Most of the time a rooster woke me up, but at times I woke up by myself." She'd visit the little hut that held a pit toilet with a wooden seat, then wash in the rondavel using a basin of water. "By the time I woke, Jenny already fetched water from the river and lit the coal stove. The water would be hot and boiling, and she already started cooking pap and meat, or pap and *marogo* [the grain amaranth].

"On days when Jenny wasn't working in the kitchen of the white farmer, I sat chatting to her while she was plaiting grass rugs to sell. I often went with her to fetch a bucket of water—I would have a bucket and Jenny would have a bucket. When we needed to, we washed our washing at the river before the midday meal. After the meal we would just sit chatting some more while Jenny was busy with her rugs. Or we would sit together and be quiet."

Petrus's paternal grandparents visited often; uncles, aunts, cousins, and neighbors dropped by. "They didn't do anything special; they just sat and talked and drank beer and got involved in whatever everyone else was doing," Sandra says. "They all seemed to have a good time together. Visitors often came round." The days were peopled and pleasant. A peace settled on Sandra.

Sometimes she helped Jenny in the white farmer's kitchen,

cleaning and washing. "I liked helping Jenny," Sandra says. "With Jenny and Pa Zwane on the farm, I learned about new things. My father-in-law had horses and he taught me how to ride. I was happier on the farm than I was at Brereton Park. I felt that I belonged. I was part of a family. When I was with my own mum and dad I spent most of my time in my bedroom or out with my three friends." Talking about that period in her life with Karien van der Merwe, she said in Afrikaans, "By nature I am a quiet person, so I was still quiet when I was with Jenny. But I was happy. I didn't think of my parents too often because I was happy with Jenny and them, and I did not think of the years at school." Once a month or so, Sandra called her mother from a public phone in Dorsbult. "My mother wanted to know where I'm staying and if I'm okay, and she said I must please take care and look after myself.

"We stayed well with Jenny; it was *lekker* [very nice]. They loved me. They were very good to me. We were very happy. I felt I was at home. They were like my own people."

It wasn't that black people were perfect; they were the same mix as everyone: good and bad, deceitful and honest, selfish and generous. "Black people can be jealous," Sandra once said, "and white people can be cruel." To Sandra, the most important thing about this community was that they welcomed her, and they didn't think anything was wrong with her.

In the Zwanes' *kraal,* as in Brereton Park, the husband was boss. Under Swazi customary law, women had no property rights, even though, Sandra saw, they worked harder than the men and made more decisions. On days when the family had meat, the women saw to it that the men got the most, but Sandra thought that honor should go to Jenny, since she toiled more than any of them. White or black, she thought, women had a tougher time than men in South Africa. But she felt she was where she was supposed to be. Her color wasn't a problem here. In fact, it was valued. Petrus's son Lucas Zwane was eight or nine when Sandra came to live with them in 1971. He often stayed with his grandparents at the Zwane *kraal.* "We were glad when she came," he told me when Sandra, Elize, and I visited him and his family in Ogies, the small Mpumalanga town where he works as a truck driver for a coal company. His children adore Sandra; most children do. The little Zwane girls wrapped their arms around her thick middle and lay their heads on her belly. They looked forward to the rare visits from their sort-of step-grandmother. "We wanted her to stay always," Lucas said. "We were very happy that my father brought a white person home." To be certain, I asked Lucas if they thought of her as white, and he said yes, then added a comment in Swazi. Elize translated: "He says it raised the family's status that a white person came to live with them. It was an honor to the family." On a later visit to Jenny Zwane, I asked her, through Sandra, whether when Sandra came to live in Dorsbult she thought of the girl as white or black. "She thought of me as a white person," Sandra translated from Swazi. She added, "Because at that time I was a little bit lighter than now. I think they accepted me as like them because I was friendly with them." Sandra emphasized that she didn't think of herself as white then.

Petrus and Sandra had been with the Zwanes for a month or two when Lisa, there visiting her children, asked Sandra to walk with her to a neighbor's house to retrieve some cups and plates they'd borrowed from the Zwanes. Calling to Jenny and Little Gogo that they'd be right back, the two young women, friends by then, walked through the trees and across a river. They found that the neighbors had made a big batch of homemade beer and cooked chicken and meat on a *braai,* a barbecue, they'd made out of bricks with a grate on top. "They gave Lisa a drink. I never tasted beer before, and I wanted one, too. We drank beer and ate meat. Then we drank more beer and ate more meat. Then we drank more beer." The whole day passed that way.

"By the time we went home, we were so drunk we could barely stand up. And we forget the dishes we'd come to fetch! When we got to the river, I was walking in front. I walked through the water with no trouble and sat down to rest underneath a tree. But Lisa was drunker than me, and she got stuck in the mud up to her knees and couldn't get out. She called for me to come back and help her, but I couldn't stand up. We could only shout to each other and laugh." Sandra fell asleep under the tree as Lisa swayed in the river mud. The next thing Sandra knew, Jenny and Little Gogo were shaking her awake. "They'd gotten worried and come looking for us. 'Where's *Mamakaboy*—Boy's Mother?' they said. A Swazi woman with children is called by the name of her first child. I said, 'Boy's Mother is in the river!' Oh, I laughed like a crow. They had to help me home, and then come back and help Lisa. When Petrus came home that night and found me drunk, he was so cross that he took off his belt and wanted to hit me. Jenny stopped him."

Petrus went to Lisa's rondavel, found her in the same condition, and smacked her before Jenny could intervene. "Lisa hit him back, and that made him angrier, and he hit her more, until she chased him away. That night he wouldn't even come to bed with me. He said, 'I'm not going to sleep with a drunk woman.'" Sandra woke up feeling as if a dog lived in her mouth. "Petrus was still cross, and I had a *babbelaas*, a hangover. *Ag*, I thought it would break my head. I didn't have a sip of liquor again for years and years."

As Sandra told the tale of the drunken wives, she became animated and confident in the way she had when she told the story of starting the fire. This livelier, laughing self, rarely displayed, seems to emerge when she relates examples of assertive, creative mischief. Recalling her small transgressive acts tickles the hell out of her.

After they'd lived a few months in his parents' *kraal*, Petrus leased land in Kromkrans, a black area about an hour's drive away, surrounded by white farms and towns. Early in the twentieth century, a group of black veterans of the Boer War bought the land from a white friend who fought with them. Kromkrans was a poor but relatively comfortable community of thatched-roof houses, sturdy brick homes, rondavels, and tin-roofed, scrapwood dwellings, surrounded by gardens, little pastures, and mealie fields on rolling hills. It had no general dealers or grocery stores, only *spaza* shops and *shebeens*. The nearest big shops were in white dorps, ten miles away. A few men in Kromkrans sold firewood, or vegetables, like Petrus, but most dug coal in nearby Ermelo, or worked in mines farther away, in Johannesburg or Kimberley.

Petrus hired men to build a stout, four-room brick house, two bedrooms, a lounge (living room), and a kitchen. He worked on it, too. He bought good secondhand furniture, including a yellow

Naugahyde sofa that Sandra loved. They hung photos of King Sobhusa of Swaziland on the wall. It annoyed Sandra to learn from her government file that in newspaper articles about her, Kromkrans is called a squatter's camp and her house a shanty. "It was a proper brick house! And I told Petrus he must build another house on our land for Lisa," Sandra says. "His children still stayed with Jenny because there wasn't enough room for them to sleep in our little house, but if Lisa had a house next door, the children could sleep in both houses and visit more often. We were good friends. She stopped trying to get Petrus back. I knew Petrus loved me, and I had no worries. Lisa got drunk too often, and she was always fighting with Petrus. I felt sorry for her, but I didn't feel it was my fault." Eventually, Lisa found a new man and a live-in job, working in a white family's kitchen in Boksburg, two hours away. But for a while, during her long visits, they were a traditional Swazi family, a husband and his two wives, like Pa Zwane.

Petrus's vegetable business was doing well, and he'd bought a cow. Sandra had a garden that she loved. "Everything I planted with my hand grew well. In summer, tomatoes, peas, lettuce, beans, and roses. In winter, everything slept but spinach and onions." Jenny and Pa Zwane visited often. Sandra was happy in Kromkrans, busy doing whatever the day brought her.

"When I was white, most things I didn't do, like cooking, washing, those things. When I was black, I was cooking, I was doing my wash myself, cleaning. When I was black, I like doing all those things. I like working. But when you are white, you just think there's someone who's going to do it. When I made those three friends in Brereton Park, and with Petrus, I don't worry about color. When I lived with Petrus, I think of myself as black. I didn't think about white people. *Ja,* I can say—because the black people liked me; they didn't say nasty things at me.

"When I was white, maybe I didn't feel I'm white—because I was happier with black people. I think that black people treated me better than white people. The way they looked at me. I just feel better if I'm with black people—they don't see me as different. I felt stronger inside when I was with black people."

19

MOTHER-CRIES

S
ANDRA FELL PREGNANT, AS THEY SAY IN SOUTH AFRICA. On her sixteenth birthday, in November 1971, she applied for an identity document as required by law, but using her mother's maiden name, Roux, rather than Laing. She asked to be classified as coloured instead of white. Concern for her unborn baby motivated the request; she was afraid that if she were classified white and her baby coloured, the child might be taken away from her. In January 1972, according to Sandra's government file, the Department of Home Affairs sent her a letter saying that because she was under twenty-one, she needed her father's permission to be reclassified. The letter was returned as undeliverable, perhaps, Sandra says, because they'd moved and now used a different post office box.

Department officials debated whether or not to contact Abraham and ask for his consent. Handwritten notes in the government file, in Afrikaans and signed with initials but not names, focus on the worry that Abraham might publicly malign South Africa and apartheid to the "outside world."

Reclassification: White to Coloured
Miss S.M. Laing

1. I do not agree with sending [a letter to Abraham Laing]
2. Judging by Mr. Laing's actions in the past, it is clear
   that he stops at nothing. It seems he sent a false report
   into the outside world with a photo of him and his
   "daughter."
3. Should we make contact with him, chances are that he
   would enrich himself further by sending more false articles into the outside world. This could be very damaging
   to our country. For example: He could say that the application form [for reclassification] was not submitted by
   his daughter and that the information filled in on the
   form is false, or that she was forced by a policeman to fill
   in her race as coloured. He would say that the Department
   still doesn't want to let him and his "poor little girl" rest.
   He would say the truth of the matter is . . . (this is where
   he could give full flight to his imagination), etc. etc.
4. I therefore suggest that we contact the magistrate at Carolina and ask him to find Miss Laing. He could ask her
   to sign an affadavit explaining how she became known
   by her mother's surname, Roux, and who her natural father is. How does she know? What is the name of the
   man she is living with as husband and wife? If Laing is
   not her father, what is her mother's address? Do her
   mother and Mr. Laing still live together, and any other
   information you would regard as being of value. The
   magistrate should be able to find her since she gave her
   address as a post box in Carolina.
5. Should the magistrate be able to supply us with such a
   statement, we could address a letter to Miss Laing's
   mother rather than to her "father." Should Mr. Laing
   publish any false reports, the Department will have a
   document with which to defend itself . . .

On the memo, someone else has written:

> I believe more damage would be done should such an affa-
> davit or statement be obtained from Miss Laing through a
> magistrate. I am not implying that Laing will try to gain
> more publicity. He would probably realize it could turn
> against him. I feel the case should rest for now.

The minister of Home Affairs agreed that a magistrate needn't be
involved. In February 1972, his office sent Abraham a letter in-
forming him that Sandra had applied for an identity document as
a coloured person, and telling him that his consent was required before she could change her race. His reply:

> March 6, 1972
> Dear Sir
>   . . . Since Sandra's natural parents are white, the race
> she submitted as coloured is incorrect. No such permission
> can be granted. She is classified as white. I refer you to your
> letter of 25/2/1967. Since she deserted her parental home
> and I do not know her whereabouts, I cannot send the form
> to her for completion. I therefore return it to you.
>
>   Yours truly,
>   A. Laing.

Abraham's letter launched another flurry of notes among officials,
once again identified only by initials. "Since our letter to Miss
Laing was returned undelivered," one wrote, "and her father, according to him, does not know where she is, the case will have to
rest until we hear from her again." Finally the minister weighed in:
"He is a heartless 'father' but a very loyal husband. He doesn't
care how Sandra now suffers. Your decision to let the case rest
until she contacts us again is good." He seemed to have felt that
Abraham ought to allow his "daughter"—the intradepartmental

correspondence bristles with snide quotation marks—to be reclassified as coloured.

On April 7, 1972, Sandra and Petrus's son Henry was born at Jenny and Pa Zwane's *kraal*. Petrus was going to visit his uncle for a few days, Lisa was away, and a very pregnant Sandra, nervous about staying in Kromkrans alone, asked to be dropped off at Jenny's. "When my water broke and I started to have pains, Jenny made me lie down on the bed," Sandra recalls. "She got on her knees behind me. She held me up and kissed me on my cheeks. I started yelling, loud mother-cries, but Jenny told me to be calm, and I was. Jenny wasn't a real midwife, but she remembered the way her mother and her aunty had helped her. Little Gogo was there, too. Jenny looked up and asked the Zwane ancestors to help me." Sandra says she thought about her own mother and for a moment felt a thorn in her heart. "I wished my mum was there with me. But at this time of my life I felt that Jenny was more of a mother to me."

The baby came quickly and then Sandra thought only of him. "Yes, the pains and pushing hurt, like someone was trying to turn me inside out, but I was so happy when Jenny caught Henry and put him on my belly. Jenny danced and clapped her hands. Then she went outside to talk to the sky and thank the *amadlozi*, the ancestors, for helping with the birth."

When Petrus came home two days later, he was very happy to find he had a new son. He chose the name Henry; Sandra can't remember why. "I think it was his grandfather. The other children came over to meet their new brother. Lisa came, too—it was nice. All day the relatives came to say congratulations. Jenny and Pa Zwane served the neighbors beer and a drink called *mocheu*, made of mealie, like porridge but soft. They can't come near, but must sit away from us. The baby's navel must fall off before they come close. Only once the cord came off could Petrus touch the baby. We believed that children would not become sick if other people didn't come close during this time. The only people who came near the baby then were me and Jenny. I stayed in bed for ten days after the birth of Henry, and Petrus slept in another room in the same house."

Before Henry was born, Jenny called Sandra *Kotee*, daughter-in-law. Now she began calling her *Mamakahenry*, Henry's Mother, according to Swazi custom. Jenny helped Sandra breastfeed Henry, which was sweet and satisfying, and she loved the feel of him tied on her back, kept close all the time.

As soon as she could, Sandra went to the nearest public telephone and rang her mother to announce Henry's birth. They'd only spoken a few times in the year since Sandra left. "She said I must bring him to show her. I should come in the middle of the day, she said, so my father wouldn't know. I was nervous about seeing her, but so proud of my baby."

Sandra hadn't traveled the road to Brereton Park or seen her mother's face since the day she and Petrus eloped. She was nervous and excited. Petrus dropped Sandra and Henry off close to the shop and then waited down the road in the parked car.

Mother and daughter hugged and cried. "She looked the same," Sandra says. "She was just sad to see me." Sannie held Henry and kissed him. "She said, 'He's a beautiful boy.' We stood outside on the *stoep* for the whole visit. Stefaan took care of customers." Sannie didn't invite Sandra into the house. She asked if Sandra was all right, and said she missed her. Sandra told her mother she missed her, too. "She said my father musn't find me because he's very angry. The visit was only ten minutes. My mum was scared my father would come. I just felt I had to show her my child. He was her grandchild. She was happy to see the baby. She wasn't angry with me and she didn't scold me. She was never really angry with me.

"Leon was still in South West Africa, she said, and Adriaan was away at his first year in Piet Retief. We couldn't visit for very long."

When it was time to leave, Sannie gave Sandra a box she'd already packed with food, diapers, and clothing for all the children. "I also let my mother know I needed my birth certificate because I wanted to get an identification document. I don't remember if she gave it to me that day, or later. Then she kissed me and said I must write or phone and that I must look after myself." Sandra walked back down the road to the car. When she got home, she discovered that Sannie had tucked her doll Melinda into the box.

Sandra enjoyed being a mother, although at sixteen she was still a child herself in many ways. "In Kromkrans, sometimes I left the baby with Jenny and went to the next street to play *zingando* with girls my own age." She and Petrus got along well enough, although he could be moody sometimes. She just stayed out of his way then. They listened to *kwela* music on the radio, bouncy, jivey, tin-whistle tunes. When the news came on, Sandra didn't pay attention. She worked in the garden, chopped wood, carried water, cooked, cleaned, cared for Henry, and visited with relatives and neighbors.

Some of Petrus's uncles and cousins belonged to the African Zionist Church; members met in people's houses or garages to sing and praise the Lord. Blacks were banned from the Dutch Reformed Church and many belonged to evangelical Christian sects. Petrus didn't go to church; he consulted *sangomas*, indigenous healers and diviners who cast spells, interpreted omens, and consulted the *amadlozi*—the spirits of dead ancestors. Sandra translates *sangoma* as "witch doctor." Lots of black Christians consulted *sangomas* then and still do, Sandra says.

Sometimes at night Petrus woke up gasping for air. He told Sandra he was plagued by a *tokoloshe*, an invisible gremlin that sat on his chest, pressing on his heart and making it hard for him to breathe. The *tokoloshi* are mischievous spirits, troublemakers sometimes summoned by an enemy. Petrus also worried that his neighbors might pay a *sangoma* to order up lightning attacks. During summer's fierce electrical storms, he feared that a bolt would come zinging down from the sky and fry him. Sandra isn't sure why he worried so. "Maybe he thought people were jealous because I was white and they believed I brought him luck." Petrus went to a *sangoma* himself for *tokoloshe* repellent and a special anti-lightning potion that he sprinkled in the corners of the yard.

Sandra's personal credo incorporates elements of both her early religious training and Petrus's faith in *sangomas*. The God she'd learned about in the Dutch Reformed Church seemed to sit in exactly the same place on the chest as the *tokoloshe*, and was just as ready to steal your breath if you should forget and break his many rules. In Sandra's view, the warding off of evil is a major component of both belief systems. In Tsakane, she consulted a *profet,* a kind of Christian traditional healer, about sore legs, and the woman told her that jealous neighbors were the cause and prayer the cure. Sandra talks to God sometimes when she's alone. "I think he's a person like us," she says. "An old white man. I thank him for helping me get things I wanted, and I ask him to look after my children." Sandra believes that miracles are possible, but not probable.

Petrus may have been anxious about curses, but Sandra felt no danger in her life. She had a scary moment when she was pregnant again and she and Petrus rode Pa Zwane's horses across the Mkomazi River when they were visiting an uncle. Her horse lost its footing and got swept away in the current, but Petrus rescued her. Pa Zwane was angry at his son for being so reckless when she was expecting, but Sandra relished the adventure and attention.

Sandra telephoned Sannie to say that her second child, Elsie, had been born on July 21, 1973, in Kromkrans, again with the help of Jenny and Little Gogo. In early 1974, when Elsie was about seven months old, Sandra brought the baby to meet her white Ouma Sannie. Henry and Jenny came, too. As they had the last time, mother and daughter hugged and cried, and once more she sent Sandra home with clothing and food. "Again, Ma said I can't stay long. She was scared my father would come home. The visit lasted less than thirty minutes. My mum gave us a cooldrink and a packet of sweets to take home. As I was about to leave, my mum said to me that they were thinking of selling the shops and moving somewhere else, but that she didn't know when the shops will be sold or where they will be moving to. She said I must look after myself. She also said that I should not make contact with her again. I was sad, but I knew it was my father's idea, not hers."

"But it was your mother who let you go when you ran away to Swaziland," I said when Sandra told me this. "How do you know it wasn't her idea?"

"It wasn't," Sandra said quietly but emphatically. That Sannie was in any way complicit in her exile is an idea Sandra will not entertain. "I thought my mum would find a way to make contact with me, and I tried not to think about her." Instead she turned her mind to the daily details of life with Petrus and her children in Kromkrans.

Sandra still needed a national identity document, required by law for anyone over sixteen. So in February 1974, when she was eighteen, Petrus drove her to the Department of Home Affairs in Pretoria to apply for one. "The person there said if they give me a white I.D., they're going to take my kids away because a white woman can't have kids who are not white. So I wanted to become coloured again." Two years after her first attempt to change her classification from white to coloured, Sandra filed an affidavit through a lawyer in Pretoria; she doesn't remember how she found him. It read, in part:

> I am happy with my boyfriend and our children. I want to obtain permission to be classified and/or reclassified as a Swazi and I do not want to be classified and/or considered white because I want to keep my children and also proceed to marry my present boyfriend. I have for all intents and purposes lived as a Swazi woman for the last four years and I have given birth to Swazi children and I intend remaining a Swazi and I pray that I be permitted to continue living as a Swazi in which group I have been accepted as a Swazi daughter-in-law. I do not intend to go back and live as a white.

Since she was under twenty-one, she still needed her father's permission to be reclassified. Once again, he refused when the authorities contacted him. The magistrate at Carolina sent Sandra and Petrus a summons, and when they appeared before him, he warned them to stop living together in Kromkrans. "He told me to go home to my parents," Sandra recalls, "and he said the children could go to a coloured orphanage. He said he would be in touch with us." The magistrate's threats worried Sandra, but she had no intention of leaving Petrus or giving up her children. She decided to drop her quest for an identity card, and the magistrate didn't pursue the matter. "At that time in apartheid, if people find you without an I.D. they lock you up," she says. "But no police ever asked me for my I.D." Somehow the newspapers found out that Sandra had requested a race classification change. Perhaps some reporter bored with being stuck out in the *bundu*, the bush, spotted the once-famous name of Sandra Laing on a docket and tracked her to Kromkrans. Or maybe the lawyer in Pretoria thought the publicity would help Sandra. In any case, an article called DAD STOPS SANDRA GOING BLACK appeared in the *Rand Daily Mail* of March 5, 1974. The *Cape Times* headlined its story WHITE GIRL RACE VICTIM PLANS TO MARRY BLACK. Sandra's request for reclassification was also covered in the Afrikaans press. SALLOW SANDRA NOW WANTS TO BECOME BLACK, *Rapport* announced. Translated, the story reads in part:

> Sandra Laing, the sallow [*blas,*yellowish or dark-brown] daughter of white parents who eight years ago drew the attention of the world to her when she was reclassified Coloured, now lives with a Bantu. They have two children.
>
> The girl, who after a political storm, was reclassified White, has now applied to be reclassified either Coloured or Bantu . . . Her being a white, a magistrate has warned her not to live with her black man. But Sandra, aged eighteen, says, "I want to stay with Petrus . . . Tell the world that is the way I want to live . . ."
>
> An obviously confused Sandra spoke this week openly to *Rapport* about her struggle for "identity" . . . She said she could not understand why she was still persecuted by white society. The same society that had always rejected her now demands of her to desert her Bantu "husband" and two non-white children. Sandra Laing and Petrus cannot understand all these matters . . .

The Transvaler, a National Party newspaper, weighed in a few days later with a piece headed SANDRA'S BANTU IS THE LAST STRAW. The article is notable in that it contains the Laings' first published repudiation of their daughter after years of supporting her in the press. An Afrikaner friend suggested to me that perhaps after the newspaper accounts revealing that Sandra lived with a black man and had children with him, they felt that they had to protect their sons by distancing themselves from Sandra, so the boys wouldn't be tainted by their sister's transgression.

"Sandra will have to make her own path through life now [. . . *eie paadjie oopkap*: chop open her own little path]. My husband and I want nothing to do with her. You and the government can decide what becomes of her now." That was said by a bitter Mrs. Sannie Laing, 57, yesterday in her shop in Brereton Park. Sandra, 18, is their only daughter, and for the past three years she has been living with a Bantu, Petrus Zwane, in a location near Carolina. Now they want to get married and Sandra wants to be classified as Coloured or Bantu.

With dark rings under her eyes and feeling very heartbroken and distressed, Mrs. Laing said that she and her husband considered committing suicide after they had read the newspaper articles on Sunday. "If it wasn't for our youngest son Andre [sic], 11, we would have made an end to our lives. But Andre needs us. My other son Leon, 28, who lives in South West Africa, is also dead unhappy about the whole affair."

. . . According to Mrs. Laing, Sandra tells lies. "She told the newspapers that I knew about her relationship with Petrus. This is a blatant lie. I never knew about the relationship and do not approve of it. She did not want to listen to her parents, and therefore she will now have to bear the consequences of her actions. My husband and I did everything in our power to give Sandra a good upbringing."

The only comment a dismayed Mr. Abraham Laing, 63, would make, was that he did not want to see his daughter at all.

But he elaborated a few days later for the *Rand Daily Mail* in a short article headlined "Mother: She has rejected us."

Yesterday, [Laing's] mother, a postmistress at Brereton Park, near Piet Retief, said: "We don't care what the Government does with her. We have tried to help her but she has rejected us." Her husband said, "I blame this on the Department of Education for pushing her out of school in the first place and the Department of the Interior for classifying her as Coloured. This, and the newspaper publicity that followed, left deep scars on Sandra's young mind and outlook."

. . . Mr. Laing said, "We can't have her at home now that she has lived so long as an African."

"I didn't know about the newspaper articles, so how could they make scars?" Sandra said, frowning slightly, when she read this story for the first time in 2001. We were working our way through her government file. "I think it was my father's idea that they didn't want to see me." Even after reading a number of stories in which Sannie is quoted as saying she and her husband want nothing to do with Sandra and that she's washing her hands of her daughter, Sandra doesn't hold her mother accountable. "Maybe my mother is saying those things because I broke their hearts when I wanted to be classified as coloured after they struggled to keep me white," Sandra says. "At the time, I didn't know about their struggle. I know now. I feel sorry for her. I feel sorry for him, too. I didn't know how hard they worked to keep me white.

"But if they told me then, I probably still wouldn't have stayed, because I was in love with Petrus."

An Afrikaner friend a little older than Sandra, a man who'd read about her case when he was a boy growing up outside Johannesburg, had an interesting take on the "Last Straw" stories.

"For the Laings to have chosen to define their family as consisting of five people, not four, would have been a rather schizophrenic thing to do," he wrote in an e-mail. "The entire society around them hinged on the removal of all such ambiguities, and employed the full force of the state and the much greater force of convention and respectability to achieve this. Cutting off Sandra was the sane thing to do: imagine the strain if they had not. Of course one can now say *ja*, but they should have been brave, they should have acted in a moral manner. But how many people here did that then, on this the most intimate level? By cutting off Sandra the Laings sought simply to disappear into society; they wanted to become like everyone else around them; they wanted to be invisible. Every time Sandra reappeared [in the press] they were dragged back into the light, where they alone then had to bear the full weight of the moral contradiction inherent in apartheid."

Almost two years after she'd last seen her mother, Sandra says, two journalists came to Kromkrans and asked her to accompany them on a trip to Brereton Park to visit Sannie Laing. She can't remember what newspaper they were from. "The children stayed at home with Jenny," Sandra says. "When we arrived at the shop where my mother was supposed to be, I found the shop to be empty and a black family in the house where my parents used to stay. I knew my parents were thinking about moving, but still I was shocked. The black people in the house knew who I was, but I could not remember them. They told me that my parents had sold the shop and moved to Pongola. They also told me that my parents now only had the one shop. I told the journalists that we would not be able to go to Pongola because my dad will also be at the shop. They took me back home and they did write a story about me, but I can't remember what paper it was for."

After the trip to Brereton Park, Sandra wrote to her mother several times. "I just wrote on the envelope 'S. Laing, Pongola.' But I got no answer."

20

BLACK SPOT

O N JUNE 16, 1976, RIOT POLICE SHOT AND KILLED
an unarmed thirteen-year-old black boy, Hector
Pieterson, at a peaceful demonstration in Soweto,
the vast black township outside Johannesburg.
Students were boycotting schools to protest a government order
that math and social studies lessons be taught in Afrikaans. After
the shooting, riots erupted in townships all over South Africa. Angry crowds set fires outside Carolina, not far from Pa Zwane's *kraal*.
The government acted swiftly to quell the resistance banning all public gatherings except sports events, postponing the opening of black
schools, and passing the Internal Security Law, which allowed the
arrest and unlimited detention without trial of anyone suspected
of "threatening public order." The suspension of civil rights was
necessary, Prime Minister John Vorster said, in order to fight the
communist threat posed by the antiapartheid movement.

Sandra, pregnant at the time with her third child, remembers
hearing about the riots on the radio, and feeling sorry for the boy
who died and the hundreds of children who were jailed, Petrus said,
in brutal house-to-house police sweeps. "But I didn't know about
political things," she says. "I didn't read the newspapers and I didn't
really listen to the news." Yet "political things" continued to affect
her life directly. At the end of June, an article with no apparent

news peg ran in the Johannesburg *Sunday Times*; it hinted at the up-
heavals to come for Sandra and her family.

BLACK IS BEAUTIFUL NOW FOR WHITE SANDRA

. . . Sandra Laing, 20, said this week:

"We are as happy as circumstances permit—but we will
be even happier in November—my 21st birthday—when we
are getting married. We have to wait until then because my
father has refused us permission to marry. I have already
applied for reclassification as a Black and I don't foresee any
problems." . . . Sandra said: ". . . I have been fully accepted by
my neighbors and regard myself as Black to the fingertips.
Petrus is a gentle, considerate husband and father. No girl
could have wished for a better man. If there's a cloud hanging
over our happiness, it's that we will probably have to move to
a homeland next year. The authorities have already warned
the people at Kromkrans that the area is White and that they
must be prepared to leave. Petrus and I have been very happy
here. It will be a wrench to go."

Sandra and Petrus were about to be the victims of a forced relocation. Kromkrans was what the government called a black spot—an
all-black community in the middle of a white area. The grand plan
was to eliminate all black spots by relocating the inhabitants.

Not long after the *Sunday Times* article appeared, notices went
up in Kromkrans announcing that the residents had two weeks to
pack up their lives. Government workers started painting big numbers on front doors, indicating that the houses were going to be
knocked down by bulldozers.

Petrus's son Lucas can't recall the exact date of the removal—
the government notices referred to it as a "resettlement"—but he
remembers the event vividly. "Government trucks and bulldozers
came and the men said, leave, we're pushing down your house. They
gave you two weeks warning. The government told you where you
must go—you didn't have a choice. My father was angry." Sandra

doesn't remember being particularly alarmed by the move. As long as she was with the children and Petrus, and Jenny was nearby, anything that happened was okay with her.

From 1976 through 1979, 7,600 people were kicked out of Kromkrans. The Surplus People's Project, an antiapartheid group that documented forced removals, estimates that between 1960 and 1983, more than 3.5 million Africans were moved—always to someplace worse—in order to suit the needs of apartheid policy, the ultimate goal of which was to remove all black people from South Africa.

This vanishing act would be accomplished, according to the program known as "separate development," by relocating as many black people as possible to one of ten so-called homelands, according to their tribal origins. Never mind that millions of families had left their traditional tribal areas generations before to live in cities, or that intermarriage often rendered tribal affiliation meaningless. Any black South African could be moved to an area that the government decided was his or her area of origin, sometimes based on the language spoken, sometimes on names or customs. It was as if all Americans with Irish-sounding last names were deported to Ireland because the government deemed it to be their ancestral home.

The plan was for the displaced South Africans to become citizens of these homelands, also known as tribal reserves, or bantustans. The homelands were crowded desolate places, with barren farmland, rudimentary housing, no industry, no jobs and little infrastructure, each run by a black puppet government controlled by South Africa. Eventually, these ten Bantustans would be granted independence, and all the people who lived there would lose their South African citizenship. Their labor would still be required—but they'd be foreign laborers. "It is accepted Government policy," said a government circular published in 1967 by the Department of Bantu Administration and Development, "that the Bantu are only temporarily residents in the European areas of the Republic for as long as they offer their labour there. As soon as they become, for one reason or another, no longer fit for work . . . they are expected to return to . . . the territory of the national unit where they fit ethnically, if they were not born and bred in the homeland." Between 1976 and 1981, the government created four homelands—none recognized as independent by the world community—and denationalized nine million black South Africans, who couldn't enter the land of their birth without a passport.

Sandra and Petrus were sent to Tjakastad—a "relocation camp," the government called it—near the Swazi border in a Bantustanin-waiting called KwaNgwane. In the distance, they could see pretty green hills, some of the planet's oldest, studded with huge, tawny boulders heaving up through the grass. Closer at hand, two thousand displaced people were already living in makeshift shelters, with no running water or even communal taps. "We fetched water from the river," Sandra says. "It wasn't far. Lots of people went with water in basins on their heads. Petrus fetched our water in steel drums. We dug our own outhouse, like everyone else." Sandra didn't know the details of the relocation; she didn't know that they'd been sent to a homeland, or what a homeland was. "I just knew black people were poor and white people had all the land. I knew that we had to build a new house and start over again."

Sandra and the children slept at Pa Zwane's *kraal* for a few nights while Petrus and some other men built a rondavel on the edge of Tjakastad. First they made a cylindrical room out of concrete blocks, and then a frame for the conical roof out of sticks. The workmen and their wives had already gathered a lot of grass and tied it in fat bunches. "I watched, but I couldn't help because I was too pregnant," Sandra says. The men spread the bunches on the roof-frame in thick layers, then sewed them to the framework with big needles threaded with string from unraveled burlap mealie-meal bags. After the thatch was sewn on, the men fastened a big flattened tin can to the very top so rain couldn't come in the smokehole. The rondavel was cozy and waterproof.

Petrus also built a temporary kitchen of corrugated tin, a small room a few yards away from the rondavel, with open space between the walls and roof. Concrete blocks kept the roof on in a wind. In the kitchen were a coal stove, a huge storage pot filled with rice, a sink with a flowered oilcloth skirt, and two shelves. He also built a tiny wooden *spaza* shop, no more than a kiosk, with a counter in front.

Henry, who was four and a half, and baby Jenny lived with Petrus and Sandra. Elsie, nearly three, stayed with her grandmother Jenny to be near her half-sister Stiena, Petrus's daughter with Lisa. Informal fostering was common in the black community. Sandra saw Elsie several times a week, and liked the way Petrus's extended family was intimately involved in childrearing. She thought it was good for the children and good for her.

The move didn't change Sandra's daily life very much: everything that mattered stayed the same. She chopped wood every day for the coal stove, and washed clothes every few days in a big tin tub that the family also used for bathing three or four times a week. In between, they washed their feet in a small plastic tub. Sandra planted a garden—tomatoes, potatoes, pumpkins, spinach, and onions—and kept chickens. Petrus also brought her baby goats to feed by bottle until they were big enough to sell. For his vegetable business, he needed only his *bakkie* and some gasoline. When he was off delivering vegetables, Sandra worked in the *spaza* shop. She felt lucky that Petrus made his living in a way that didn't require him to spend eleven months a year away at the mines and factories, like a lot of the men in Tjakastad. And she felt lucky that the family had plenty of vegetables, milk from the goats, bread and jam every day, meat at least twice a week, eggs, cheese and margarine regularly.

The rondavel was fine. They'd brought the couch, the bed, and a good table from Kromkrans, and she hung a rug on the wall with a picture woven into it of windmills and tulips along a Dutch canal. Petrus began building a brick house next to the rondavel, the nicest they'd ever had, with a big kitchen and three other rooms. Although getting kicked out is never a good thing, Sandra says, she was happy in Tjakastad. Elsie and Henry were lively and smart, and little Jenny, born with the help of the grandmother who shared her name, was strong and happy. "We stayed well, and Jenny was a big, beautiful girl."

Petrus, however, remained angry about the relocation. Lucas

Zwane recalls that his father and other people from Kromkrans complained that the government would never move white people around like this, sticking them in some godforsaken place with bad land and no water taps. He was better off than other men in Tjakastad, who felt that the government, by restricting access to jobs and housing and denying them freedom of movement, had reduced them to slavery and made it impossible for them to provide for their families. Some steeled themselves and kept working. Others responded to the pressure and poverty by drinking, or smoking *dagga*, marijuana, introduced to South Africa by the Portuguese in the sixteenth century. Many took out their frustration on their wives.

Petrus became more and more irritable. He'd always been a jealous man, Sandra says, but now his behavior was ridiculous. "When the neighbors' brother walked from their house to the outhouse, Petrus would say, 'Why is that man walking up and down like that? It's just to look at you!'" At first, Sandra wasn't bothered. She was flattered, in fact. "I just thought it meant he loved me and didn't want anyone else to have me."

When Little Jenny was seven months old, in May 1977, she became feverish. Sandra and Big Jenny tried "rubbing out" the baby—massaging her with Vaseline and Haarlemensis, an old-fashioned remedy that Sannie used to sell at her shop. "Then Jenny got *kopstuipe* [literally, head seizures]—a high, high fever and the soft spot of the baby goes in."

In KwaNgwane, fifteen doctors served 200,000 people; Sandra was lucky to find one for Jenny. There'd been a big cholera outbreak, but the doctor said that wasn't the problem. Sandra doesn't know what caused the seizures. "He gave her medicine because she was vomiting and her tummy was running. But she got sicker. When she was sick two days, Petrus went to a *sangoma* lady two streets from us. When he came back, Jenny was panting, and when she stopped doing that, we saw that she was busy dying. Petrus tried to use the *muti*, the medicine the *sangoma* gave—it was something to burn on a plate, some herbs maybe. But Jenny died that night. *Ag*, we were so sad! I cried for days and days. Jenny came to sit with me.

"Petrus went to buy a small coffin, and we buried her the day after she died in the Tjakastad cemetery. We prayed and sang songs in Swazi. It was a small funeral; I just made tea and sandwiches for the family. Jenny stayed with me a couple of weeks, maybe a month. Oh, I was sad."

Petrus, Sandra believes, blamed her for Jenny's death and thought she somehow failed to protect the baby. He began to drink excessively, and he thought all men were looking at Sandra. He didn't like it when she was alone at the shop and men came to buy "house beer," then sat outside the shop drinking. Sandra didn't mind because it meant more money. "He accused me of fooling around with the men who came to the shop, and the man who lived next door. He used to park the car far away from the shop and sneak up on me to try and catch me. I wasn't cheating on him. I loved him."

A journalist from England came to film Sandra and Petrus. Antony Thomas had already spoken with Mr. Van Tonder and others in Piet Retief for the documentary *The South African Experience: The Search for Sandra Laing*. He interviewed Sandra and Petrus, and filmed them going about their lives in Tjakastad. Petrus insisted they be paid for their time and trouble, and Thomas gave them enough to expand the small *spaza*. That's the first time Sandra remembers earning cash for telling her story.

Antony Thomas told Sandra that he was going to Pongola to find and film her parents. She didn't see the documentary Thomas made until almost fifteen years later. In it, Thomas surprises Abraham and Sannie in their general dealer store and asks them if they're related to Sandra Laing. "She's our child," Abraham says in English, a polite smile never leaving his face. But he won't answer any questions about her. "I'm not prepared to talk about her," he says. Thomas asks Sannie whether she hears from Sandra. "Yes, I hear from her," Sannie replies, in a small voice, glancing at her husband.

"Do you visit her?" Thomas asks.

"No," Sannie says.

"Why not?"

A sad half smile and another sideways glance at Abraham. "My husband doesn't want to see her."

The film aired in England, the rest of Europe, and the United States, but not in South Africa. Television had arrived in 1976, over Hertzog's dead body, but the government banned *The Search for Sandra Laing* as "objectionable," and it wasn't shown there until after the fall of apartheid. Nevertheless, a few enterprising reporters once again tracked down Sandra after the film was shown abroad. A piece that ran in the *Rand Daily Mail* in early October 1978 contains several inaccuracies but gives chilling hints of Petrus's decline that corroborate Sandra's memory of his behavior:

SANDRA FINDS HOME IN A HOMELAND

South Africa's harsh racial laws have driven Miss Sandra Laing, 21, a long way from the comforts of her white family. Today she is the barefooted mother of two small black children, tending her vineyard in the Tjakastad Kwa-Ngwane homeland near the Swaziland border.

The reporter recounts what he calls Sandra's "fall from cushioned privilege," misstating the location of her school, her age when she ran off with Petrus, Henry's birthdate, and the name of her dead daughter. He continues:

The *Rand Daily Mail* visited the couple at their Tjakastad home and found them full of beans and bounce, involved in building a new four-room home next to a shop they own . . . Mr. Zwane, standing nearby, eyed our car suspiciously as it neared them. At his side was a ferocious-looking bullmastiff called "Bull."

After establishing our identities, Mr. Zwane started driving hard bargains. "You just can't come all the way from Johannesburg to write a story about me and not pay for it, man," he started. "How much have you got at least? Look, there were others here before you and they paid R300 with a smile to get my story and Sandra's. Now you, as my black brothers, I'm prepared to treat leniently with money—how much are you prepared to pay?

"If you have no money on you, you'd better drive back to Johannesburg and speak to your bosses well about this story. You are working and get paid for this, and there's no reason why I should not capitalize on our story—we are a struggling family and we need every cent to establish ourselves in this new territory," he said.

Payment of R80 loosened Mr. Zwane's tongue and he spoke his heart out about the troubles besetting him in this "new place" . . . Looking furtively around him, Mr. Zwane dropped his voice to a whisper and said, "The trouble with us here is not classification and color issues.

"I am having loads of trouble from men who want to snatch Sandra away from me. I cannot leave her for long at home or at the shop before some local men start pestering her with proposals of marriage and a happy future."

The reporter goes on to state, incorrectly, that Sandra and Petrus visit her parents often, and that the Laings dote on the children. But he seems, Sandra thinks, to have caught accurately something of the man Petrus was becoming:

As the *Mail t*eam left, Mr. Zwane was thinking aloud about applying for a firearm to ward off his ardent rivals for Sandra. His last bitter words to us were:

"They all want her because they think she brought me good luck in business and family life. Go back to Johannesburg and come to us with more money and I will tell you the grand plans we have for the future."

Petrus began beating Sandra when he was drunk, which was often, working himself up over an imagined infidelity or sign of disrespect.

At first he slapped her. Then he began hitting her with a *sjambok*, a whip traditionally fashioned from leather thongs or rhinoceros hide. Petrus's was made of tough, black tire rubber. "He beat me until my skin turned purple and blue, on my back, shoulders, and head," she says. Her back was always full of deep *sjambok* cuts; blood ran in streams from her head. "I washed my head over a big tin bowl of water. Henry was only five at the time. He took the bloody water and threw it outside. Henry was very angry with Petrus, because he always saw when Petrus beat me. It happened often. He never hit the children, just me."

Petrus drank away the money meant to stock the shop, and then got angry with Sandra when the shelves were bare. Often they were down to a few African cabbages, like big green heads, and half a loaf of brown bread. "I remember once my arm was blue when I went to visit Jenny. She asked me, 'Why is he doing that?' and I said, 'He drinks the money for the shop.' She talked to him and told him he must stop, but he didn't.

"Petrus was a good man," Sandra says. "Just the drinking was bad. He beat me blue and purple. After, he'd make a cloth in hot water with salt and say, '*Ngujacolisa, Mamakahenry, bengida kiew aye geyippinde, yuwe ogekwa tisayo.*' I'm sorry, Henry's mother, I was drunk. I don't do it again. But you made me angry."

Sandra worried that somehow his anger was her fault; she wasn't sure how. Men beat their wives, it was too often a part of life, Sandra saw, whether you were an Afrikaner woman or a black one. It was just something women lived with. But Petrus was going too far. Sandra thought there was a good chance he would kill her.

Jenny sometimes told Swazi tales as she braided her rugs. The children loved listening to her stories, and so did Sandra. She remembers only one of them, about a lazy dassie, also called a hyrax or rock rabbit, a little animal that looks like a pointy-nosed woodchuck. When the gods were handing out tails, the dassie was too lazy to go and stand in line. He asked the other animals to pick one up for him. But by the time they finished getting their own, the gods were all out of tails, and that's why the dassie has only a stump. The moral of that story is a famous Swazi saying, *Imbila yeswela umsila ngekula yetela.* Sandra translates it as, "If you don't do things for yourself, you might get nothing." Maybe that story was on her mind when she decided it was time to run away again.

21

THE NEXT ESCAPE

P ETRUS HAD A FRIEND, DAVID RADEBE, A MECHANIC FIVE years older than he, who split his time between Tjakastad and KwaThema, a black township south-east of Johannesburg. David had a wife and grown children there, but he liked the countryside. When he came to the shop for groceries and beer, he was calm, pleasant, and kind, and always had time for a chat with Sandra. She confided in him about the beatings Petrus gave her. David was sympathetic, although he didn't intervene or put in a word with her husband. "That wasn't the way men did with men," Sandra says. She began to daydream that David would rescue her from Petrus. "I slept with him twice because I hoped that would make him help me," she says. "I didn't love David; I still loved Petrus. But I was afraid that he would beat me to death without meaning to. I asked David if he would take me to KwaThema with him. I'd never been to KwaThema. I didn't know what it was like, but I thought it had to be better than that side. David knew the beatings were getting worse and worse, so he said he would take me."

On a chilly winter afternoon in late June or early July 1979, while Petrus was off with the car in Barberton or Nelspruit picking up supplies, Sandra locked the shop, placed the key on the seat of the *bakkie*, and hurried the children to David's house. Henry was seven and Elsie was six. They took only the clothes on their backs, a plastic bag with toothbrushes and a few toys, and a bit of cash that Sandra had been taking from the shop till and hiding in the kitchen under her rice pot. She didn't want to pack anything, so Petrus wouldn't notice right away that they'd left.

The three of them hid in David's house all day. Very late that night, he drove them to KwaThema, about four hours away. "I told Henry and Elsie that we're going because Petrus is hitting me all the time," she says. Sandra felt great sorrow at leaving her dear mother-in-law Jenny and her stepchildren without saying good-bye, but she believed her survival depended on slipping away that very minute.

David brought Sandra and the children to stay with his sister Sophie, who lived with her husband and three children in KwaThema. The Laings—the children always kept Sandra's last name—stayed in a one-room shack behind Sophie's house. In return for food and shelter, Sandra helped with the housework. For a bit of extra cash, she cleaned other people's houses and took in laundry.

KwaThema was built in 1952, on empty grasslands twenty-five miles southeast of Johannesburg, to house mine and factory workers employed in the nearby small towns of Boksburg and Springs and black people forcibly removed from white areas in Johannesburg.

The townships were an experiment in social engineering, all laid out according to the same grim specifications—situated far enough outside cities so they couldn't be seen, with tiny, cheap, featureless matchbox houses, often made of asbestos and without indoor plumbing, set in rows so riot police could fire between them easily in case of an uprising. The dirt roads were wide enough to allow a tank to turn. Surrounded by an expanse of empty ground, officially known as parklands but referred to privately by administrators as "machine-gun belts," townships lacked the simple blessings of shade or a winding street.

But by the time Sandra arrived in 1979, KwaThema had spilled out of its grid. The inhabitants had eased its angles with gardens and ornate fences, planted trees, built illegal backyard huts

like the one behind Sophie's house, and tossed up ragged squatter camps of cardboard, flattened cans, and corrugated tin. The
crowded township had the feel of a giant *kraal*, dilapidated but in-
tensely alive. Restrictive laws bred fierce competition for scarce resources, petty jealousies, crime, and violence. The same conditions
engendered generosity and a strong sense of community, of *ubuntu,*
a word that literally means "humanness" in Xhosa and Zulu.
Ubuntu is the indigenous African humanistic philosophy reflected
in the saying "A person is a person only through other people."
Sandra defines it as "to share with people." Sometimes *ubuntu* ex-
isted more in theory than in practice, but it was a useful ideal. A
center of strong support for the banned African National Congress,
KwaThema was rowdy and jivey, with a nervous energy absent in
quiet, rural Tjakastad.

A low fog of smoke hung over the township, generated by
coal stoves and the coal-burning tin heaters people lit outside with
kindling and then carried into their small homes when the coals
began to glow. So many people in one place, to make such a big
cloud, Sandra thought. KwaThema intimidated her a little, but
she felt she'd done the right thing by coming, the only thing she
could think of.

A few days after Sandra left, Petrus came looking for her. "Some
people in Tjakastad had told him they'd seen me walking with the
kids toward David's," Sandra says. "He went to the police station
in KwaThema and came with the police to David's house. I was staying that time with Sophie, David's sister. The police looked all over
the house, in the wardrobes, with Petrus and David. David's woman
was upset. Petrus was very mad. David said to the police, 'Ask him
if he's married to the person he's looking for.' They did. Petrus said,
'No, but she is my wife. I took her from home.' The police said, 'We
can't help you. This person isn't your wife, she's just a girlfriend.'
David told me that night.

"Later, I found out Petrus went to the witch doctor, the *sangoma,*
and took my doll Melinda to help the witch doctor get me back.
That time when I was sleeping at Sophie's, I could hear Petrus call
me at night in my dreams: *'Mamakahenry, Mamakahenry!'* Always I

er a story about Sandra's expulsion appeared in *Die Beeld*, an Afrikaner newspaper,
ith African and foreign reporters and photographers flocked to Brereton Park. Her
ner, Abraham Laing, hoped that sympathetic press coverage would help Sandra's case.
re and below Sandra, age 11, with her mother, Sannie, in 1966.
imes Media Collection, Museum Africa

Abraham and Sandra, 1966.
© *IMAGES24.co.za*

Sandra and her baby brother, Adriaan, age one, 1966. Brother Leon, seven years older than Sandra, was away at school when these pictures were taken.
© *Times Media Collection, Museum Africa*

Sannie Laing in 1966 with her two younger children, Sandra and Adriaan, born ten years apart.
© *Times Media Collection, Museum Africa*

The Laing's housekeeper, Nora, holding Adriaan, with Sandra, 1966.
© *Times Media Collection, Museum Africa*

Sandra in 1966, age 11, during the time Abraham was preparing a case to be heard before The Supreme Court.
© *Times Media Collection, Museum Africa*

...dra and Sannie in Brereton Park, circa 1966.
© *Associated Press*

Sandra skipping rope in Brereton Park, some time before the 1967 Supreme Court decision about her race classification.
© *Times Media Collection, Museum Africa*

Sandra in the storeroom of the Brereton Park Shop after being expelled, posing in her school uniform with the correspondence course books sent for by her father. Sannie looks on.
Photograph © David Goldblatt

Abraham Laing in his shop, 1966.
© *Times Media Collection, Museum Africa*

Sandra, 18, holds two-year-old Henry; Petrus holds eight-month-old Elsie in Kromkrans, 1974.
© *IMAGES24.co.za*

From left, Elsie, Henry, and Sandra Laing and Petrus Zwane in front of their rondavel in Tjakastad, where they were relocated by the government in 1977. Sandra, 22, is pregnant with her third child, Jenny, who died in infancy.
Photograph © by David Goldblatt

Sandra in her Tjakastad kitchen, behind the rondavel, 1977.
Photograph © by David Goldblatt

The coal stove in Sandra's corrugate
tin Tjakastad kitchen, 1977.
Photograph © by David Goldblatt

Sandra, left, and a neighbor
wringing laundry outside the
Tjakastad kitchen, 1997.
Photograph © by David Goldblatt

Tjakastad in 1977
a year after the
forced relocation
that brought Petru
and Sandra—and
thousands of othe
black families—to
barren spot near t
Swazi border.
*Photograph ©
by David Goldblatt*

Sandra holding Steve, nearly two, with Anthony, 6, at the gate of the ramshackle rented farmhouse with no electricity, 1989.
© IMAGES24.co.za

Sandra and Jenny Zwane, 85.
©Photo by Anthony Fabian

Sannie and Sandra Laing, reunited in 2000 after a 27-year estrangement.
hotograph by Elizabeth Sejake © Sunday Times

Sandra and her family in Tsakane, 2001. From left, Prins, Sandra, Anthony behind Steve, and husband Johannes Motlaung.
© Photo by Anthony Fabian

Sandra at the count
of the Rainbow
Tuck Shop.
© *IMAGES24.co.za*

Sandra's
three-bedroom
house in
Dalpark,
January 2002.
She revels in
owning "a
place where no
one can kick
me out."
© *Photo by
Anthony Fabian*

Sandra, family
and friends at
her 50th
birthday party
November 20
Sandra, left,
watches as
Johannes, righ
lights the
candles; Steve
18, center, loo
on holding
Prins's son.
© *Photo by
Anthony Fabian*

heard him call me. One night I nearly answered him, and then I woke. David said that if I had answered him in the dream, I would have woken up in Tjakastad. I believed him. Witch doctors can do such things."

Sandra soon discovered she was pregnant. David wasn't at all interested in the baby that was coming, she says, and she saw less and less of him. "I thought, he helped me get here and now I must find some other kind of help." She would need a real job, and that required an official identity card. In September 1979, Sandra again applied to the Department of Home Affairs, asking to be classified as coloured. She took a combi to Pretoria and signed yet another affidavit, which stated, in part, "I don't accept myself as a white and I feel more at home among Coloured and Black people." The clerk said she should hear in a month or two. As soon as she got reclassified and found work, Sandra thought, everything would be all right, or close to all right. At least blood wasn't pouring from her head and the children had food to eat.

Sandra and the children had been at Sophie's two months when Elsie came down with a high fever and a swollen throat. "Sophie told David to take us somewhere else because she didn't want Elsie to die in her house. She asked him, 'Who will bury the child?' A funeral is a big responsibility. People spend money on a good burial. They invite people and have to feed all of them. Sophie had only a little money, and I had none." David moved them to the house of a cousin in Duduza, a township about ten miles away. *Duduza* means "consolation" in Zulu. The township, built after a 1973 forced removal, was yet another collection of matchbox houses and makeshift shacks, most without running water, electricity, or plumbing. Sandra took Elsie to an *inyanga*, a traditional herbal healer, in Duduza. "Elsie still had a high fever and something growing in her throat that kept her from eating," Sandra says. She was terrified that she was about to lose another child. The *inyanga* covered her finger with cloth, dipped it in a medicine called *rooipoeier*, red powder, made from cayenne pepper, and put it down Elsie's throat to kill the infection. "By the very next day Elsie was much better, and could eat soft food. Her strength returned."

David's cousin said she didn't have room for Sandra and the children, so David moved them yet again, to the home of his uncle Thomas Mehunu, who lived with two wives and two daughters in Balfour, yet another township about thirty miles away. Sandra's second son, Prins, was born in their home on March 23, 1980. After Prins came, Sandra began using birth control for the first time—contraceptive shots in her hip every three months, administered at a local clinic.

David didn't contribute to the baby's support, but he did find the family a more stable home in the coloured township of Geluksdal—the name means "Happy Valley" in Afrikaans—near KwaThema. Mrs. Lena Smales, the mother of a friend of David, took them in. "This was really the first time I knew coloured people," Sandra says. "I thought of people as black or white. Coloured didn't mean anything to me." Though the Piet Retief School Committee had petitioned to classify her as coloured, and though she had applied for the designation herself, Sandra had never encountered coloured culture, which, like the black and white cultures with which she was familiar, had its own distinct customs and attitudes, anxieties and advantages, specific privileges and restrictions under the law. In some ways, life in a coloured community felt very familiar to Sandra; everyone spoke Afrikaans—during apartheid, more than half of all Afrikaans speakers were coloured—and attended the coloured branch of the Dutch Reformed Church. People classified as coloured were second-class citizens, but they still had more freedom of movement—no pass required—and better jobs, health care, and education than blacks. Some coloured people identified with the oppressed black majority and were fiercely active in the antiapartheid struggle, but others identified with the white minority, so much so that in the 1994 presidential elections, most coloured voters in the Western Cape, presumably worried about their place in a black-majority government, voted for the National Party, which had imposed the painful hierarchy of color in the first place.

Geluksdal was less crowded and people were better off than in KwaThema; the houses were larger, and there were no squatter camps.

"Mrs. Smales was a nice lady," Sandra says. "When I came from Balfour, the kids wore the same clothes every day, and their shoes were too small. They were going barefoot even in winter." East Rand winters can leave a skin of ice on ponds and puddles. "Their heels cracked with the cold. Mrs. Smales bought them tekkies [sneakers]. We had no money. David didn't even buy Prins's clothes when he was a baby."

This is the way Sandra remembers what happened next: She and the children stayed for a while with Mrs. Smales and her husband, and then with a church friend of the Smaleses, a lady in her nineties named Ouma Katrina, who lived alone. Sandra can't recall why they left the Smales home. To pay for food and rent, she cleaned houses and did laundry and ironing. Henry and Elsie attended school in Geluksdal. Prins had to go to a public hospital twice—once when he burned himself by knocking over a kettle of hot water, and once for a bout of pneumonia.

When Prins was nearly a year old, Sandra became ill. "I began having terrible pains in my womb, and I bled all the time," she says. On a visit to the Geluksdal public clinic, she met Aunt Connie Carelse, who volunteered there and belonged to the same church as Ouma Katrina. Aunt Connie and one of the white nurses at the clinic, Sister [Nurse] Ferreira, took an interest in Sandra and the children.

Aunt Connie offered a different version of their first meeting when Sandra and I visited her in Geluksdal in June 2001. A fierce churchgoer and relentless uplifter of the coloured community, Aunt Connie began the conversation by cheerfully extorting a small donation for her one-woman feeding scheme; she delivers sandwiches every day to children in Geluksdal schools and daycare centers at her own expense, and the *bakkie* she uses needed repairs.

Aunt Connie remembers spotting Sandra from afar before they met face to face. In 1980, workmen began digging along the road from KwaThema to Geluksdal, preparing to bury huge concrete storm pipes, six feet in diameter. Sections of pipe were piled a few hundred feet from the road, ready to be installed. Riding the bus near the construction site one day, Aunt Connie says, she saw in the distance a young woman emerging from a drainpipe. She thought she'd imagined the woman, but a few days later she spied her again. She told her husband, Uncle Peter, to watch for the young woman in the pipes the next time he rode the bus. He saw her, too, and this time she had two children by the hand. So Aunt Connie went hunting for the woman and her children. She found them, she says, living in one of the drainpipes.

"When Sandra told me who she was," Aunt Connie said, "I recognized her name. It was well-advertised in the newspaper. According to the newspapers, she was born into a white family but they disowned her. You know, we come from Jan van Riebeeck, and some of our children look white, and some of them look black and some's got straight hair and some's got *kroessy* [frizzy] hair, and some's got broad figures and some's got slim figures and all this. I don't know if it comes from the forefathers and going backward. It just doesn't matter.

"When Sandra went for food and water, she left the children and told them to play near the pipes and to stay out of sight. I insisted that they leave the drainpipe and come with me, and I found them a place with Ouma Katrina."

As Sandra remembers it, she went from Mrs. Smales' to Ouma Katrina's without Aunt Connie's intervention. "I don't remember staying in the pipes," she says. "Maybe I stayed in the pipes, but maybe I didn't stay in the pipes. I don't think so. The kids did go play in the pipes. Maybe Aunt Connie saw them and thought we were staying there?" Sandra doesn't trust her patchy memory. But Aunt Connie's memory isn't 100 percent trustworthy, either. She got a few things wrong in our chat, confusing Petrus, whom she never met, with David, and confidently misstating several details of Sandra's childhood. Later, I asked Sandra's daughter Elsie if she remembered a time when they lived in some pipes; she frowned and nodded. "It was not nice," she said. She's not sure how long they stayed there. "Not long, I think." She would have been about seven years old. Her mother brought them food, Elsie says, from where, she doesn't know. "We just played, but if we see it's getting dark and my mum is not here, we were crying. At night we had just one or two blankets for me and Henry. My mother didn't worry about it but she just covered us. I was very sick that time." But Henry, who was nine then, doesn't recall living in the pipes, just playing there sometimes. Possibly at some point in their shuttling from place to place, Sandra took the children to play in the pipes while she cleaned houses, and then picked them up at the end of the day. Elsie may have conflated two frightening episodes: the earlier illness and playing alone in the pipes. In any case, both children were unhappy about their move from Tjakastad to Kwa-Thema. Elsie missed her half sister Stiena, and she was upset that she had to repeat a year in school because her teachers in the East Rand considered rural schools inadequate. "And I was missing my father, even if he did drink. He was a nice father. I remember him. He was a friendly man." But Elsie had seen her father hitting her mother; it frightened her and made her cry. Sandra always told the children the truth, Elsie said—that they couldn't go back because their daddy was hitting her.

Whatever the order of events, whether or not she lived in a drainpipe or left the children to play in one while she cleaned houses, Sandra's life had begun to feel like a fever dream. She was constantly ill and worried; she longed for Petrus, but the old Petrus, the one who didn't beat her. Then she got bad news. At the local clinic where Aunt Connie volunteered, the doctors told Sandra she'd have to go to Coronation Hospital, a public facility in Johannesburg, for some tests. "At the hospital, a test showed I had cancer," Sandra says. "I was twenty-five. The doctors told me that they were going to remove my womb." A second biopsy confirmed the first diagnosis, she says. "The doctors told me that after the operation I'd be in the hospital for a long, long time. I was sick, I had no job and Ouma Katrina was very old. I didn't expect her to take care of my children. I had no money to give her and I didn't know what was going to happen to me."

Aunt Connie and Sister Ferreira visited Sandra at the hospital. They both felt strongly that Sandra should give up custody of her children to the Department of Welfare, which would then put them into foster care. "I didn't know what else to do," Sandra says. "That time I didn't think to go back home or let the kids go to Jenny. I was still angry with Petrus and didn't want them to go back. It was a hard decision, but I had to let them go. I was struggling. The doctor told me I had cancer in my womb, and Ouma Katrina couldn't take care of the children. I thought it would be better if the welfare took the children." She wept and begged Aunt Connie and Sister Ferreira to explain to Henry and Elsie that she had no choice. What Prins would think, poor baby, she didn't know.

As the date for surgery approached and Sandra's health and spirits deteriorated, Aunt Connie decided to try for divine intervention. She and Uncle Peter and two other women from their church undertook a vigil, praying and fasting in Sandra's hospital room for twenty-four hours. "After they went home, I was retested," Sandra says. "The cancer was gone." She believes that a miracle occurred. Perhaps the cancer went away; perhaps the miracle was that the doctors gave her a more accurate test the third time. Either way, she says, she's thankful that Aunt Connie and her friends prayed on her behalf, and she regrets that the miracle didn't arrive a little earlier, before her children went into foster care.

"By the time I left the hospital, the children had already been taken," Sandra says. "I moved in with Aunt Connie and Uncle Peter. The lady from the welfare took me to show me where my children were. I was very sad, because they were at another place." Sandra cries every time she tells this part of her story. She says that putting her children in foster care was one of the hardest, saddest things in her life.

The children had been sent to the Van Rijn Place of Safety, an East Rand children's home run by what was then called the Department of Welfare, to wait for a foster-care placement. It's still there, a clean and spacious facility, with a pool and a playground and razor wire coiled atop the perimeter fence that separates it from the industrial area around it. Elsie thinks they stayed there three weeks. "It was a nice place," she says. "We played with other children, and the people were nice, but we worried about my mother and missed my father."

Sandra was able to visit her children a few times at the home; then the welfare department found a foster family. Elizabeth and

Churchman Morris had three children of their own and a simple, pleasant house with a yard, very near the elementary school in Reiger Park, a coloured township outside the industrial town of Boksburg. It was about half an hour by combi from Geluksdal. The Morrises would get a monthly stipend from the government for taking in the children—less than what white foster parents received, but more than what black foster parents got.

"Mrs. Morris was visiting us for two Sundays," Elsie recalls. "Me and Henry told the welfare that if people took us they musn't split us, they must take us all together. And so the Morrises took us all three. I was worried about my mum, but they told us that if we go there to the Morrises, maybe in a month or so my mother is going to come back and get us." It would be nine years before Sandra was able to reclaim her children.

22

LIPSTICK SOUP

SANDRA VISITED THE CHILDREN EVERY OTHER WEEKEND, staying over at the Morrises and helping with the housework. "The kids thought Mrs. Morris was all right," Sandra says, "but her kids didn't want to wash the dishes or clean, and Henry and Elsie must do that. They wanted me to bring them home, and I had to explain over and over why they couldn't stay with me."

The three children were very close, but the separation from Sandra wasn't easy for them. "It's hard growing up without a mother and father," Elsie says. "The kids at school say, 'I'm going home now to my mother and father,' and we can't say that. Ma just came to visit us on weekends. Not every weekend, because she doesn't have enough money. But when she got money, she'd come to visit us.

"At first, living with the Morrises was all right, because we were little. We were looked after there, but some things were nice and some things were not nice. Sometimes she don't handle us as if we're her own child. Sometimes on holidays, when school was closing, we asked if we can go to our mother's and she said we must stay there. On holidays me and Henry must clean the walls and the ceilings early in the morning and I must wash the washing.

"For a long time I didn't understand. Then I did, but it took a while, until I grew up. I was really heartsore. Last year I told the

188

people in the Loving Circle of Prayer at my church, I told them everything, and they prayed for me and my mum. I needed someone bigger to talk to then. I can talk to my mother now, but not when I was little." Henry was sometimes sad and angry at being with the Morrises, Elsie says. She doesn't know if he still feels that way, and when I ask him several times about that period in his life, he says he has no memories at all.

Sandra wanted her children back, she says, but didn't know how to go about it. "At first I thought that when you gave your kids up, you never got them back. But I was sick and I couldn't take care of them, so I had to let them go. Then welfare said I could have the children back when I've got a job and my own place to stay." This conversation with an official seems to have taken place at the Van Rijn Place of Safety, just before the children were moved from there to the Morris house. "I always went to visit the kids, but I didn't try to get them back because I didn't have my own house. I was staying in a room the whole time, so I thought I couldn't have them."

Sandra Laing was officially declared a coloured person in September 1981—the second time she'd been given that label, and the third time the director of the Census had changed her race. Her government file shows that a series of civil servants heartily endorsed the decision. "I support [the] application fully," a bureaucrat named Badenhorst wrote in Afrikaans. "She is coloured and nothing else. I don't think the media will be *krapperig* ["scratchy" or "crabby"]—she now requests the change herself." Another official added, in a handwritten note at the bottom of her approved application, "By so doing, the last official chapter in the history of the classification of Sandra Laing will hopefully have been written."

Of course, the only reason that Sandra wanted to change her race classification to coloured was so that she could keep her children with her and stay with Petrus—and now she'd left Petrus and her children were in foster care. The one good thing about being granted a coloured I.D. was that now she could get a job other than housecleaning and laundering. Sister Ferreira knew somebody at the Vanda Cosmetics factory in the nearby town of Springs, and Sandra became a lipstick maker.

She was one of two women assigned to each of three big electric pots filled with thick, warm liquid of various shades of pink, red, or coral, a sort of lipstick soup. Sandra and a partner worked with a big iron mold, something like a hinged waffle iron, but with deeper indentations, shaped like individual lipsticks. The women held the mold under a spigot in the pot, turned the spigot, and filled the mold with lipstick soup. Then they closed it, moved it to a cooling table for a few minutes, scraped off any oozing goo, and put the mold in a big fridge. When the lipstick hardened, they opened the mold, removed the cylinders of lipstick, and dropped them into tubes. They seared them briefly with a gas-bottle flame to make the lipsticks shiny, popped tops on them, and packed them in boxes. Each day they made 1,500 to 2,000 lipsticks, and sometimes more.

The factory, which also made face creams, foundation, powder, mascara, and perfume that always smelled good to Sandra, employed a few hundred people. Sandra made friends with three black women on the lipstick team. Joyce, Ollie, Daphne, and Sandra ate lunch with the men who cooked the lipstick and brewed the perfume. Sandra thinks her friends knew her story from the newspapers, but they never asked her questions about the past. The group chatted about kids and money and romance. Sometimes the talk turned to politics, but Sandra says she never paid attention. She didn't talk about her problems at these lunch gatherings, but sometimes in private she told the women that she was sad about not being able to get her children out of foster care.

With her new friends' encouragement, Sandra, now twenty-six, pierced her nose and wore a little fake-gold stud. While she was shopping for groceries in Springs a man struck up a conversation. Simon Nkosi, who worked as a driver for another factory nearby, came from Driefontein and remembered her parents. He had an easy, teasing manner; he reminded her of Petrus, whom he'd known slightly. Sandra started seeing Simon. Aunt Connie didn't like her dating a black man. "Sometimes I would go to KwaThema for the weekend to be with Simon, and Aunt Connie would say, 'I can't stop you, but I don't want you to go, because I don't want you to get pregnant.'" When Sandra was in the hospital, the doctors had discontinued her birth control shots; after her release, the clinic doctor had inserted an intrauterine device, but it hurt and she had it removed. "Then I used the pills," she says, "but maybe I forgot them a lot. I didn't ask Simon to wear a condom because men didn't like them." During the happy years with Petrus, her body felt like her home. After she left him, Sandra felt disconnected from her physical self, and she didn't pay close attention to what happened there. She didn't pay close attention to much of anything, except visiting her children regularly, and holding the mold carefully as hot lipstick poured into it. Sex with Simon was another kind of fog.

"I didn't want to upset Aunt Connie, but I didn't want to obey her, either," Sandra says. So she moved out, to her own place in KwaThema, a room behind the house of an old couple. The rent was low and she could cook in their kitchen. She had enough space for a wardrobe and a bed where all three children crowded in with her when they visited on school holidays. Aunt Connie and Uncle Peter said they were sorry to see her go, and they stayed friendly.

Sandra fell pregnant, just as Aunt Connie had predicted. Simon already had another girlfriend, besides the mother of his children; Sandra was once again the other other woman. But to her surprise, Simon asked her to marry him. The wedding, in December 1982, was a five-minute ceremony in an African Zionist Church—"just Simon, me, and the priest. After the wedding, we lived together, but not long. He went back to his girlfriend. I don't know why. Maybe she went to a witch doctor for him."

Simon left before Sandra's third son, Anthony, arrived on April 26, 1983, the first of her children to be born at a hospital. Sandra wished she could take him to show her mothers, Jenny and Sannie, but she'd lost touch with Sannie, and she couldn't afford the trip to Jenny's place. "Simon was the same as David after Prins was born; he didn't give money to buy milk or food for the baby. I had to go back to work a month after Anthony was born to make money. I left the baby with Simon and his woman during the week, and took him home on weekends. Two weekends a month, Anthony and I stayed with the Morrises, if I had the money for taxi fare to Reiger Park." On holidays, all the children came home with Sandra and filled her little room.

When Anthony was a baby, Sandra experimented briefly with drinking too much. "I always fetched him on Friday, but sometimes we'd work weekends at Vanda, and if I was working on Saturday I couldn't fetch him. Those weekends, after work I would go for a joll with my friends from Vanda." She remembered the lovely, bubbly blankness of that day long ago when she and Lisa drank beer, the way she fell asleep beneath the tree and woke to find Lisa stuck in the mud, how they laughed until their faces ached. She went to *shebeens* with her Vanda friends, downing brandy and passing out at home. "When I was drinking I didn't think about Petrus. I drank so I wouldn't have to think about painful things." She stopped cold, she says, because she knew it wasn't good for her children to have a mother who drinks.

More than four years had passed since Sandra and her children fled Tjakastad with David's help. She missed Jenny and the sober Petrus, and she knew Elsie and Henry did, too. So she asked a friend from the lipstick factory who had a car if she could hire him to drive her and three of the children to Jenny's place in the country, a four-hour trip. She left Anthony with friends. "When I went to look for Jenny in Dorsbult, they told me she is in a village outside Lochiel, in the hills near the Swazi border. So I went there. She was so happy to see us she danced and cried. Pa Zwane died, and Petrus's sons Boy and Kiki didn't want to farm, so Jenny had to leave." Her new village was a scattering of houses made of wood and mud with cement floors and tin roofs, nicely situated in rolling hills covered with mealie fields and pine trees.

Jenny didn't ask Sandra why or how she'd left. "But she told me that she had tried and tried to get Petrus to stop drinking and beating. That meant she understood why I had to go, and she didn't blame me." Petrus was living with another woman by then, but when Jenny sent word to him in Tjakastad he drove over immediately and swept Sandra and his children into his arms. He was on his best behavior, not drinking at all. Henry and Elsie wouldn't let go of him.

All of Petrus's other children welcomed Sandra and their step-siblings. Elsie was especially glad to see Stiena. Petrus turned his world-mending smile Sandra's way, and said over and over how much he missed her and the children. He told her that he had come looking for her, and that he had brought her doll Melinda to a *sangoma* to try to charm her home. "So I knew that was why I heard him calling me in my dreams," Sandra says. They slept together, and she felt whole, returned to her body; the cobwebs in her head blew away for the first time in a long while. "But he never said he was sorry for the beatings." When it was time to leave, Petrus begged Sandra and the three children to stay. They could send for Anthony, he said. Sandra need never go back. He cried, and so did Sandra. But he didn't quite explain what would happen to the woman he lived with now, and Sandra felt she couldn't take the risk that he might become violent again.

She left glad that she'd seen Jenny, but being with Petrus again had cut a fresh furrow in her heart. Elsie and Henry were agitated and angry with her. They saw only that she was prying them away from their father in order to return them to a home that wasn't theirs. They forgot, for the moment, about the drinking and the beatings and the basins of bloody water, and found little comfort in Sandra's explaining yet again why they had to stay at Mrs. Morris's, about whom the two older children still had mixed feelings, although little Prins was very attached. He says, as an adult, that he considered himself to have two mothers, and he mourned Mrs. Morris deeply when she died in 2004. "Some holidays Mrs. Morris didn't let them come to me," Sandra says. "She made them clean her house. It happened more than once. I didn't complain. I just thought because she was looking after them, maybe she has to do it. Mrs. Morris said that welfare wouldn't give them back until I had a house. Then she told me I would never get them back, and I believed her. Mrs. Morris always used to say to the children and to me that I would never get my children back—Mrs. Morris never gave a reason for why she said so."

One day when Sandra was recounting this period in her life, which we'd already explored several times, I asked her exactly what the welfare people said when she spoke to them about getting her children back. "I didn't ever go to the welfare," she said. "I knew welfare wouldn't let me have the kids if I was living in a room, so I didn't even ask."

"The whole nine years?"

"*Ja,* I didn't."

"Why not?"

"Because the kids were under Mrs. Morris, they weren't under me."

This was a new narrative wrinkle. "Did you ever ask Mrs. Morris if you could have them back?"

"No, because I knew what she would say. She was all right because they were brought up well. She didn't treat them badly, not all the time—just when she didn't let them come to me on holidays. My kids did ask me to take them away. But they also believed Mrs. Morris when she said I wouldn't get them back."

"Is it possible," I asked Sandra, "that a part of you didn't want the kids back—for perfectly understandable reasons, because you were depressed and afraid you couldn't care for them properly?"

"No," she said quickly and firmly. "That's not possible." Ambivalence, her own and that of others, is difficult for Sandra to acknowledge. And depression is not a word she ever uses to describe her emotional life during her first years in the East Rand. It was hard, she says. I was *hartseer,* heartsore. I suffered. I was sad.

But depression seems one appropriate label for her state. Another might be "complex post-traumatic stress disorder," a syndrome named by Harvard psychiatrist Judith Herman. The kind of psychological and physical trauma Sandra experienced—community ostracism, playground persecution, unjust punishment, perceived emotional abandonment, threats of violence from a parent, incarceration, forced relocation, and spousal abuse—can engender dissociation, the shutting down that began when she was a girl. This state of psychic numbness is characterized, Herman says, by "emotional detachment and profound passivity, in which the person relinquishes all initiative and struggle." Those who experience early trauma are often left prone to shame and self-doubt. "They lose their trust in themselves, in other people . . . Their self-esteem is assaulted by experiences of humiliation, guilt, and helplessness." Although dissociation may be helpful at the time of the trauma—"one of nature's small mercies, a protection against unbearable pain"—it can leave the sufferer with a number of physical and psychological symptoms, among them memory loss, guilt, and "paralysis of initiative."

If you don't buy that diagnosis, you could simply say that even before she was tormented at school and then expelled—before the court case; before she witnessed her mother's aborted suicide attempt; before she ran away from home, was arrested, and went to jail; before her father threatened to kill her and himself and her mother broke off all communication; and before her husband beat her nearly to death; when she was simply a confused schoolgirl whose parents and teachers insisted that she couldn't possibly have seen what she knew she saw—Sandra had canceled some part of herself. Early lack of adult validation had a corrosive effect on Sandra's faith in her powers of perception; as a result, she shut down most of her observational and analytical skills. That's how she was able to remain unaware of the political turmoil all over the East Rand, sometimes right in KwaThema: the disappearance of activists taken away and killed by the Special Branch, the secret security police, antiapartheid demonstrations that ended in police shootings and mass arrests.

Sandra seems to have been forgotten by the press for a seven-year stretch, until February 1985, when the *Express* ran an update on the woman who, as a child, the reporter noted, "had become a symbol in the public imagination of all that is iniquitous about apartheid." Sandra was twenty-nine, working at Vanda, renting a room from the Thabede family of KwaThema for R25 a month and giving the rest of what she earned to her children, according to the reporter. Sandra doesn't remember the interview, but she remembers the family. "There was an old man I called Grandfather, his wife, Mother Thabede, and three sons. I was happy with that family. I missed the other children, but saw them every second weekend." The reporter notes that none of her four children live with her. "Three, Mr. Zwane's children, have been taken over by welfare . . .

she cannot have them back until she has a house in Geluksdal. She doesn't know how to get a house.

"Her fourth child, Anthony, nearly two, lives in KwaThema with his father, Sandra's estranged husband. She can't have him with her because she has to work to save money for her children."

Before Anthony turned two, Sandra and Elsie went to Simon Nkosi's place by taxi to pick up the boy for a Christmas visit. He was dirty and his trousers were torn, and Sandra was afraid that Simon and his girlfriend weren't giving him enough to eat. "They weren't looking after him well. We found him outside. Simon was inside the house, busy with people. We left with Anthony and never brought him back." She asked her neighbors to watch him while she was at work. Prins was four, and Sandra was concerned that he would wonder why his baby brother could stay with her all the time but he couldn't. "Prins didn't show me he was sad, but I worried," Sandra says. Elsie remembers asking her mother, " 'Why is Anthony living with you and we are there with Mrs. Morris?' She told us again that she'd gotten sick and we have to go to that house, but not to worry because someday we would come to live with her." Later in 1985, Sandra was laid off from Vanda and supported herself by doing temporary work in other factories, cleaning houses, and taking in laundry and ironing. She preferred working to thinking too hard about everything that made her sad, things she didn't understand how to fix.

The Prohibition of Mixed Marriages Act was repealed that year. The Dutch Reformed Church issued a statement saying that mixed marriages were not, after all, scripturally prohibited, but that the cultural differences might create serious problems for a mixed couple. This seemed like a good sign to freedom fighters. But at the same time that one of apartheid's most important pieces of legislation was undone, Prime Minister P. W. Botha jailed unprecedented numbers of antiapartheid activists, invoking the Internal Security Act, passed after the Soweto riots of 1976, which allowed unlimited detention without trial of anyone suspected of "threatening public order." Also, one of the first instances of the hideous township practice of "necklacing" was reported, in Duduza: Suspected police informers were ers were punished by vigilantes who jammed an old tire over their heads, doused them with gasoline, and burned them alive.

Sandra paid no attention. She had just enough energy and enterprise to put one foot in front of the other, to work and to worry. Sometimes she felt she had betrayed Petrus and her parents; sometimes, but very rarely, she allowed herself to feel that they had betrayed her. She told herself that placing her children in foster care had been her only choice. She wondered if her mother and father thought she was a bad person. Sometimes she missed her white family, and often she missed Jenny.

Vanda called Sandra back to work in January 1986. She found yet another place to live, a room in the house of a nice old lady called Ouma Letty back in the coloured community of Geluksdal. Neighbors looked after Anthony during the day. Sandra doesn't remember why she left the Thabede family in KwaThema; she recalls little from this period. Her work friend Joyce asked Sandra to join her on a train trip to visit relatives in Cape Town; she and Joyce left their children with Joyce's parents. Sandra bought her first bathing suit, and they went to a beach for non-whites where Sandra saw the ocean for the first time. It made her feel "small and happy." She dated a man named Jacob, a truck driver, another charming, unfaithful tyrant, and the affair came to nothing. She stopped seeing him because he wasn't nice to Anthony.

Sandra still missed Jenny, and in 1987 decided to pay her another surprise visit. She missed Petrus, too, but on the long drive to the countryside—again she paid her work friend to take her—she steeled herself against falling for him, no matter how much he cried. When she and the children arrived, Jenny embraced them, this time weeping tears of sorrow, not joy. Petrus had been killed in a fight a few months earlier. He'd been selling homemade liquor in front of his house when he got into an argument with a drunken customer who hit him on the head with a *knobkerrie*, a fighting stick. Though Petrus was a flawed man, though she was forced to flee him, Sandra considered him the love of her life, and she mourned him deeply. So did his children.

Back in the East Rand, she sleepwalked through her days at the factory. A colleague told Sandra that a friend of his had seen her on the bus they all rode to work and wanted to know if he could talk to her. Johannes Motlaung asked the friend to tell Sandra he was a good man with a steady job as a truck driver for a factory that made gun and train parts. "But I had enough with men," she says. "I stopped taking that bus."

Johannes waited a bit; then he spoke to Sandra at the shops near work, introducing himself, mentioning their mutual friend, asking after her health. "I could see she was a good somebody," Johannes Motlaung told me in 2001. "I read about her in the papers, and I wanted to meet her." His first language was Sotho, but he spoke fluent Zulu and pretty good Afrikaans. He was all right, Sandra says; he seemed interested in what she had to say, and patient enough to wait until she said it. Maybe he'd take care of her, and do a better job of it than Petrus or David or Simon had. Johannes began courting Sandra in 1987, picking her up after work, visiting her in Geluksdal, staying overnight with her in the room behind Ouma Letty's house. Sandra was technically married, but if she didn't have Anthony as proof, she'd swear she dreamed Simon. In fact, she never saw Simon again, although Anthony sometimes visited him, and she learned of David Radebe's death, in the mid-1990s, from a newspaper.

Johannes neglected to tell Sandra that he, too, was married and living with his wife, who was dying of cancer, and their two children. "When I found out, I was already pregnant," Sandra says. "Or maybe it was after the baby was born. My neighbor told me that someone told her he'd had a big wedding. I asked him why didn't he tell me he's got a wife. He said he did want to but I got quickly pregnant and he couldn't tell me because he was scared I'd get angry and get sick. Jacob, my old boyfriend, saw me pregnant and said, 'Why didn't you give *me* a baby?' That's how men think."

She took only a short leave from work to give birth to her fourth son, Steve, in 1988, and to have her tubes tied. Sandra loves all her children and regrets none of them, but she felt she had done her share of populating the world.

Her room in Ouma Letty's house was too small for two little

boys, so she rented a dilapidated farmhouse on the road leading to KwaThema, with no running water or electricity but plenty of space. She can't say why she felt able to find a house then but never before; she thinks it might be because Johannes helped with the search and paid most of the rent. The white man who owned the place charged ten times what it was worth. Sandra made R400 a month at Vanda, and the rent was an extortionate R300. But Sandra eventually sublet the house, little more than a shell, and some makeshift rooms in the yard to boarders, and she and the children moved to a slightly more comfortable outbuilding. Johannes divided his time between Sandra and his sick wife and first family, but he helped out with rent and food. Sandra brought in extra money by making beer or buying it in bulk and reselling it in brown bottles. "I liked being with Johannes," she says. "He was quiet, and he didn't beat me."

The farmhouse was terrible, but it was a house. Right after she moved in, her older children came for a visit. Henry was seventeen, Elsie fifteen, and Prins nine. "Henry said I must go to the welfare and tell them that the children didn't want to stay at the Morrises anymore." On Monday, Henry and Sandra went to the welfare office in Reiger Park, a trip that had taken her nine years to make. "Henry told welfare he didn't want to stay, that Mrs. Morris treated her own children better and it wasn't all right to stay there anymore," Sandra says. "Welfare didn't come look at my house. They just asked me would I look after the children and I said yes." Elsie remembers arriving home from school that day and being surprised to see her mother standing at the gate. "She told us she was coming to fetch us for good. I was really, really glad. I cried. She said she doesn't have money to give us and I said, 'Ma, it doesn't matter, as long as we are together.'"

23

WE ALL GOT THE SAME

SIXTEEN YEARS HAD PASSED SINCE SANNIE LAING TOLD Sandra not to contact her again. Sandra occasionally thought about trying to reconnect with her parents, but the task seemed as daunting as getting her children back from Mrs. Morris. What if they refused to see her? She knew they'd moved from Pongola to Amsterdam, the farming community where Sannie grew up. Sandra says she had an address for them there, but she can't remember how or when she came by this information, except that it was before she moved to the farmhouse with her children. Once the family was all under one roof, she felt strong and settled enough to find her mother and father.

In 1989, Johannes borrowed a car from a friend and drove her to Amsterdam. "We went straight to my parents' address," Sandra says. "Nobody was there. The neighbor told us the owner of the house had a shop in [the center of] Amsterdam. We went to the shop and the man there said he bought the shop and house from the Laing family, who moved away; he didn't know where. But he said the Laings have family that side [in the area], and he showed me. That's where I found my cousin Susanna. Johannes stayed in the car, and I went to the door holding Steve. Susanna peeped out at me through the window and asked what I wanted.

I told her I was looking for the Laing family. She asked who I was that I was looking for the Laing family, and I told her that I was Sandra. Steve and I went into the house. I asked her where my parents were, and she told me that my father had passed away in 1988.

"I felt sad and shocked. I had wanted to ask him for forgiveness before he died. Susanna told me that my mother was now in Pretoria, and she gave me her telephone number there. She let me use her phone and I called my mother and talked with her for the first time since '73.

"She was surprised to hear from me. First she wanted to know where I got hold of her number. Then she told that my father had been very ill and that he had passed away from throat cancer. She asked for my address because she wanted to send me something. I thought it would be money, but I didn't ask her. She said that I must not think that Leon and Adriaan received the most, so I knew from this that she meant money. She wanted me to know that we all got the same.

"She asked how many children I now had. I told her five. She kept asking where I was staying and if I was okay. I didn't tell her about Jenny the baby. I didn't ask her where she was, but I did ask my mother why they didn't let me know that my father had died. She said that they didn't know where to find me."

After the call, Sandra chatted with Susanna, while Johannes stayed in the car. "I was about an hour with her. She sent her husband to fetch her mother, Tannie Marie, from the old age home. Tannie Marie was happy to see me. It was a good visit. They told me that Leon had got married."

Sandra never called her mother back at the number Susanna had given her. "I didn't think my mother wanted me to," she says. She might eventually have worked up the nerve to do so, but a few weeks after the telephone conversation from Cousin Susanna's house, Sandra received a letter from Sannie, which she still keeps carefully on a shelf in her bedroom closet. Here is Sandra's translation of the letter:

Hello, Sandra:

> . . . I send you a little bit of money that you got from your dad. Sandra, it is a little money because the doctors and hospital took it all . . . I hope you will understand that Leon and Adriaan got the same and be happy that I did send you something.
>
> Leon is moving to Cape Town and the rest of us fly on the 26th . . . When I'm there I will write you and give you the address . . . You mustn't ask for more money. There isn't more money. Too many bills to pay. You must stay well and look out for yourself.
>
> Many regards from Mamma

The chilly little missive, which came with R1500, was postmarked Cape Town. Sandra later discovered that her mother was nowhere near Cape Town; one of her brothers had posted the letter on a visit so Sandra couldn't track down Sannie. "I was happy to get something from her, but sad that I would never see her again," Sandra says. "I thought it was Leon's idea not to put the address. I thought because my father's not there anymore, now Leon was going to tell my mother what to do." I asked Sandra why her mother emphasizes the fact that there's no more money and tells Sandra not to ask for any. Had she ever asked her mother for money before? Sandra says she hadn't.

On the drive home from Amsterdam, Sandra couldn't stop thinking about how she would never have a chance to patch things up with her father. She also became convinced that the reason Sannie hadn't arranged to see her after the phone call was that her brothers wouldn't allow it. She still thinks that was the case. Sandra firmly rejects the idea that Sannie might have decided on her own not to make contact; she believes strongly that her mother was repeatedly coerced into cutting off communication first by Abraham and then by Leon. How does that fit in, I asked her, with the only big decision Sannie clearly made on her own—stopping Abraham from sending the police to retrieve Sandra when she and Petrus eloped? Sannie did that, Sandra says, because she understood that her daughter would be happier with Petrus, and she wanted to protect her from Abraham's wrath. What about the newspaper article in which Sannie says, "My husband and I want nothing to do with her"? Sandra believes she said that because she was afraid of Abraham. And anyway, she points out, newspapers sometimes say things that aren't true.

Although the telephone conversation with Sannie and the letter that followed weren't especially warm—maybe *because* they weren't—Sandra began to think constantly about finding her mother. "But I didn't know how to find her. I had no telephone, no transport, no money." She'd been laid off from Vanda again and took whatever temporary factory work she could land; Johannes contributed to the household and split his time between his dying wife and Sandra. Sandra had thought she would be happy if only all her children were with her. Indeed, she was greatly cheered and relieved to be reunited with them. But now, before she slept and when she woke, her mind gnawed at the notion that nothing would be right until she saw her mother.

24

THE PERILS OF
HARMONIZATION

SANDRA'S NEIGHBORS DANCED IN THE STREETS WITH JOY on February 2, 1990. Prime Minister F. W. De Klerk was releasing Nelson Mandela from prison after twenty-seven years and officially recognizing the African National Congress, banned since 1960, and other anti-apartheid organizations. Here was the first real sign that the grip of the National Party was loosening, and that apartheid might someday end.

Hundreds of people from KwaThema were signing up for buses to Johannesburg, where Mandela would be welcomed at a huge rally, and some of Sandra's friends invited her to come along. "I had to say I didn't know who Mandela was."

In talking with Sandra over the years, I'd become used to her willed absence from the political life of the nation, and I understood its causes. But this statement took me by surprise. "How is that possible?" I asked her, truly astonished. Nelson Mandela was the revered hero of the freedom struggle and had been for nearly three decades. No one was more famous in South Africa, and the East Rand was an active hub of underground support for the ANC.

"I didn't know of him because I didn't watch TV, read newspapers, or listen to the news."

"Your friends never talked about him?"

"I didn't listen to talk about politics."

As one longtime KwaThema resident put it when he learned that Sandra hadn't heard of Nelson Mandela, "Man, you'd have to wear a blindfold and put stoppers in your ears not to know about Mandela!" That's not a bad description of Sandra's state in those days. I hadn't realized the extent of her disconnection in the years after she left Petrus. Now I imagined that she saw the world then at a watery remove, as if through a diving helmet.

She wasn't entirely numb, of course; she retained enough awareness and initiative to survive, to keep her family from disintegrating, and to find wherever she went a community of friends and caretakers drawn to her essential sweetness. But the sealing of her powers of perception, an effective defense in girlhood, had stopped protecting her. Instead, it had devolved into a form of self-punishment, robbing her of a sense of worth and a belief in her ability to shape her own fate. "If, to survive, a child is required to ignore certain things," the psychoanalyst Alice Miller writes in *Banished Knowledge*, "the chances are that she will continue to be required to ignore those things for the rest of her life. The life-saving function of repression in childhood is transformed in adulthood into a life-destroying force." That force drained her of initiative to such an extent that she was unable to retrieve her children for nearly a decade; to maintain a relationship in which she wasn't the other woman, the one with the less legitimate claim on a man's love; and to stay in closer touch with her beloved Jenny.

Her jubilant KwaThema friends, she says, were eager to tell her about Madiba, the clan honorific by which Nelson Mandela is commonly known in South Africa. She was glad to learn that the world had such people in it. "But it was sad, too. Madiba and the others struggled to end apartheid, but still it wasn't over." Reporters came to find Sandra at the farmhouse; they wanted to ask her what she thought, in her capacity as a symbol of apartheid's abuses, about Madiba's release. "I just said to them all I'm glad Mandela's out, but it's too late for me."

A year later, reporters returned for Sandra's comments on the repeal of the two laws most responsible for shaping the infernal infrastructure of apartheid and her personal woes—the Population

Registration Act, which required racial classification, and the Group Areas Act, which mandated residential segregation and had resulted in the uprooting and dispossession of millions. "For me it is 25 years too late," she told the *New York Times.* "I cannot turn back the clock."

A piece in the Sunday *Star,* "Confessions of a Human Classifier," profiled an anonymous Durban woman who had spent thirty-two years on a race classification appeal board. "I don't tell my friends at the bowling club what I did," the former classifier is quoted as telling the reporter.

> "I say I was the registrar of births, deaths, and marriages. Who is anybody to judge another? We broke up families. All the time I was working in the department I was very glad I was white . . . I did feel pity at the time but it was a job. I had to earn my living . . . we didn't make the final decision, we just made the recommendations. Humanity didn't come into our recommendations. We had to stick to the rules—the tragedy didn't influence us. We would have situations where children with the same parents landed up with different classifications . . . I am an Afrikaner through and through. But race classification was wrong. I am not proud of what I did. But I can't say I am ashamed. There was nothing we could do about it. I'm just glad it's over."

In less than a paragraph, the anonymous classifier neatly summarized the general moral stance of National Party supporters, a fortunate minority facing the end of a system that had blessed them: I felt pity, but I had to earn my living. Race classification was wrong; I'm not proud of it. But I'm not ashamed. There was nothing we could do.

Sandra's grade-school roommate Elize Lötter didn't run across any of the stories quoting Sandra, and she often wondered what had become of her former classmate. In the early 1990s, while Sandra was living in the ruined farmhouse and dreaming of finding her mother, Elize was working as a corporate "harmonization officer," helping employees adjust to a racially integrated workplace. Fluent in Afrikaans and English and comfortable speaking Swazi and Zulu, Elize had taught elementary school for several years, but had switched to working in human resources. She became one of South Africa's first diversity trainers, teaching workers of all races how to cope with the end of apartheid as Nelson Mandela and President F. W. De Klerk negotiated a peaceful transfer of power from nearly 4 million whites to some 35 million black, Asian, and mixed-race South Africans.

At one multinational company, Elize prepared shop stewards for the coming transformation. Not surprisingly, the whites had the hardest time adjusting. During a training session, Elize says, a fellow Afrikaner was especially outraged at the thought of having to share a sink and a cafeteria with black people. "He said, 'Are you telling me I have to use the same bloody basin as a black? I have to drink from a cup that a black has used?'

"I said, 'Hang on. Who cleans the basin in your home?' 'Our maid,' he says. 'And who cleans your water glass?' 'The maid.' 'And is she black?' 'Of course,' he says. 'So a black person can put her hand in your glass to clean it, and you can use it all right, and she can clean your basin with her black hands, but a black person can't clean his hands in the same basin as you?' He stood up with his face red and his fists raised—I thought he was going to hit me—then he turned and walked out.

"Later he came back and apologized. He said to me, 'You're making me think, and I don't like it!'"

25

SCREENING

ONE OF THE JOURNALISTS WHO CAME TO FIND SANDRA at the ruined farmhouse made a surprising offer: A German television company wanted to fly her to Hamburg so she could speak on television about her life. By that time, she'd been in the public eye so long that media coverage of Sandra had become news itself: A reporter reported on the fact that she was being reported on. SANDRA LAING TO TELL WORLD OF RUINED LIFE ran the headline in the magazine *South* for September 1991.

> One of the most famous victims of apartheid, Sandra Laing, is to travel overseas where she will tell the world how, in spite of the scrapping of racial laws, her life has been left in ruins. Although the laws have changed, it has made no difference. She remains poor and downtrodden. The legacy of the laws which classified her first white, then, at age 11, black, then white again and then finally black, continues to determine her friendships and family relationships. Even today her mother, Mrs. Sannie Laing, will not see her. ". . . I hope this trip will bring some happy moments to my gloomy life," Laing said . . . "I'm looking forward to the journey. It will be my first trip . . . out of South Africa. To me this place has been one big hell for 25 years."

Sandra's white family must have seen the interview, which she doesn't remember giving—there are few she does—because not long before she was scheduled to leave for Germany she got a letter from a man named Jan Kruger, who said he was a friend of her mother's. Sannie Laing, he wrote, was very upset by recent newspaper and magazine articles mentioning Sandra, and had threatened to take her own life. (It's interesting to note the number of times Sandra's parents reminded her—and the press—that she was potentially lethal to them.) Kruger wrote that he knew Sandra didn't mean to hurt her mother, but the past is over and she should look to the future. If Sandra promised not to talk to any journalists again, the letter said, Sannie would send her address so Sandra could write to her. This was the first but not the last time the family offered to bargain for Sandra's silence. Here, the dangled reward was knowledge of Sannie's whereabouts. And Sandra might have agreed to the transaction, except that the letter, she insists, came with no return address. "I didn't answer because there was no address on the letter," she maintains adamantly. "I didn't know where to send an answer."

The journalist who arranged Sandra's trip to Germany, Amina Frense, now a news producer at SABC television, had lived in Germany in the 1970s and seen *The Search for Sandra Laing.* She remained curious about Sandra, and in 1990 found her through journalist friends; she did some pieces for the German production company that now wanted Sandra to come to Hamburg. They'd pay her way, of course, and give her a fee.

Before the trip, a German camera crew followed Sandra as she took her son Anthony to school. "He was eight or ten years old," Amina says, "and we asked her, 'When you were that old, you were removed from school, and now you're taking your child to school. How do you feel?' Her answer was, 'I feel heartsore.' That was her answer to a lot of things. She told us she was denied an education and development, denied a life; that's what she felt very bitter about. She would have been a different person. She would have been able to look after herself and give the kids a better chance."

That people overseas were interested in her seemed odd to Sandra, but she was glad for the chance to fly in an airplane for the first time. "The clouds looked like soap foam," she says, "and Hamburg looked like Johannesburg without black people." The interview took place in a studio under painfully bright lights, with a man who asked Sandra questions in English about everything that had happened to her since she was kicked out of school. She felt she couldn't remember enough to make him happy.

Amina stayed in touch after Sandra's trip to Germany. "Sandra was definitely damaged by what happened to her," she says today. "She was quiet and withdrawn. She didn't articulate very much but that she was hurt inside and she wanted to find her mother. We tried searching the telephone directory and actually got some numbers that might have been her brothers'.

"But I was cautious. I got approached by a number of foreign networks that said, Find her mother, and we'll pay you generously, whatever it takes. But I didn't feel like I wanted to do that. It was a major responsibility; she couldn't go to Cape Town and find her mother herself. If the brothers found out that she was trying to contact the mother, they were probably going to hide her even further. What if she found them and they chased her away? I didn't want to be responsible for that type of thing unless I could be responsible from A to Z—take her there, and if it's a failed attempt, be there for her, counsel her. And I didn't have the energy for that, so I didn't pursue it."

Johannes's wife died in December 1991. His five children, the oldest in their late teens and the youngest seven, were informally adopted by his sister-in-law. Johannes finally moved into the farmhouse with Sandra permanently, although he visited his children daily. His brother told him that there were "bank houses"—government-subsidized rentals, sometimes called council houses—available in Tsakane, a newer township very near KwaThema, tidy, tiny brick homes with yards. In May 1992, Sandra and Johannes moved from the crumbling farmhouse to the small two-bedroom house where I first spoke with her.

Tsakane had the same drawbacks as any township. Bright anti-crime lights on huge stanchions bleached the sky at night and only seemed to make the crime—glue-sniffing, robbery, brawling, the occasional murder—easier to see. Schools were crowded and substandard. The township had no real grocery stores, just *spazas*, tuck shops like the one Sandra and Petrus ran in Tjakastad; no park, just a big square of hard-packed dirt where kids played soccer.

But it had advantages, too, besides running water, electricity, and indoor plumbing: a good, gossipy crowd of neighbors, plenty of playmates for the younger boys, a nearby clinic, lots of combi taxis. Informal enterprise thrived: tuck shops, roadside bicycle repairmen, an old tank truck converted into a snack bar, panel beaters—auto-body shops—in small sheds. "One settler, one bullet," someone had painted on a shed wall, the slogan of the Azanian People's Liberation Army, the military wing of the Pan-African Congress, a liberation organization that unlike the ANC's policy didn't allow whites to join.

Six people moved into the tiny Tsakane house: Sandra, Johannes, Henry, Prins, Anthony, and Steve. Elsie had a room in Reiger Park near Mrs. Morris's. The kitchen was nearly invisible, just a pass-through from the back door to the little parlor, but Sandra liked cooking there for the family. She planted beets, carrots, tomatoes, beans, and lettuce in the yard, as well as roses and lilies to lift her spirits.

When you're driving down to the East Rand from Johannesburg on Highway N-17, you pass some nice housing tracts, very suburban Los Angeles, bordered with palms, pines, and blue gum. Between them lie open grassland and the sprawl of contiguous townships; factories, slag heaps, and mineheads, those erector-set ironwork arrays that mark the spot where workers descend to harvest mineral wealth of various sorts. You know when you're getting close to the turnoff for Tsakane because suddenly, instead of industrial smokestacks, you see what looks from a distance like a djinn's palace, shimmering white, an arrangement of vast tents, tilted and bent at Dr. Seuss angles, outlined in ice blue, hot pink, and acid green neon. Up close, it's just as cartoony, Vegasy, circusy. This is Carnival City, a casino, arena, and cinema that looks pretty at night from afar, but mighty weird set among the mine waste, the squatter-camp scatter, and rows of tiny township houses, the whole creating the effect of a somewhat dystopic theme park. The casino was built in 1991, after the Separate Amenities Act was repealed, so from opening day a person of any race could enter. Sandra had never been inside when I met her, and neither had any of her neighbors. But they liked seeing the casino glow on the horizon, and dreamed about hitting a jackpot on the slots.

Sandra went back to work at Vanda in 1994. She couldn't look after the vegetable garden anymore, so she put in a lawn and kept only her flowers. The children were happy in school, Johannes was no trouble to her, and both of them had jobs. And on April 27, 1994, they did something that she would never have thought possible: They waited in line for two hours in order to cast a vote for Nelson Mandela in the first free, multiracial elections in South Africa's history. Mandela was elected president of a black majority government and power was peacefully transferred. "If my father was alive that day," Sandra says, "maybe he would say South Africa's going to die because of a black president."

Amina Frense drove down from Johannesburg after the elections to tell Sandra, who had no phone, that Peter Ustinov, the British actor and writer, wanted to interview her for a television program about South Africa. She returned with Sir Peter, a camera crew, and a copy of the 1977 documentary *The Search for Sandra Laing*. The family crowded into the sitting room of a neighbor who had a VCR, and Sandra was filmed watching herself on film for the first time.

As sad, tinkly music played, she saw the store in Brereton Park, and the house, first shown abandoned and in disrepair, then whole again, the way it looked on the day she left with Petrus. There she was as a ten-year-old, soon after being expelled, sitting on the knee of her smiling father and running into her mother's open arms. Sandra could almost catch the sunny smell of Sannie's freshly laundered apron. She began to cry. There was Adriaan as a baby in Sandra's arms, clinging to her neck. There she was chasing a goose, and laughing with her parents on the grass. Sandra's children watched intently but said little. Sandra cried quietly with longing and regret.

The school at Piet Retief appeared on the screen, and Sandra's stomach churned. Antony Thomas had filmed the scene eleven years after Sandra's departure, but little had changed, including Van

Tonder and the mole on his cheek. Then came a shock—a shot of Adriaan at about the age Sandra was when she was expelled. She recognized her brother immediately, before Thomas identified him. He looked like her, but paler and with close-cropped hair. He was eating in the hostel dining room, at ease among the other children. Seeing him on the television screen, Sandra felt not like a grown woman who had given birth six times, but like a child nearly suffocated by sorrow and a sense of injustice. "I thought, why can he go to school with no problems?" she says, "He's just a little bit lighter than me. Why didn't they kick *him* out?" (Some possible answers: In a pigmentocracy, a little bit lighter matters a great deal. The publicity attending Sandra's expulsion was so painful to all concerned that no one wanted to relive it. By the time Adriaan came along, ten years after Sandra, Afrikaner parents in Swaziland were used to sending their kids to Piet Retief; Willy Meyer no longer had to defend his urging them to do so.)

On-screen, two nuns at St. Dominic's, Sister Flora and Sister Jordana, said that Sandra was a shy and troubled girl who seemed happier with black people, like the school's driver. "She brought many problems with her," one said. Then the film showed Sandra's mother and father in their Pongola general store, which she'd never visited. Her mother was saying to the camera that it was Abraham who didn't want to see their daughter—just what Sandra had always believed. Finally, she saw herself as a young mother in the Tjakastad rondavel with toddler Elsie on her lap. Her old home looked at once dismal and wonderful from the distance of years. And then her handsome Petrus was alive again on film, saying, about the people in Piet Retief, "What they did was bad, but that's not my business. All I can say is thank you for giving me my wife."

When the film ended, Sir Peter asked Sandra and the children some questions; she was too dazed for the event to register. "It was nice to see everyone, but very sad," she says. She longed for her mother more fiercely than she had since she was a child away at school. "I wanted my mother to forgive me for leaving home," Sandra says.

Vanda moved to a much smaller building and laid off many

workers, including Sandra. She worked short stints at various factories; at the Drink-a-Pop plant, her job was to open damaged boxes
of soft-drink mixes and pour the flavored powders—cola, orange,
strawberry, peach—back into big drums. She wore a cap and mask,
but the powder still invaded her nose and coated her hair. When
she bathed at night, the water looked like fruit juice. Work was spo-
radic, so when another German film crew wanted to shoot a story
about her, and offered R1,000 to interview her and film her with
her family, white and black, she said yes. Sandra didn't enjoy telling
her story, she says, but she needed the money.

Without writing or telephoning first, she led two journalists to
her cousin Susanna's door in Amsterdam. Susanna was startled and
angry. "She looked through the window," Sandra says, "and when
she saw me and the two men with their cameras she told us to go
away and that she would call the police if we do not leave. We left."
Sandra was embarrassed; it hadn't occurred to her that Susanna
might resent the invasion of her privacy. She wasn't concerned about
hurting Susanna's feelings, however. Sandra was worried that she'd
cut off a possible avenue to her mother.

26

Bold is to Beautiful
as Truth is to
Reconciliation

O
NE OF THE BEST THINGS ABOUT MOVING TO A HOUSE
with electricity was that Johannes bought Sandra
her first TV. She became, and remains, passion-
ately involved in soap operas, a national addiction.
Her favorite is *The Bold and the Beautiful*; she worries about the char-
acters as if they were neighbors, especially Brooke, the designated
bad girl, who has married most male members of the featured Forrester clan, and has required more than one paternity test to determine the origins of her four children. "Nobody likes her," Sandra
says. "I wondered, Why doesn't she just leave town?"

Sometimes Sandra seems to know more about the history of
Ridge Forrester and Brooke Logan Forrester Forrester Chambers
Forrester Forrester Jones Forrester Forrester Forrester Marone (I include the annulments at Sandra's urging) than she does about her
own. That may be part of the show's allure. Sandra was handed
down such a meager store of family lore, so few tutelary tales to help
her make sense of the world, that the soapies seem to substitute.
(Or at least provide a frame of reference; when Sandra described her
first sexual encounter with Petrus, she said, "He was like a man and
in charge, but gentle, like Ridge.") Furthermore, *Bold* offers the very
attractive recurring theme of reversible loss: Ridge didn't perish in
the fire! Taylor wasn't really shot! And maybe since it's painful and
difficult for Sandra to plumb her own psyche, she practices on

Brooke. Perhaps that last is too fancy a conjecture, but Sandra does
seem more comfortable talking about what motivates Brooke than
what motivates her. At the very least, soapies take Sandra's mind
off her own problems by offering woes that, however melodramatic,
are guaranteed to be resolved, albeit with deliciously agonizing
slowness.

Though nothing beats *Bold* in Sandra's book—it's the most
popular American soap in the world, with 300 million viewers in 100
countries—she's very fond of other American serials and South
African soapies (shown at night, so working people can catch them)
like the multilingual *Isidingo*, *Generations*, and *Sevende Laan*, in
Afrikaans. "I didn't like to watch *Molo Fish*," she says, naming a more
political miniseries about the effects of apartheid on a coloured
activist exiled to Canada. "It's about the time I was born, about
apartheid. I don't need to see that."

She did, however, watch a real-life apartheid drama unfold on
television in 1996. Nelson Mandela urged the nation's new multiracial Parliament to create the Truth and Reconciliation Commission (TRC), which would hold a series of public hearings,
chaired by Nobel Peace Prize winner Archbishop Desmond Tutu,
investigating human rights abuses committed between March 1,
1960, and May 10, 1994. Survivors of those abuses and the families of dead victims were given the chance to tell their stories, formerly suppressed by the government. Perpetrators from all sides
of the struggle who publicly disclosed their crimes, admitted guilt,
accepted responsibility, and expressed remorse could apply for
amnesty. Mandela and a majority of Parliament felt that forming
the TRC was preferable to either convening a Nuremburg-style war-
crimes tribunal and insisting on harsh punishments, or moving forward without acknowledging three hundred years of the persecution
of black people by white. "There is not a single person who has not
been traumatized by apartheid—even the perpetrators," Tutu said.
"We have to pour balm on tortured souls."

A million South Africans, most of them black, tuned in to the
weekly *TRC Special Report,* a program that excerpted and analyzed
the hearings. Sandra didn't follow the TRC hearings as avidly as she

did the soapies; they were far too real and painful. "I watched some," she says. "I heard how white police killed black people, and some black people killed white people.

One mum said, "Please, can you find me even just a little bone of my child so I can give him a decent burial?" Like most viewers, Sandra, was haunted by the testimony of a security police colonel who told how he and his colleagues abducted a young black activist, gave him knockout drops in a cup of coffee, shot him in the head, then burned his body. And because it takes several hours for a human body to burn, they had beers and a *braai*, a barbecue, next to the pyre.

TRC commissioner Pumla Gobodo-Madikizela, a professor of psychology at the University of Cape Town, was particularly struck by how much the government kept from ordinary citizens, including the extent of the fierce and lengthy covert war waged against apartheid's opponents by secret government forces. Testimony revealed that an extralegal government secret security force, the Special Branch, had not only enlisted township spies to foment black-on-black violence but was itself directly responsible for several thousand deaths, crimes the government had previously denied. "This lends some small degree of credibility to the defense of South Africa's whites who say that they didn't know what was going on, that the government hid much of it from them," Gobodo-Madikizela writes in *A Human Being Died That Night*, an extraordinarily compelling book about her prison interviews with the head of a secret-police death squad. He's now serving a prison sentence of 212 years for the state-sanctioned murder of antiapartheid activists. "On the other hand, white South Africans couldn't help but know that they benefitted from a morally corrupt form of government."

That government shielded itself from guilt, says Gobodo-Madikizela, a clinical psychologist, by keeping secrets from itself. "Killing apartheid's opponents became South Africa's dirty little family secret that everyone could see but no one openly talked about for fear that the house of cards called apartheid might come crashing down.

"There were two South Africas: white and black. Similarly, there was the public world and the private world, the open and the covert. And they were rigidly separate. What happened under cover of covert action was fine, so long as it did not come out in the open. The two spheres were not to collide. White South African bystanders were able to live with the brutality against blacks because it was being carried out in relative secret, in that 'other' world. Everyone engaged in an 'apartheid of the mind,' in psychological splitting."

In order to live with consciences intact, the white beneficiaries of apartheid had to ignore a great deal, or hold several conflicting ideas in their heads simultaneously. The vaunted Afrikaner struggle for freedom was built on the enslavement of others. Laws said to be based on Christian ideals violated the Bible's basic code of justice (Do unto others . . .), never mind Kant's categorical imperative (A law is just if you'd apply it to yourself just as you apply it to others). Separate development, the banishing of millions of South Africans to distant Bantustans where they barely avoided starvation, was touted as "a policy of good-neighborliness." A minority based its control of the majority on notions of racial purity that were known—even by eugenicists and social Darwinists—to be impossible to achieve. Whites blamed the poverty of blacks on the blacks' own fixed, inherent, biological limits, and the poverty of whites on fixable environmental factors. The Immorality Acts prohibited interracial sexual liaisons; a mixed-race population of one million proved they took place regularly. To survive these contradictions, many South Africans mastered the art of knowing and not knowing at the same time—of not seeing what they saw. Sandra Laing and her parents were among them.

Some people thought the TRC was helpful and healing; some thought amnesty was too good for the guilty. Afrikaners were most likely to grumble, "Why rehash the past? It's over." An odd opinion coming from people who are still actively fuming over the Boer War.

Some critics of the TRC called it a big, meaningless show. Bishop Tutu felt that the hearings couldn't possibly be considered "an exercise in airy feel-goodism" in a country where the formerly oppressed and the former oppressors had to live together. "If we look only to retributive justice," he said, "then we could just as well close up shop.

Forgiveness is not some nebulous thing. It is practical politics. Without forgiveness, there is no future."

Sandra agreed with him. She had come to feel that her own future happiness depended on receiving forgiveness from her mother. Her life was on an even keel. Elsie married a nice man she met in church, and Sandra paid for Jenny to make the four-hour taxi trip for the wedding. Henry, who had a good job as a technician in the quality-control department of a scientific glass company, married a high-school classmate. Prins dropped out of high school to work as an airport baggage handler, and Anthony and Steve were in school. Johannes still had his job as a driver, and Sandra earned extra money babysitting for neighbors' children. But the first thing she thought about in the morning and the last thing she thought about at night was how she could find her mother. Then, in 1998, the means to do so knocked at her door.

27

"A Decent White"

ARIEN VAN DER MERWE, A PRODUCER FOR THE SABC television current-events program *Special Assignment,* was asked by her bosses to make a half-hour segment about Sandra's life. "The funny thing is I never knew about Sandra until I was asked to do the story," Karien says. She read up on the Sandra Laing case and was touched and intrigued. When she met the woman at the center of the story, she was worried. Sandra was so shy and tongue-tied during their preliminary interviews that Karien was afraid, she said, that she'd have to make a silent movie.

"*Ag,* you were a plank!" Karien, Sandra, and I were drinking instant coffee in the backyard of Sandra's Tsakane home in the South African spring of 2001, sitting on kitchen chairs under a blossoming peach tree. Two little girls from next door came over and draped themselves across Sandra like bandoliers.

"I thought, my God, I can't film her! She barely speaks! The Sandra you see today is a different person to the one I met that day."

A pretty woman with short, blonde hair and a melodious, smoke-and-honey voice that sounds especially good on the air, Karien is impulsive, engaging, and an intrepid and accomplished television journalist. She's compelled to fill silences with chatter, providing Sandra with soothing white noise, as it were, and Karien finds Sandra's placidity terrifically comforting. The two are the same age, and they were both raised by white, middle-class, Calvinist, Afrikaans-speaking parents who delegated a good deal of child-rearing responsibilities to an affectionate black housekeeper.

Karien is chagrined to recall firmly believing, as a girl, the National Party claim that if black people weren't separated into tribal homelands, they would kill each other. When she was eighteen, she was an exchange student in southern Illinois. "I gave the most naïve interview to the *St. Louis Post-Dispatch*," she told me, and she shared the clipping, though it mortifies her today.

Asked about apartheid, South Africa's strict system of race separation, Kareen [sic] said comparisons with America's racial situation are difficult to draw. "Apartheid works in South Africa, but it would never work in America," she said, adding that "integration will never work in South Africa." Whites are of several national origins and the blacks who compose 75 per cent of the country's population have their own tribes, she said. South African blacks are more tribal and less experienced in politics and government than most American blacks, Kareen says. They are allowed to vote only within their own "kingdoms," which are large areas set aside for them within South Africa. Their role so far in the national parliament is strictly advisory but "it's slowly changing," she said. She predicted a much greater role for blacks in the government and society in the future.

However, most buses and hotels are still segregated by race, she said, although such restriction in the past as separate park benches have been abolished. Racial intermarriage is prohibited by law. Kareen gives the white view in support of this: with 25 per cent of the nation white, "if you have intermarriage, we will die out." While racial restrictions in South Africa often have government backing, the US has many similar restrictions enforced just as strongly by sheer social custom, Kareen says.

"I was taught—and I believed—that the black tribes had a violent history and still fought amongst themselves," Karien says. Certainly a campaign of Zulu expansion in the nineteenth century had led to intertribal battles—but that was long over. In the 1980s, the Xhosa-dominated African National Congress clashed violently with the Zulu-led Inkatha Party, but the TRC revealed that the police had paid Inkatha to foment trouble. "I believed that they liked living in their own homelands and didn't want to mix with one another, that each tribe was too proud of its own heritage and identity, and that keeping them separate in home-lands was for their own protection." When she discovered, dur-ing her stay in the States, the real history of South Africa, she says, "It was the loneliest feeling in the world."

Karien says she has difficulty reconciling her affection for what's admirable about her Afrikaner roots from distress over what's reprehensible. "They've been brainwashed by apartheid," she says about some of her *volk*. "If they'd grown up differently they wouldn't think like that. Deep in their hearts, they're decent people." I can see her confusion in action. On the one hand, she's risked her life covering stories about township violence. On the other hand, this otherwise rational and politically progressive woman, afraid someone might try to convince me that English-speaking South Africans were more enlightened about race issues than the Boers, offered this flustered defense of her people, with-out any consciousness of its ironies: "They say that they're so lib-eral, the English, but we Afrikaners were much more sensitive to the blacks! In Durban the English put their maids in tiny, dirty kitchens, and fed them bread and jam for supper. We gave our maid a big, comfortable kitchen to work in, and she ate just what we ate!"

In the course of doing research and preliminary interviews, Karien got to know Sandra, tended to her, nagged her like a sister, watched soapies with her, and became her friend. They had a great deal in common: They spoke the same language; they had gone to the same sort of school and learned the same lessons in church. "And I knew what it felt like to be an outsider," Karien said, "I wasn't English enough for Durban, where I grew up, and I wasn't Afrikaner enough at college."

Karien decided that one way to enliven Sandra for television would be to film her in Brereton Park and Piet Retief. The idea alarmed Sandra at first; seeing those places on tape had been hard enough. But like a fresh and reckless wind, Karien gathered Sandra up and plunked her down again in her past. Karien sees now that she took a great risk with Sandra's psyche, but she didn't think about that at the time, she says. Luckily, her strategy paid off for both of them.

Karien says exactly what she thinks, which Sandra seems to find salutary, but it can be startling for an outsider. "I don't remember hating blacks, but I remember being afraid of them," she once said when the three of us were in the car. She always insisted that Sandra sit in the front seat. During apartheid, blacks weren't allowed to sit in the front seat of cars driven by whites, and she was afraid that people would think we had forced Sandra to the rear. "And I remember thanking Jesus that I wasn't born black. Sandra's parents would have felt she came from the devil. To have a child who's dark is the worst possible thing that could happen to them. But they loved her. Maybe they moved away out of the community so they could be safe. But the world caught up with them."

Sandra asked to bring her youngest son, Steve, on the journey to her girlhood home. He was eleven then, the same age as Adriaan in the 1977 documentary. They set off in a minivan driven by a cameraman. "We stopped for lunch in Ermelo, the town where Sandra and her father had been told to leave a restaurant," Karien recalled. "She was afraid to go into the Wimpys there, even though she knew apartheid was over. She didn't want Steve to feel any discomfort. She finally agreed to go in, but insisted we sit in the corner where nobody could see us." They had no problem. Things had changed, even the name of her old province; since 1994, it was no longer the Eastern Transvaal but Mpumalanga, Swazi for the "land of the rising sun."

First they went to Brereton Park. The house had been torn down, and a black family lived in the disintegrating shop, a different family from the one Sandra had encountered in 1976, when she arrived with journalists to find her parents had moved. An old man who worked as a foreman on a timber crew remembered the Laings, and told her that the black customers always thought of her as a white child, despite her looks. The sounds and smells of Brereton Park had stayed the same: birdsong, the squeak of the *kraal* gate, the sighing of the wind, the rhythmic thudding of cows munching grass. The jacaranda leaves cast feathery shadows, and the orange and yellow butterflies danced as they had when Sandra was small. The yesterday-today-tomorrow tree still bloomed beside the former shop, but the forest behind the house where she and Petrus secretly met had been cut down for lumber long ago.

Sandra laughed when she showed Steve how to let the calves suck his fingers, and she wept when she smelled the yesterday-today-tomorrow. She cried more on that trip, she says, than she had in all the years since leaving home. At times, she feared she'd never stop. But she was glad, ultimately, because the tears opened a clogged stream of memory and began to dispel the fog in her head.

They visited Jenny in the countryside, and as usual, Sandra was made instantly happy by the sound of her mother-in-law's raspy voice. The cameraman filmed Jenny and Sandra speaking in Zulu. Only a snippet appeared in the finished program, but the conversation was important to Sandra.

"When you came to live with me, I was very happy to see you. I was very happy!" Jenny clapped her hands together. "I was very happy to help you give birth to Henry and Elsie." She clapped her hands again and shouted, "*Jabula!*" Happiness!

"Petrus asked me to go and see your mother. I personally spoke to your mother and she said I must please look after you. I was very happy that you became my child and that you gave me grandchildren. I now live here alone, and if it wasn't for all my furniture I would go and live with you."

"You always came to visit us in Tjakastad," Sandra said.

"Yes. When I came the dogs barked and you came running to me, shouting, 'Here comes Mama!' Yes, Sisi [a Zulu endearment]. Even now I am still happy when I see Sandra."

Sandra asked Jenny the question that had been gnawing at her, "Do you think my mother turned her back on me and threw me away?"

"No. Your mother never rejected you. She was only scared of

your father and what he might do to you and her. But when he wasn't there she always wanted to see you and talk to you."

"What happened when you told my mother I was in prison in Carolina?"

"Petrus sent me to your mother to tell her you were in jail. Your mother told me she had heard. She had received a telegram. She told your father, but he wasn't interested. Your mother said there was nothing she could do, because she had to listen to your father. Your mother just asked us to take care of you when you got out."

"What do you think my mother would say if she could see me now? I last saw her when Elsie was still a baby."

"Your mother will be very happy to see you because you are still her child."

"What do you think of my father? Was he strict?"

"I didn't know him, but your mother told me he would fight."

"At the time I left home with Petrus," Sandra said, "[my father] was very angry with me, and he said he never wanted to see me again because I chose Petrus above him. What do you think of the fact that my father turned his back on me because I chose Petrus?"

"I understand him. It is okay. He may not have wanted to see you again, but Petrus loved you. Now Petrus is dead and your father is dead. There is nothing we can do." The two women stood silently together. Sandra cried, and Jenny consoled her. Then she told Jenny, "I don't know where my mother is, but they will find her for me."

From Brereton Park, Sandra and Karien went to Piet Retief by the same dirt road that Sandra had taken the first day of school. Van Tonder had retired and Schwartz had died. Sandra was relieved; she didn't feel ready to face either of them. Very little in the town had changed, and neither had the school buildings. But Piet Retief Primary was in one way transformed: Since 1994, the conservative Afrikaner boarding school had been racially integrated. True, the Afrikaans-medium students were all white, most of the English-medium students were almost all black, and no white students were living in the hostel. Still, Sandra was amazed to see black and white children playing together on the same athletic field where she'd been called Kaffir, Blackie, and Frizzhead.

The school permitted Karien to film a group of hostel residents, coloured girls of eleven and twelve, chatting with Sandra. The documentary shows them listening with tear-filled eyes as Sandra tells her story of being expelled. When she finishes, they hug her and pat her on the back tenderly, responding with solemn empathy. "You're really strong to handle these things," one says. Another urges Sandra, "Don't feel ashamed about what has happened. You are welcome here. This school has changed. When we fight with the white children, the teachers help us; they tell us color doesn't matter and we should be friends." A particularly bright and confident girl looks into Sandra's eyes and says, "God has changed this world, for a long time things have been changing. And next time we will carry the world. Make it a lot happier." That night, at the motel, Sandra was too drained to speak. Karien and the cameraman went off for a drink. Sandra sat with Steve, watched her soapies, and cried. But afterward, she says, she felt more hopeful than she had in a long time.

The last stop of the trip was the cemetery in Pretoria where Abraham Laing is buried. Karien filmed Sandra visiting her father's grave for the first time. Sandra sobbed and spoke to him out loud. "I just wanted him to forgive me for leaving home and not being at his funeral," Sandra says. "The angry part of me was very small at that moment." The comment is notable for being one of the very few times that Sandra has acknowledged having an angry part.

When she saw the empty half of the headstone waiting for her mother's name and the plot of earth that would someday receive her body, Sandra's longing for her mother was stronger than it had been since the day she left home, she recalls. "I thought I couldn't go on with my life until I see her." She says so on camera.

On their travels together during the making of the television show, Karien promised to help Sandra find her mother. She knew it wouldn't be easy, because she'd already tried to talk to Sandra's brothers for the segment. While she was doing some background research for the film, a sympathetic employee in a government bureau—a woman familiar with Sandra's story from the newspapers—slipped Karien the brothers' tax identification numbers.

Once she had those, a friend of a friend who worked for Internal Credit Control, the tax department, was able to look up their addresses and telephone numbers on the computer.

Karien called Adriaan Laing first. He told her that he and his brother weren't interested in speaking to her or in seeing Sandra—and that they definitely didn't want her to find their mother. Sannie had suffered three strokes, Adriaan said, and they were afraid the shock of seeing Sandra again might kill her. Leon was protecting their mother and had put her in a safe place where neither the media nor Sandra would find her. Adriaan felt strongly that Sandra had betrayed the family by running off with a black man and choosing to be classified as coloured, after his parents had put so much effort into keeping her white. It was her choice, he kept saying to Karien, that she was no longer their sister. He said that if his wife and children were to find out that Sandra Laing was his sister, it would destroy their family. Adriaan sounded especially bitter about Sandra's having spoken to the media, and the incident with Susanna and the German film crew seemed to gall him the most. The brothers' view, Karien said, was that Sandra went to the media every time she needed money.

After she and Sandra visited Abraham's grave, Karien tried to talk to Adriaan in person. She knew he worked as a mechanic for a trucking company in Pretoria, so she drove there and looked for him. She recognized him from his photograph as an eleven-year-old in Antony Thomas's documentary. He had very short frizzy hair and skin lighter than Sandra's, but was clearly her kin. Adriaan Laing told Karien he would ask Leon one more time about talking to her. Later, he called from a phone booth to say the answer was no. Sandra was only after money from the media, he said again, and didn't care about her mother or the family. Adriaan begged Karien, "as a decent white," to please understand and leave them alone.

Though she didn't approve of the brothers' political stance, or share their interpretation of Sandra's actions and motives, Karien began having doubts about whether she should interfere in the Laing siblings' complicated relationship. And she felt sorry for the brothers. She didn't condone Adriaan's attitude toward his sister, she says, but she understood its context; she didn't think it was right that his neighbors would make his life hell if they learned he had a sister who was classified as coloured, but she knew they would. Karien promised Adriaan that she wouldn't help Sandra find her mother. "I told Sandra that I decided I shouldn't mix in family business, that there'd already been enough media meddling," Karien said. "We'd hit a dead end, and so I let it drop." But a few weeks later, Karien began to feel remorseful about her decision, and wondered if she'd done the right thing. "I thought about it and prayed about it, and I decided Sandra's right to see her mother was more important than the promise I'd made to Adriaan." Karien found a way to reconcile what she felt were two conflicting obligations, to Sandra, out of friendship, and to Adriaan, because she'd promised him: She would continue the search for Sannie behind the scenes, but as a friend, not as a journalist. A freelance reporter she knew, Karen Le Roux, would help publicly with the search, making inquiries as a sort of media beard. For her troubles, Le Roux would get an exclusive story if there was ever a reunion of mother and daughter.

The search continued fitfully throughout 1999. Karien, Karen, and Sandra decided one day to drive to the town three hours from Johannesburg where Leon lived and owned a tire shop. Karien and Sandra waited in the car while Karen went in and pretended to shop for tires. "She told us that Leon came across as a very bossy and stubborn person, and that she wouldn't want to get on the wrong side of him," Karien says. "She thought he'd grown up to look a lot like his father." They drove to Leon's home and Karien rang the doorbell; only the housekeeper was in. She told Karien that Sannie was in Upington, a town in the Cape province, and that she was very sick. "I called all the old age homes in Upington and couldn't find Sandra's mother," Karien says. "Leon seemed to have coached the helper to give that answer if anyone came around asking."

Karen Le Roux continued to make inquiries. Early in January 2000, through "a friend who is an ex-police officer," as she later wrote in the *Sunday Times*, she learned that Sandra's mother was living at the Amandashof Retirement Village, outside Pretoria, less than an hour's drive from Tsakane.

28

REUNION

TWO WEEKS INTO THE NEW MILLENNIUM, ON A HOT Friday afternoon, Sandra stood at the entrance to a visiting room in the Amandashof Retirement Village, twisting a white handkerchief, dizzy with anxiety. "I thought maybe my mother will say she won't see me," Sandra says. An inner door opened and a nurse appeared, pushing an old woman in a wheelchair. The chair came to a stop before Sandra. Sannie Laing sat with her eyes downcast. Her thin, stroke-skewed face looked fragile and sinewy at the same time. "I was afraid she was still mad at me," Sandra remembers.

While they searched for her mother, Sandra told Karien over and over that once they found her, any outcome would be all right; it was just the uncertainty that was driving Sandra crazy. She didn't want her mother to die before she could find out how Sannie really felt about her, and she didn't want to live with the regret of never having asked for her forgiveness. That Sannie might be the one requiring forgiveness was not a thought that occurred to Sandra at the time. She promised herself that if Sannie truly didn't want to see her again, as she had seemed to say in her last cold letter, she would accept her mother's wishes and go on with her life. "But Ma looked up," Sandra says, "and I saw that she still loved me."

A photographer snapped pictures, and Karen Le Roux took notes for the story that ran in the *Sunday Times* on January 23, 2000:

> The moment she has been aching for for nearly 30 years has arrived . . . for a couple of breathless seconds their eyes lock, then Sannie Laing opens her arms and Sandra bursts into tears, even before she stoops down to accept her mother's embrace . . .
>
> "At last. My daughter, Sandra." The soft words of Sannie Laing. A mother who did not know whether her daughter was dead or alive.
>
> Sandra holds on tightly to her mother's shoulders. It takes a few minutes before she is able to utter her first words. "Mammie. Mammie . . ." Sandra settles close to her mother. Now Sannie really looks at her daughter, disbelief mingling with unutterable joy on her face. "Can it be true? Is it really my daughter? Who brought my daughter to me? Tell them thank you. Thank you very, very much."

Sandra confirms that this is what happened, except for two things: she can't say for certain whether Sannie's face revealed "unutterable joy," and she *can* say for certain that Sannie knew very well that her daughter was alive.

Karen and the nurse left Sannie and Sandra alone. "It wasn't necessary to ask her for forgiveness with words," Sandra told Karien van der Merwe in Afrikaans, after the reunion. "I just knew she had forgiven me and I didn't feel the need to talk about it. I think that if I had found my mother and she'd been angry with me for running away, I would have kept coming back and begging for her forgiveness until she gave it. Maybe Jenny was right—my mother didn't reject me."

Sannie seemed pleased to see her daughter, but confused, Sandra says. She appeared to be suffering from some sort of dementia. "That day she wasn't well. She asked me the same thing over and over—where I'm staying, how did I come there, and said that if she had a place she'd take me in." She asked about Sandra's children and said she would be glad to see them; she complained about the food at the home and said that there wasn't enough. When Karen and the photographer rejoined the pair, Sannie was telling Sandra how much her perm had cost, and commenting on her wardrobe: "And here I am, in one of my oldest dresses on this happy occasion." Then she said to Sandra, "Now tell me again about the children."

Adriaan Laing happened to call Sannie at the retirement home during Sandra's visit. When the nurse reported that Sandra was there, he was furious, but the nurse told him that his mother had a right to see her daughter. "Adriaan must have called Leon," Sandra says, "because he then phoned and told the sister that they mustn't let the photographers take pictures. The sister said if my mother wants to take a photo with me, they can't stop her."

Two weeks after the first visit, Sandra brought her family to meet Sannie. They came in two cars, one belonging to Elsie's husband, Jafta Allies, and one to Henry's sister-in-law. "It was Henry, his wife, Sharon; Elsie and Jafta; Johannes, Prins, Anthony, Steve, and me. We met in a sitting room. They brought my mum out in a wheelchair and put her in a chair. The first thing she said was that she's glad to see the kids. She teased me about getting fat. We stayed only half an hour because she wasn't well. Sister said she hadn't slept. Jafta took photos of all the kids with her, one by one, and then a group photo. She asked the kids where they are staying; she asked me where I am staying. Her memory was failing. She said she wished she'd had as many children as I had. She also spoke Zulu to the black ladies who worked at the home. All of us drank tea with her, and then we left. She told me I must look after myself. After, the kids said they were glad to meet her."

Sandra's brothers were unhappy about the reunion story that ran in the *Sunday Times*, and another the next day in the *Daily Mail & Guardian*. "I wrote to Leon after the first visit," Sandra says. "I said I want them to forgive me for leaving home, I want to be friends, and I want to see them. I didn't ask for money. He didn't write back to me himself. He had a man named Jan write to me. He was a friend or a lawyer." She doesn't know if he's the same Jan who'd written nine years earlier, offering Sannie's address if Sandra would stop talking to the press. "The letter said Leon would give me money, R300 a month, if I would never see my mother again and keep quiet and not talk to reporters.

"I wrote this Jan back and said all these years I didn't see my mum, I can't stay away now. I said I do need money, but I'll keep seeing her whenever I have money for transport." In the letter to Jan, Sandra, who didn't have a telephone, included the phone number of a neighbor.

"Then Leon called. It wasn't a good call. He was angry. He said I broke my parents' hearts. Since I left home, my mother and father weren't happy again, always crying. My mother got sick and started having heart attacks. My father didn't want her to see me, and that made her sick, too. Leon said I must lie on the bed that I made for myself. He said I must forget about them. I chose to leave home, he said. I chose not to be their sister.

"I didn't answer him. I just listened. Then he said about Adriaan that the story people saw in the newspaper about me and my mother, the kids at school were talking about it to his kids, and his life wasn't the same anymore since people found out I left with a black man.

"Leon was angry, but he wasn't rude. Then he said about the time Karien and I went to my father's grave: 'You said on TV, "If I can see my mother just once, I can go on with my life." Do you remember? You've seen her now, so leave her alone.' He said it's me that's making her sick.

"I said to him I will try to stay away, but I don't promise anything. Leon did send money for five or six months, by postal order. That time I didn't have transport and so I didn't see my mum. When I did go see her, someone at the nursing home phoned Leon to tell him I was there. He stopped sending the money."

Nearly five months after Sannie and Sandra were reunited, in June 2000, Leon spoke to a reporter from the *New York Times*:

Leon Laing says he is sorry for the pain of the past, but he insists that history cannot be undone. The siblings will probably never know whether their family had a black ancestor somewhere, as some suspect, or whether their mother had an affair with a black man, as others believe. But even in the new South Africa, Mr. Laing says, his children would be humiliated if their white friends and neighbors suspected they had African ancestry. So he pretends his little sister was never born and begs reporters to help him keep the secret.

"I've got my wife and kids to think of. You understand? I have to keep them safe."

In July 2000, Sandra was interviewed for a BBC radio series, *No Triumph, No Tragedy*, about people with disabilities. "Nobody in their right mind would see being black as a disability," says host Peter White. "[But] under the peculiar and obscene tenets of apartheid, a physical characteristic . . . was used to include and disempower, in the same way that disability is often said to do . . ." Sandra told White:

My two brothers blame me for all of this. My eldest brother got two children. He adopted them. My mother told me that his wife can't get children. Maybe he is scared that he is going to get a child that looks like me.

An interview with Sannie Laing appeared in the *Sunday Times* more than six months after their reunion in the nursing home. Sannie is quoted as saying:

In those early years before she went to school, I was not too concerned about her future. I was not fully aware of the cruelty she endured because of her skin color and springy hair. She only casually mentioned the teasing. Today I know that she must have carried a lot of pain in her own little heart.

I was shocked when Sandra eloped with Petrus. Abraham was furious. He felt he had defended Sandra and she betrayed him. He was horrified that she had married a black man . . . A sadness hung over me.

. . . I never rejected my daughter. The rejection came from my husband. Today I think he was furious not so much because she married a black man, but because she didn't confide in us and just ran away . . .

My sons have made their decision and do not want to see Sandra, but it would be wonderful if we could reunite.

Sandra didn't see her mother again for several months. She insists that she couldn't afford to make the trip; Johannes was only working part-time then, she says, and they barely had enough money for food, rent, and clothes for the children, let alone cab fare or gas money. She could barely manage the seventy-four cents for a public phone call from Tsakane to Amandashof. I pointed out that her son-in-law's car could easily have been commandeered again. "I didn't want to bother Jafta to take me," she says, "and I didn't have money to give them for petrol."

The next visit Sandra made to her mother, in September 2000, was in the company of British filmmaker Tony Fabian, who'd heard Sandra on the radio in England and was deeply moved. "My first response was tears," he says. "I felt I wanted to make reparations for what had happened to her." He also thought Sandra's story would make a compelling film—not a documentary, but a dramatized feature. He tracked Sandra down through his contacts in the film industry.

Tony met with the whole family in Tsakane about the movie he proposed to make and was able to offer enough money for the rights to her story that Sandra's financial worries ought to have been over. Sandra and the family found Tony to be a kind and fair person, and agreed to the project. Tony drove Sandra to see her mother at the nursing home. "I left them alone together," he says. "But before I did, Sannie said, " 'Promise me you'll look after her for me.' "

When Sandra couldn't visit her mother, she telephoned or sent cards. She didn't see Sannie again until July 2001, when Karien brought her for a visit. The nurse warned them that Sannie had suffered two bad falls and several small strokes since they had last seen her, and that they shouldn't expect too much. Sannie's face was black and blue; she had a large bump on her forehead and stitches above one eye. She was confused and barely recognized Sandra. "Are you still alive?" she mumbled. Sandra had to put her ear close to Sannie's mouth. She made little sense. She asked if Sandra had brought her any money; she said that she needed to iron her clothes, that she was turning one hundred years old that day, that her husband had died two years ago. "She was sick that day, she wasn't right. I don't think she knew who I was," Sandra says. While Sandra sat with Sannie and smoothed her hair, Karien chatted with the nurse and mentioned that she and Sandra were hoping to ask her mother to tell her, once and for all, whether Abraham was her real father. The nurse said she thought it highly unlikely that Sannie would have had an affair with a black man. She doesn't like black people, the nurse said. "*Sy kan hulle nie voor haar oe verdra nie.*" She can't bear to have them near her. Karien felt that Sannie was so confused it would be cruel to ask her. The nurse also told Karien that when the special assignment segment aired in 1999, Sannie denied having a daughter, but she was happy when Sandra came.

Sandra cried all the way home, and told Karien she had a feeling she'd never see her mother again. When Sandra phoned the nursing home a week later, they told her Sannie was sick and had been taken to a hospital. "The next time I phoned, she was a little better." Three weeks went by before Sandra called again. "They told me she'd died two weeks before."

Sandra feels certain that her brothers hadn't let her know about her mother's death because they didn't want her at the funeral. Hurt and furious, she comforted herself with the thought that her mother was in a better place, that she could rest, that she died with a contented heart. Sandra wondered aloud to Karien and others whether Sannie had willed herself to stay alive until she saw her daughter again. Maybe she deteriorated after their reunion, Sandra suggested, because she'd been hanging on to make peace with her daughter and stop living a lie that Leon and Adriaan demanded from her. These conjectures made Sandra feel better in the weeks after her mother's death. The one thing she was sure of, Sandra told Karien, was that her mother had been glad to see her.

Though Sandra grieved for Sannie, the relief of feeling forgiven had already begun to lift the weight that flattened her heart for years, and to release complex emotions, long suppressed.

"Only after her mother died," Karien says, "did Sandra admit to me that she couldn't relate to her. Her words were"—Karien speaks them in Afrikaans and then translates into English—"'She didn't feel as though she was part of my family.'" Sandra told Karien that although she felt her mother loved her, they were in some ways strangers to each other. "She said they belonged in two different worlds: 'It didn't feel right, like she maybe isn't my mother, because all these years I didn't see her.'

"But it opened another door for her," Karien says, "because it's as though she came to terms with who she is and no longer thought, 'I don't know if my mother wants me.'"

Sandra seemed free to see how much her newly lightened heart belonged to Jenny, who had taken over the job of raising her when Sandra was a teenager and had welcomed her exactly the way she was. Both her white mother and her adoptive black mother had tried their best for her, Sandra thought, but it was her black mother who held her when her children entered the world, and it was her black mother who comforted her at Petrus's grave.

Three months after Sannie's death, Sandra, Karien, and I visited Jenny in the hills outside Lochiel. Her three-room, tin-roofed house, built from boards with smooth mud plastered between them, had no electricity or plumbing. At eighty-two, she carried her own water in a bucket from a communal tap, chopped her own firewood into kindling for her coal stove, and tended a small field of mealies. She supplemented her old-age pension by making and selling beer; she also paid in beer when she needed to hire workmen to repair the house or help her in the mealie field. Jenny was delighted with the surprise visit and welcomed Sandra as a beloved child.

Sandra brought Jenny a newspaper file photo of Petrus from the recent spate of articles about her life. Jenny looked at the image of her son, sighed, and spoke to the picture in Swazi, half to herself. Sandra translated: "She's saying, 'Oh, if I could stand him up and breathe him awake!'" Jenny led us to Petrus's grave on a nearby hillside, a stone-covered mound, and we went to work pulling the weeds poking up through the piled stones. Jenny talked to her son in Swazi as she tended the grave. "She's telling him he has visitors." Sandra said. "She's telling him the news, and saying that he must look after me."

We sat on a bench in Jenny's kitchen while she boiled water for tea on the coal stove and told stories of teenage Sandra's arrival in the Zwane *kraal*, how comically inept she was at fetching water and gathering wood. Sandra basked in the teasing, relaxed and laughing. But as we drove away from Jenny's place, Sandra began crying. "Petrus would still be alive if I hadn't left him," she said. "*Ag, shame*," Karien said. "That's just not true." Karien told Sandra that Petrus might have gotten himself killed, anyway—and that if she hadn't left him, no doubt it would be her grave Jenny was cleaning, not his.

Sandra knew a shortcut back to the main highway and flawlessly guided us along unmarked, unpaved back roads she'd last traveled with Petrus nearly thirty years before. Sandra may have spent some time lost emotionally, but never spatially—she's always had an extraordinary sense of direction. She never forgets a route, always knows where she is, and even though she doesn't drive, she can give detailed directions to places all over Mpumalanga and the East Rand. In Tsakane, Johannes kept a coop of homing pigeons; Sandra called them doves. We were in the yard a few months after her mother's death and she told me, "A dove is the animal I would most like to be. I love doves. They are free. They can always find their way home."

After her mother's death and the visit to Jenny, Sandra began having what she calls the laughing dream, several nights a week. In it,

Petrus is alive, and they're together in her mother's shop in Brereton Park, or the ruined farmhouse on the KwaThema road, a place he never saw. They're not making love or even kissing. They're laughing and laughing and laughing, and she feels a new space open up in her heart. Sometimes it remained open after she woke.

29

DURABLE GOODS

S ANDRA'S STORY FIRST BECAME A COMMODITY THE DAY that someone, most likely her father, traded it to the press for sympathetic coverage after she was expelled from school in Piet Retief. Two years later, in 1968, Abraham threatened to peddle the tale to the movies if the government didn't come up with compensation for the Laings' suffering and humiliation.

They didn't pay; he didn't sell. No hard currency changed hands until the 1970s, when the press caught up with Sandra as a young mother, first in her flourishing Kromkrans garden, then in a hardscrabble Bantustan. She never hawked her tale the way she might a pile of pumpkins or a tub of house beer; it's just that reporters occasionally tracked her down, asked questions, and offered small infusions of cash that were a big help.

Sandra wouldn't have chosen this particular cottage industry; she feels it cost her more emotionally than it ever brought her financially—until December 2001, when Sandra's story earned her what she wanted most in the world: a permanent home, one that she owns, "a place where no one can kick me out." With the money from a book advance negotiated for her by Tony Fabian and a year's option on film rights to her life, she was able to pay cash for a spacious, well-made house in a mixed-race residential development that's a twenty-minute drive from the old Tsakane house, which would almost fit into the largest of the three new bedrooms.

The new development is free of annoying crime lights, though not of crime—mostly break-in robberies and carjackings, one involving a murder. But it's safer than Tsakane, and the houses are much more stylish and substantial. Sandra's salmon-coloured stucco house with black trim, a landscaped front yard, and a built-in brick barbecue out back wouldn't look out of place in a middle-class southern California housing tract. The friend of Elsie's who told Sandra the house was for sale, a widow named Sabina Matroos, lives directly behind her and has a built-in swimming pool. In fact, Sandra's new neighborhood, with its bottle-brush bougainvillea, could be an L.A. suburb, except for the presence of a squatters camp about a mile away across a grassy field, a jumble of cardboard and corrugated tin structures nearly always wreathed in woodsmoke haze. Until about fifteen years ago, this was an all-white area. After the end of apartheid, a few white families stayed, but the majority of the residents now are coloured and Indian, with a scattering of black families.

The new house deeply delighted Sandra. She felt it was meant to be hers the first time she toured it and saw that next to the front door grew a yesterday-today-tomorrow, her favorite tree. Sandra wished that Sannie had lived to see her house, and wondered whether her brothers would ever visit it.

She paid Prins and Anthony to paint the place inside and out, and held a big housewarming party—a roof-wetting, it's called in South Africa, after the ritual celebrated at the raising of a thatched rondavel. Family, friends, and new neighbors gathered for a *braai*. Soon after, Sandra surprised and pleased herself by finding an excellent school for Steve without anyone else's help, and she was able to cover the first quarter's fees with the money left over from the house purchase. She was relieved; Steve had fallen behind at the township school, partly because he didn't pay attention and partly because the teachers sometimes didn't show up. Small for fifteen, Steve played with younger boys and was extremely attached to his mother, an overdependence she couldn't help encouraging a bit. He was her baby, and she did best with babies. In the crowded Tsakane house, he'd slept in the same room as Johannes and Sandra, and he continued to do so in the new place. Johannes was annoyed.

In fact, Johannes wasn't terribly happy with the move at all. He hadn't wanted Sandra to buy the new house because it was too far away from the factory where he worked. Her decision to do so anyway became a source of tension: Johannes was the man of the house, but Sandra wasn't heeding his wishes. He began spending weeknights at his brother's house to be closer to work, and he refused to contribute to Steve's schooling. Sandra was especially hurt that Johannes gave clothing, cell phones, and money to his two younger children with his late wife but not to their son. The couple didn't fight, but they'd never been more distant—and Sandra hadn't kicked Steve out of their bedroom.

Henry and Elsie were settled comfortably with their spouses nearby; both of them had cars. Jafta was a computer programmer; Elsie wanted to work but her husband didn't approve, so she spent most of her days with Sandra. Henry's wife, Sharon, was an office administrative assistant, and Henry still worked as a quality control technician. During the week their son Naijan, nearly two, stayed with Sandra. Prins was twenty-one and unemployed; he spent most of his time sitting around at home listening to music, or hanging out in sports bars playing video games and drinking, on money Sandra gave him. Prins often snapped at Sandra and had perfected a gangster glower, but was tender and attentive to little Najean. Anthony, nineteen, devoted himself to weight lifting and prayer meetings. He talked about attending a *technikon*, a technical college, in order to become a recording engineer, but he didn't apply. Like his older brother, he'd had no luck finding a job, and to Sandra's alarm, he'd been joining Prins at sports bars.

When Prins and Anthony pestered Sandra for cash, she found it impossible to say no. Not only did she feel it was a mother's duty to share her good fortune, but she felt she owed them something for the hard times growing up, and they knew how to work her guilt.

The boys escalated their spending, mostly on clothes, sports equipment, and beer. Then Sandra launched her own brand of recreational profligacy.

With the house paid for and Johannes contributing from his salary, even a reduced share, the family ought to have been able to live comfortably for several months on Sandra's book and film earnings. But Sandra quickly encountered the strange arithmetic that so often governs windfall after hardship: Although she could get by on nearly no money, she couldn't get by on a lot.

In post-apartheid South Africa, so many lottery winners burned instantly through riches meant to last a lifetime that they're now required to take a class in money management before they can collect their loot. Sandra could have used such a course. The first danger sign was the Great Knickknack Crisis of '02, engendered by Sandra's new infatuation with Home Choice, South Africa's largest shopping catalogue. A splurge on decorative ceramic doodads, curtains, bedding, and kitchenware soon maxed out the account Sandra opened for herself, so she opened a couple more in her children's names. The situation ultimately required a frantic 5 A.M. phone call to Tony in London for an advance on Sandra's next option payment, followed by a tearful promise never to live beyond her means again.

Within a few months, Sandra fell more deeply into debt—partly because she kept buying things she knew she couldn't afford, but also because of cultural dislocation. For example, her electricity was turned off because she didn't pay the bill—but she hadn't realized she needed to, she says. In Tsakane, Sandra had purchased power the way many poor South Africans do—with a prepaid card good for a certain number of hours of electricity, printed with a code number that she punched into a keypad in her home. When the amount on the card ran out, the electricity was cut off. Like most township dwellers, she learned to ration electricity use down to the nanosecond; she knew exactly how much television she could watch each day if she wanted the refrigerator to keep running.

When Sandra moved into the new house, the electricity was

on. She thought it was part of the deal because white people lived in the neighborhood. Sandra believed that white people got their light and power for nothing—not so outlandish an assumption in a country where, until a little more than a dozen years ago, economic privileges, from the best job to free textbooks, were regularly bestowed on whites and denied to blacks. By the time she understood that people of every hue must pay for electricity, the power was off and she had to borrow money to restore it. She'd already tapped out Karien van der Merwe. Sandra never asked black or coloured people to lend her money, she says, because she knew they were struggling themselves.

So she turned to Elize Lötter, her old boarding-school roommate. Elize had reentered Sandra's life briefly in 2000, after reading about Sandra in the *Sunday Times* and sending a letter that she hoped would eventually find its way to her friend. "Many years have passed and I know that there is no way that you could remember me," she wrote.

> All my life I had wondered what had happened to you, as I always wanted you to know how much what we had experienced back at the boarding school in Piet Retief had impacted on my life . . .
>
> Sandra, you became a major source of inspiration to me, determined to become one of the whites to assist to bring about change in this country in my own way just as a normal citizen. My determination to become instrumental in uniting people of various cultures took me on my spiritual journey knowing that much of this was born from having known you . . . You are unaware of the fact that many people's lives in this country has been touched through you. I want you to know that all the pain that you suffered was not fruitless and all along there were some of us who did care about you. I always remembered the fight you put on and quite often said to myself if you could fight them then I could do the same . . .

Elize went on to tell Sandra that she'd taught school for several years and then, in 1988, took a job as a safety trainer at Eskom, the national electric company. When the dismantling of apartheid began in 1991, she was chosen as one of only three whites among a group of forty-seven participants in a management development program. "The most difficult year of my life started as I became a sort of an outcast in my community," Elize wrote to Sandra. "Whites saw me as a traitor to them, some black people thought that I was now siding with the black people as it was now politically better to be black." She began taking on extra corporate consulting jobs, specializing in harmonization and cultural diversity workshops, and used the money to create a successful program linking township schools with schools in England that sent books, computers, and supplies. "Change is happening and slowly I can see that no child will ever have to experience what you had to go through," Elize wrote. "You were the one who planted the seed within me many years ago to tackle something even in a time when the country was not ready for what I tried to do."

The letter was eventually forwarded to Karien van der Merwe, who arranged for the three of them to get together near the end of 2000. Elize was right; Sandra had no memory of her at all, but liked her and was interested in her stories about their school days. They didn't see each other again, however, until after Sannie's death. Sandra thought Elize had abandoned her, but Elize was going through a difficult divorce. When she got back in touch with Sandra, she became an important and consistent force in her life, pledging to devote one day a week to the Laing family for a year, offering any sort of help they needed. About ten years earlier, Elize had left the Dutch Reformed Church and become a follower of Sai Baba, an Indian guru whose motto is "Love All, Serve All." Barely five feet tall and weighing less than one hundred pounds, Elize has two grown children from the first of her three marriages, a voice pitched like a piccolo, an Afrikaner accent as thick as boer sausage, big hair, a small ego, and an extraordinarily good nature.

Elize drove Sandra to the hospital to visit her stepdaughter

Stiena, and helped her cope with Stiena's death from cancer at the age of thirty-two. She guided Anthony and Prins through filling out job applications. But she devoted most of her time with the Laings to trying to help Sandra get a grip on her spending. Elize pointed out to Sandra that the film and book money wasn't going to last forever, and then she'd need a job or some other source of sustainable income. Sandra said she couldn't take a job because she needed to watch Najean but what she'd really like to do someday was run a shop, as her parents had—maybe a little spaza, a tuck shop, out of her house.

But first there was the electric bill to square away, and then the phone bill. Sandra's first-ever telephone was turned off when she couldn't pay the puzzlingly massive bill, nearly ten times higher than it ought to have been. Prins and Anthony and their friends, she discovered, had run up hours of long-distance charges. She didn't ask the boys to pay her back; instead, Elize loaned her money. Sandra got a prepaid plan and put a lock on the phone. She wore the key around her neck.

Tony, concerned about Sandra's future, suggested to her that she put the money into a trust account, out of which she would receive a monthly sum. That way, he said, she could live comfortably, and the money would last longer and earn interest. Sandra agreed. "But once the payment became imminent," he says, "Sandra changed her mind and said she wanted it all at once. It was her money, she said, to spend as she saw fit. Contractually, I had no choice but to give it to her." Sandra assured Tony that she would use the money responsibly.

Elize left for a ten-day business trip to England. In her absence, Sandra received a large lump-sum payment enough for the family to live on for nearly a year—and launched a frenzy of acquisition that cleaned her out completely before Elize returned. The principal purchases were a faux French colonial dining-room set—table, chairs, and sideboard—for R50,000, at least three times what it was worth, and the down payment on a burglar-alarm system, bought on credit. She instantly fell behind on payments, and couldn't come up with the next installment of Steve's school fees.

The shopping spree, Elize thought, gave Sandra a way to prove her worth. A dining-room table suggests abundance and evokes the image of an intact and happy family. Furthermore, its presence says the owner has the means to acquire such furniture. A burglar alarm sign in the yard announces to the world that she has things worth protecting, and suggests she deserves them.

Sandra extricated herself from the burglar alarm contract. Elize tried putting Sandra on a budget; she tried signing her up with a free personal financial advisor at the bank, but neither plan worked. Though Sandra told Elize she didn't have enough money for groceries, she hired a woman to do her ironing and a team of six gardeners with power mowers and hedge trimmers to tend the yard. Then she was possessed by the desire for a swimming pool, and began inquiring about having one built on credit. "It was always my dream," she told Elize—who promptly pointed out the pool fifteen feet from her back door that she was welcome to use any time. She also pointed out that Sandra had never once used her neighbor Sabina's pool. Elize called in Karien, who'd taken a little break from Sandra because she was tired of being hit up for loans all the time, and together they talked Sandra out of her pool plans.

In using possessions to prove her worthiness, Sandra may have been unconsciously enacting an article of her girlhood faith. Among adherents of the Dutch Reformed Church, material wealth was considered a possible outward sign of God's grace. It's likely that Sandra also understood the power ascribed to ritual objects by traditional diviners and healers. She was familiar with the way *sangomas* use animal bones and ceremonial fly whisks to summon the help of ancestral spirits, and she knew they regularly added power objects to their armamentarium in order to expand their command of supernatural forces. Sandra felt the numinous power of tchotchkes, and was able to activate the mysterious forces of consumerism, but she didn't know how to control them. Like the sorcerer's apprentice, she was drowning.

Sandra's spending could also be considered a kind of political statement, though neither conscious nor healthy. South African social critics have wondered in various media commentaries whether the end of apartheid, like the fall of the Berlin wall, has brought far too great a focus on the freedom to shop. Eve Bertelsen, a professor of media studies at the University of Cape Town, scrutinized magazine ads aimed at black readers and found that many appropriated the messages and symbols of the struggle against apartheid, conflating political choice and the freedom to choose among products. "In these ads," she writes in an essay that appears in *Negotiating the Past: The Making of Memory in South Africa*, "positive social identity is strictly tied to the acquisition of commodities . . . 'You've won your freedom. Now use it. Get a Foschini's credit card today.'" Bertelsen points out a curious by-product of the free-market philosophy embraced by South Africa's new political leadership: Consumer capitalism, she says, is replacing old markers of identity, such as occupation and class, with new ones: "Distinction is increasingly conferred by possessions and appearances . . . While [the] poor and unemployed may not be able to afford to buy, their desire for commodities is just as great . . ."

When Elize asked Sandra the reason for her spending sprees, she said simply, "I needed things."

Whatever her motivations, conscious and un-, Sandra seemed to have shifted most of her trust and hope from people to material objects. Perhaps durable goods made up for unendurable wrongs. Maybe she'd had it with delayed gratification. One plausible explanation is that stuff and money felt like love. She often said that the fact that her father left her money proved that he really did love her.

Sandra began to brood about whether her brothers loved her. In February 2002, Sandra left a telephone message for Leon, hoping to talk with him for the first time since the uncomfortable conversation in which he offered to pay her to stay away from Sannie. She wanted to tell him about her house, and let him know she thought of him often. Elize practiced with her what she'd say if Leon called back; above all, Sandra mustn't ask him for money, or Leon would think that's all she wanted from him. Leon returned the call. Sandra told him she was a homeowner, and he told her there was a small amount of money coming to her from their mother's will. Sandra said to Leon, "You'll always be my big brother and I love you.

I think of you often." Leon said he thought of her, too, and wished God's blessing on her. It seemed that a door was opening. Then Sandra slammed it shut. Despite Elize's coaching, Sandra couldn't help herself; she asked him to send money. Leon was understandably annoyed and felt confirmed in his belief that Sandra was chiefly motivated by greed; he sent her R1,000 and told her not to call him again. Afterward, when Elize asked Sandra why on earth she'd put the touch on Leon after all their discussions about how he was likely to respond, she said, "I just needed to know if he really cared about me. If he gave me money, then he cared."

The talk with Leon deepened Sandra's conviction that she was in the wrong for leaving home and required his forgiveness. Now that she'd managed a reconciliation of sorts with Sannie, her brother's refusal to see her seemed to take precedence as her chief source of sorrow.

30

UNRELIABLE NARRATORS

A FTER THE UNHAPPY PHONE CONVERSATION WITH LEON, Sandra asked Elize if she'd take her to visit Sannie's grave, next to Abraham's, for the first time. "I just told my mum out loud that I'm sorry I couldn't come to her funeral. I didn't know." Then Sandra became more and more agitated. "But there was fresh cement around the headstone, as if it had been removed and placed back into position," Elize recalls, "and because of that, Sandra became convinced that her mother wasn't really dead, that Sannie was still alive and being hidden from her by her brothers." Maybe she wasn't invited to the funeral, Sandra said through her sobs, because there was no funeral. Elize had never seen Sandra so upset; she was screaming with sorrow and outrage. To calm her, Elize took her to the cemetery office to see the registry of graves. Finally she convinced Sandra that her mother was really dead, but Elize could see that her friend needed help. "She was gaining more and more weight and she said she wanted to slim down." Elize says. "Her blood pressure was up, she chewed her fingernails until they bled, and she was terrified about paying her bills, though she wouldn't stop spending. She was sad about her mother, and obsessed with having her brother forgive her. She said she was very unhappy." Elize resolved to find Sandra a therapist.

The concept of therapy was vaguely familiar to Sandra from

the soapies. Elize described the therapeutic process as talking to a wise advisor who helped people solve problems, and Sandra liked that idea. A friend of Elize's recommended an Afrikaner woman whom I'll call Louise van der Bijl. In an e-mail that Elize forwarded, Louise described herself as a clinical hypnotherapist, reiki and karuna ki master, and energy therapist, and a member of the Association for Past Life Research and Therapies (USA). Reiki and karuna ki, I learned, are Eastern healing practices that purport to manipulate the body's energy fields, as defined by traditional Chinese medicine. Past-life therapy worried me. Sandra's present incarnation seemed enough of a handful. Louise told Sandra that she'd see her once or twice per week for sessions that might last up to five hours each, and that in cases as severe as hers, the therapy could take a couple of months. The earth's orbit shifted slightly as generations of psychoanalysts spun in their graves.

Sandra immediately liked Louise and felt comfortable and comforted by her; she was also pleased that Afrikaans was Louise's first language. Though Sandra asked about hypnosis—she'd seen it done on *The Bold and the Beautiful,* Louise felt she'd benefit more from talk therapy. Louise told Elize after two sessions that she felt she and Sandra had established a solid, trusting connection. "She said she would work with Sandra on building up self-esteem and confidence and losing weight," Elize says. "She thought that as Sandra worked through releasing her pain and blocked-up emotions, the weight, which she called emotional baggage, would also go."

Louise told Sandra and Elize that she would "work out of love," reducing her regular fee and postponing payment until Sandra saw real results. Sandra enjoyed spending time with the motherly, supportive Louise and bestowed her highest accolades: "all right" and "very nice." Twice a week for four weeks, in long, intense sessions, they talked about Sandra's childhood, focused on her strengths, and worked on affirmations—Sandra, for example, wrote "I am a winner" in Afrikaans on her bedroom mirror with a magic marker. Sandra said she enjoyed the exercises. She told Karien that therapy was hard, but she liked it a lot.

Louise had Sandra perform a ceremony in which she burned

candles in honor of her parents and then let go of her anger toward them. Elize wondered to me if perhaps Sandra would benefit more from letting go of her anger if she were first helped to recognize that she felt it. A British friend of Elize's once said that the most amazing thing about Sandra was that after everything that's happened to her, she has no anger. That surprised me. I saw a churning urn of burning (repressed) rage manifested in self-destructive choices, passive-aggressive behavior, chewed fingernails, desperate spending, and the extra hundred pounds she was carrying. I worried that as a therapized, feminist, kvetcho-American, I might be projecting, so I checked out my perceptions with women of color who knew Sandra. "No anger?" said one, a level-headed ANC stalwart who'd been imprisoned in the 1980s for her activism. "What? The girl is *piiiissssed!*" But like many people who've suffered physical or psychological abuse, Sandra seems unsure about whether she's entitled to anger and spends more time feeling guilty than wronged.

After a month and a half, Louise van der Bijl said she was seeing results, which meant it was time to stop working out of love and get paid. Neither Elize nor Sandra could come up with her fee, so that was the end of that.

Sandra told Elize she felt cheated by Louise, but she didn't seem terribly upset. And she was interested when, a few months after Louise's defection, Elize said she'd heard a therapist on a radio talk show who sounded good for Sandra: a white Frenchwoman in her late fifties we'll call Sylvie Picard. Sylvie used massage and "healing touch" to help people solve problems. When Elize called and told her Sandra's story, Sylvie volunteered to lower her fee. Elize decided to pay for the therapy, though it was a financial strain for her, and also offered to drive Sandra from the East Rand and back for each weekly visit to Sylvie's Johannesburg home.

Sandra loved the massage, a novel experience; she felt a profound relaxation that seemed to help her retrieve more childhood memories. Sylvie reported to Elize, who waited in the living room, that in the middle of their first session, Sandra had seen her mother and father, and they were asking her to please forgive them so they could be released to go where they need to be. Though Elize wasn't sure exactly what "seeing" her parents meant—she assumed it was the same as "picturing" or "imagining"—this seemed like a positive step since it suggested that Sandra had accepted the idea that her parents, and not just she, required forgiveness for past actions. When she left that day, Sandra said, "Thanks, Sylvie. I know you are the person who can help me."

Sandra began to express some anger at Sannie and Abraham in conversations with Elize, who cheered her on. "I told her it was perfectly human and okay to feel that her parents had hurt her, so that she could move on with her life." More and more details from girlhood came back to her—her classmates hiding her shoes in the shower, shopping with Sannie for her first school uniform—and she spoke of anxieties she'd never articulated before, such as her concern that because Prins is darker than Anthony he feels less loved. Saying these secrets out loud, first to Sylvie and then to Elize, seemed to calm and strengthen Sandra. But Sylvie was something of a bully; she'd ask Sandra questions and answer them herself, and she kept having "visions"—she'd say she could "see" Sandra in the past, doing this or that, and she insisted that Sandra see it too. That was too weird for Elize. "The whole idea of this process was to help Sandra realize that in life we have different choices as to how we're going to approach pain or difficulty," she told Sylvie. "You can choose to lie down and allow the whole world to run over you, or you can choose to say, 'This happened to me for a reason, and what is it that I want to do with this?' We can only be a tool to assist Sandra. At the end of the day, the choice is hers." But Sylvie kept focusing on her visions; I saw her in action on one visit, when she invited me, Elize, and Sandra to stay for lunch after Sandra's fifth healing sessions. She asked Sandra to tell us about the things they'd discussed.

"Sandra," Sylvie asked, over salad Niçoise, "do you remember when you walked with your father down this little alley, where there were rocks, somewhere by the house?"

"Yes, I remember—I think we were walking from the shop and we were coming home, and I fell in front of my father. And then he pushed me with his foot, and he said to me why are you so stupid, why am I always falling, I must walk behind him. It was still before I was sent to school."

"And he said something else to you, too. About your brains."

Sandra's voice grew stronger. "He said, 'You're so stupid, you have no brains.'"

"He said you have the brains of?"

"He said I've got brains like these people. And he pointed to the kitchen where Nora and Miriam was."

This was a memory of abuse far more specific, and uglier, than Sandra had previously shared. Later that afternoon, while Sandra and I were in my hotel room watching soapies—this was the mini-vacation during which she remembered that her parents quarreled—she said, during a commercial break, "I don't remember my father pushing me with his foot, but Sylvie said he did."

"Sandra," I asked, "was it Sylvie who remembered that you fell, or was it you?"

"She said to me, 'I see you walking over small stones,' and then I remembered I fell, and what my father said."

"What about your father saying to your mother, 'Is she my child?' Did Sylvie have anything to do with that memory?"

"She said to me, 'I see your parents quarreling—what are they quarreling about?' And then I remembered what he said."

Okay, I thought, that's an innocuous-enough trigger. Whose parents don't quarrel? "And Mr. Van Tonder punishing you by locking you in the closet?"

"She said, 'I see you in a dark place,' and then I remembered."

"*Ay-yi-yi*," I said.

"But most things I remember myself."

The next day, Sandra and Elize had a chat about Sylvie, her visions, and her habit of answering questions directed at Sandra. They decided that Sylvie was not, after all, the right therapist for Sandra, although the massage was delicious, and Sylvie had played a part in helping Sandra rediscover pieces of her past.

Perhaps too big a part? How much did Sylvie's "visions" influence Sandra? People can certainly be made to remember things that never happened. In a well-known 1993 experiment, psychologist Elizabeth Loftus of the University of California, Irvine, used complicit family members to implant in teenagers and children false memories of having been lost in a shopping mall when they were younger. The subjects not only quickly accepted the false memory, but added "remembered" details. In 2005, Loftus repeated the experiment, this time convincing adults, once again with the help of relatives in on the deception, that as children they'd gotten sick on a certain food and thus no longer could stomach it.

But a number of studies in which subjects record their daily experiences and are later tested on them have yielded different results. "These studies show a good deal of forgetting, but not much misremembering," writes Ulric Neisser, professor emeritus of psychology at Cornell University and co-editor of *The Remembering Self: Construction and Accuracy in Self-Narrative.* "There are very few overt errors or confabulations . . . The fact that *some* memories can be dramatically mistaken doesn't mean that *all* memories are wrong." Sylvie's prompting—and Sandra's vulnerability to suggestion—may have muddied the waters, but they didn't negate Sandra's growing memory bank, which expanded both before and after Sylvie's theatrics. An exponential burst of recollection followed Sandra's purchase of her home; feeling safe and rooted seemed to allow her to withstand a clearer picture of the past. And sometimes Sandra's memory was jogged by seeing a person or place from long ago. For example, she remembered the story of getting drunk and falling asleep under a tree after we paid a visit to Petrus's wife Lisa, whom Sandra had called "Selena" in the first few weeks we talked together. Then she realized she'd been using the wrong name; Selena was an alcoholic woman who rented one of the outbuildings at the crumbling farmhouse on the KwaThema road. The associative link was their drinking.

Sandra and I visited her mother-in-law Jenny in her rural village several different times. Near the end of the third visit, sitting on a bench near Jenny's coal stove, Sandra asked me if I'd like to go meet Lisa. Of course, I said, rather surprised. Sandra had never hinted that she knew what had become of her fellow wife. Was it far? Could we drive there? Lisa lived down the road from Jenny, not a quarter of a mile away. It may be that Sandra had forgotten that Lisa lived nearby, or that she didn't feel comfortable with my talking to Lisa until that moment, or that she didn't realize that it was important to our enterprise. Perhaps in the state of dissociative flatness from which she was emerging, it was hard for her to pick out what was important. When I first met Sandra, she was as likely to speak animatedly and in detail about dinner as about, say, her sons' schooling. More likely, in fact, since there are no hopes, or complications, or disappointments attached to dinner.

Whatever the reason, I was pleased to have the chance to meet Lisa, who died in 2006 after a long illness. You could see that she was once a beauty, but she'd become bloated and blurry with drink. She had an appraising glance and an appealing laugh. I asked her, through Sandra, "Were you mad when Petrus ran off with Sandra?"

"What do you think?" she answered with a snort. Then she grinned. "Of course I was angry. But we became friends, this one and me. Petrus was a good man. He only hit me three times, when I smoked. The boys squealed on me." She and Sandra found that remark very funny. Then, on the drive from Lisa's to our hotel in nearby Badplaas—the same hotel where Sandra and Abraham had spent a week years ago—Sandra remembered the day she and Lisa drank too much when they went to fetch borrowed dishes, and Lisa got stuck in the river mud.

The trigger for Sandra's additions and revisions to her story wasn't always as apparent. When she'd been living in the new house for a while, after she'd spoken with Leon, Sandra suddenly told me that she'd written to her father in 1987, and that he had answered her letter. For years she'd been saying that she'd never communicated with her father again after running off with Petrus. Now she said, "I think it was when they were in Pongola that I wrote. I just said that I miss them very much and I wanted to see them if they wanted to see me. And I gave them my address. That time I was staying with Ouma Letty in Geluksdal, before I hired the farmhouse. I gave my father that address. He did write back. He told me they were selling the shop in Pongola and moving to Amsterdam. He gave me the address of the house in Amsterdam. He just said he and my mum are missing me very much. Maybe he did want me to visit—why else did he put the house address in?"

"So that's the address you and Johannes went to, when you found your cousin and learned that your father had died?" I asked her.

"Yes."

"Why did you wait two years to go?"

"I don't know. Maybe I was still angry with him. Because all these years he didn't want to see me, he wanted to kill me, why now he wants me?" When she's in the grip of strong emotions, Sandra's English syntax goes askew.

"I wonder why you never mentioned the letter from your dad before now," I said.

"Maybe I forgot."

"Do you have the letter?"

"No, I lost it."

"You've taken such good care of your mother's last letter."

"No, I lost it." She paused. "Maybe I was angry."

Was there ever a letter, or merely a deep wish for one? People trying sincerely and assiduously to remember accurately, even people unencumbered by the freight of trauma, might not manage, because recollection involves at least four slippery components, Ulric Neisser says in *The Remembering Self*. He notes that narrative memory consists of: "1) actual past events and the *historical self* who participated in them; 2) those events as they were then experienced, including the individual's own *perceived self* at the time; 3) the *remembering self*, that is, the individual in the act of recalling those events on some later occasion; and 4) the *remembered self* constructed on that occasion." Most of us can't help but construct a slightly different remembered self at different times, depending on who's listening, what's at stake, and how we're feeling at the moment of telling.

Did Sandra's story of the letter mean she was strong enough to think about a squandered opportunity for reconciliation, or did it mean that she desperately needed to construct a life story in which she wasn't exiled forever? For the person who has been the victim of trauma, the remembered self may oscillate more dramatically as it emerges from hiding. "There cannot be a final and complete reconstruction of trauma," says TRC commissioner Pumla Gobodo-Madikizela, "Yet each version told by the victim reflects the various phases of progression with the traumatic material—or regression, depending on the intensity of experiences that reawaken the trauma in the victim's life and the resources available to deal with them—and is true to the victim's experience."

That may explain why some of Sandra's stories change a bit with every telling—as with her recollections of how and when she first became aware that she looked different from her family. Sometimes the details shift because of who's listening and what kind of mood Sandra is in. Sometimes they change because of new information or her growing ability to withstand old hurts. And sometimes the reason for the change is unclear.

For example, in many taped conversations with me and in recent newspaper articles, Sandra has insisted that the police drove her home the day she was expelled in 1966. Most press accounts from the 1960s reported the same thing, though a few articles from that time mention the principal, the head of the hostel, and a school inspector. But in the 1977 film by Antony Thomas and on *Special Assignment* in 1998, Sandra said that Mr. Van Tonder drove her home. When I ask Sandra about the different versions, she says simply, "I tell the story the way I remember it each time."

And if there were policemen, was one black and one white? Before Sandra told me that detail in November 2001, she'd never mentioned it in any previous account. I asked the retiring magistrate of Piet Retief whether the police took Sandra away from school and, if so, whether one of the officers was black. He said his office had no records of Sandra's 1966 removal from school. But he passed along the telephone number of the man who served at the time as sheriff, then an officer of the court who functioned more as a bailiff than a policeman. I asked Elize Lötter if she'd telephone the man, Tommy Swart, who has since died, and ask him in Afrikaans whether he knew who brought Sandra Laing to her parents that day. "I don't want anything to do with it. Fuck off," he said, and hung up.

Elize, Sandra, and I tried to clear up the policeman/Van Tonder/

black cop/white cop issue. Elize wanted to talk with two Afrikaner women her mother's age—in their late seventies and early eighties—whom she hoped would tell her more about the day Sandra was expelled, and how the community treated the Laings in the days before and after. Tannie Annetjie was a friend of Elize's parents; Tannie Issey Grobler was for forty years the secretary at Piet Retief Primary. Both are still robust and androgynously handsome, and their homes are decorated in a style that's been dubbed by some South African wag "Boere Baroque"—Afrikaner kitsch featuring needlepoint Vermeers, wooden shoes, heavy clawfoot furniture, and at Tannie Issey's, a prominently displayed print depicting the Battle of Blood River with plenty of Zulus biting the dust.

Tannie Annetjie was pleased to see Elize and asked after her mother and sisters. She greeted Sandra but addressed no questions to her. Elize tried to ask Tannie Annetjie several times about what the town thought of the Laings, but the old woman changed the subject rapidly. When Tannie Issey answered her door and saw Elize, she was delighted; she took Elize's face in her hands and said she looked just like her mother. Tannie Issey was not delighted to see Sandra—her face snapped shut—but shook her hand.

After some small talk—accounting for the health and welfare of relatives and friends, noting that Sandra and I had visited Willy Meyer, formerly of the Piet Retief Primary School Committee—Tannie Issey also let us know, in Afrikaans and in English, for my benefit, that she still feels burned by Antony Thomas's documentary about Sandra, filmed twenty-seven years earlier. "He tricked us," she said. "He made the town look bad." To Tannie Issey, it seems, the story of Sandra Laing was not about the gross injustices of apartheid, or a town's irrational fear of racial pollution, or the ruination of a little girl's life. It was about the betrayal of good *volk* for no good reason. In Tannie Issey's version of history, the people of Piet Retief were the victims of Sandra, and not vice versa.

When Elize asked Tannie Issey about the day Sandra left school, she said she knew nothing except that Sandra never came back; nor could she recall the events leading up to her departure. "I didn't know what was going on in the headmaster's office behind closed doors," she told Elize. "Perhaps someone from the Department of Education, a school inspector, took Sandra home." We thanked Tannie Issey for her time and she offered the South African autopilot polite response in English and Afrikaans: "Pleasure," she said.

Finally, we asked a young officer from the Piet Retief police force about the black policeman Sandra remembered. He laughed and said, "God, no—they would never send a black constable to a white school!"

I hoped to determine definitively whether or not there was a black policeman, but in the meantime, it seemed worthwhile to consider the significance of this detail.

Two Yale colleagues, literary critic Shoshana Felman and Dori Laub, a psychiatrist who treats trauma survivors, relate an enlightening story in their book *Testimony: Crises of Witnessing in Literature, Psychoanalysis, and History*. "A woman in her late sixties was narrating her memories as an eyewitness of the Auschwitz uprising of a group of Jews to an interviewer from the Video Archive for Holocaust Testimonies at Yale. 'All of a sudden,' she said, 'we saw four chimneys going up in flames, exploding. The flames shot into the sky, people were running, it was unbelievable.' Many months later, there was a conference of historians, psychoanalysts and artists watching the videotaped testimony. The historians claimed the testimony was not accurate and should be discredited because it was untrue. Historically, only one chimney was blown up, not all four. The psychoanalyst who had interviewed the woman profoundly disagreed. He said the woman was testifying not to the number of chimneys blown up but to an event that broke the all-compelling frame of Auschwitz where Jewish armed revolts just did not happen and had no place. She testified to the breakage of a framework. That was historical truth."

Sandra's accounts of being removed from school, though sometimes contradictory in detail, testify consistently to that same kind of breakage: Someone with terrifying authority took her home from school when she was ten. This frightening event was precipitated by some difference in her that she felt but didn't comprehend. Her relatively recent recollection of being escorted by both a white and a black policeman suggests that she understands now, even if she didn't then, that matters of race lay at the heart of her predicament, and that in the South Africa of 1966, she stood between two worlds.

Nations, too, rewrite their stories, in healthy and unhealthy ways. For years, white South Africans insisted—and some twenty-first-century South African schoolchildren still learn from outdated textbooks—that the nation's vast central plain was empty when the nineteenth-century *voortrekkers* arrived; that Bantu migrants from farther north in Africa had arrived at the same time as the white man, so that neither had prior claim on the country (and furthermore, since blacks weren't fit to govern, the white minority had every right to control the black majority). After the end of apartheid, that narrative was corrected to align with archaeological and DNA evidence showing that the Bantu migrants probably arrived around 100 A.D. One way the apartheid government was able to keep the myth of the empty land alive was by suppressing physical evidence of Iron Age settlements near Johannesburg. Now the site is a national monument, although plenty of textbooks haven't made the switch, and plenty of people, among them Willy Meyer, refuse to believe that black people have prior claim to the land.

Another salutary, though more traumatic revision of South Africa's narrative came with the Truth and Reconciliation Commission hearings of 1996, meant to restore publicly memories deliberately obliterated by the apartheid regime. Historians and Gary Minkley and Ciraj Rassol of the University of Cape Town praise attempts to write "history from below," to tell the stories of the formerly disenfranchised, but caution against a tendency to assume that every member of the oppressed majority was an antiapartheid hero. For many, they point out, there was no political activism, just a daily struggle to survive.

A related form of misremembering has emerged in the new South Africa. A growing number of people insist that they were opposed to apartheid all along, and that they didn't vote for the ruling National Party. Says ANC member of Parliament Pallo Jordan, "Many a time, visitors from outside South Africa will tell you, 'I don't understand how apartheid came into being; every white person I've met says they were not responsible for it.' But the fact of the matter is that the apartheid government was voted into office by the white electorate of this country in 1948 with a small majority. But thereafter they returned it with bigger and bigger majorities well into the 1980s."

A third twist of history is the nascent phenomenon of South African whites celebrating branches of the family tree that would once have been hidden. "Mixcd blood was denied for many years, left out of family histories," says Anne Lehmkuhl, a genealogist who for more than two decades has been helping South Africans trace their roots. "Nowadays there's more openness, and having a slave or two in your white genealogy is seen as the in thing."

31

HAZARD LIGHTS

A S WE WERE DRIVING BACK FROM TANNIE ISSEY'S IN A thunderstorm, on a dark country road—one of the old shortcuts Sandra remembered, near some trout fishing camps—my cell phone rang. It was Leon Laing calling to say that he absolutely refused to speak to me.

The week before, I'd sent him a registered letter explaining the book project and telling him that not only would I like to be able to present his story in his own words, but Sandra had questions that only he could answer, about Laing and Roux family history, Sandra's childhood, and their parents' true feelings about her. Adriaan was too young at the time to remember his parents' relationship with Sandra, though he lived through the aftermath of her departure.

I pulled over on the muddy shoulder. Rivets of rain pinged on the roof of the rental car. The red hazard lights seemed to kindle the elephant grass in flashes. Sandra panicked and erupted in nervous giggles. "Don't tell him I'm here!" she whispered. I nodded. Elize was in the backseat.

"It's been forty years," Leon shouted, his voice torqued with exasperation and pain. "Will it ever be over? Will anyone forget? Why does anyone care about my sister's story?

"I said to her, if you keep up with the media, forget about talking to me—it's just for the money." Leon and the white people of Piet Retief talk as if Sandra had gotten rich from telling her story, although until she sold the book and film rights, she never got more than a pittance from the press. The idea that Sandra profited from her family's humiliation seemed to be connected to the Piet Retiefers' lingering resentment over the Antony Thomas film. A South African screenwriter working with Tony Fabian telephoned a teacher who was a colleague of Van Tonder and asked for impressions of Sandra's nemesis. The man laughed and said, "*Wat verkoop sy julle nou weer? Hoeveel betaal julle haar die slag?*" What is she selling you now again? How much are you paying her this time?

"It's always poor Sandra, poor Sandra," Leon continued loudly. "What about her brothers, who were left alone to suffer? The other children said to me, 'What is your mother? What is your mother?'" They meant, Elize said later, Is she a whore who sleeps with *kaffirs*?

I said that it seemed to me Sandra was a child at the mercy of forces beyond her control or her understanding, and that he and Adriaan, too, were children at the mercy of forces beyond their control and understanding. At that Leon calmed down almost instantly. The rage left his voice, but the sadness and anxiety stayed.

"My parents gave up everything to keep her white. And how did she repay them?" he said. "Sandra made her choices and she has to suffer the consequences.

"I don't understand why anyone is interested in this story," he said again. "What's so interesting about Sandra?" I said that the story is bigger than the individual people in it, that it epitomizes the craziness and cruelty of race classification, that it teaches us the consequences of setting up a society based on exclusion and untruths. Leon was silent for a moment. "My brother, poor kid—I call him kid, there's seventeen years' difference between us—whatever you do, don't call him. His wife and children mustn't find out." Surely they knew; Leon told Sandra Adriaan's children were teased at school about the connection. "Look, it's still a very, very bad thing in this country to have a black sister." Why? I asked. Another silence.

"No one," Leon said, "can understand how terrible things were for my parents and my brother and myself." All the more reason, I suggested, to tell his story. He said he would think about whether there was any reason to speak to me again. I told Leon that a former classmate of his was in the car with me. "Elize Lötter, do you remember her?"

"Who?" he said.

"Oh, I can't pronounce her name properly," I said. "Here—" and quickly handed the phone to Elize. They spoke for nearly thirty minutes in Afrikaans as the rain pelted down. A couple of trucks passed us, but no other vehicle. Finally, Elize and Leon said goodbye. I started up the car and drove until we hit a main road and could stop for debriefing at a Wimpys.

"Leon said his mother would receive telephone calls," Elize said, "from people threatening her and calling her names and swearing at her for having had a black child, and awful letters, as well. He said this came from people within the so-called Christian community. They were shunned, the family. He says the media keeps on taking up the story and it's like a"—she asks Sandra in Afrikaans for the English word she wants—"a scab that starts, and just when it's healed they scratch at it again. He and Adriaan can never find peace. And his feeling is that it was Sandra's choice to have left home.

"He kept saying, 'Sandra made her choice, Sandra made her choice.' Surely he understands she didn't just suddenly wake up one morning and say, 'Hey! I'm a little white Afrikaner girl! I think I'll run away with an African!' Leon can't see now that a lot of the messages Sandra got from her parents led her to act in the way she did. The brothers think she felt no pain, only they did. Everyone sits with the thought: I was hurting, but the other one thinks I've been through nothing." Sandra listened but said little.

Three days later, Leon Laing called me again. This time it was to say he'd thought about it and he absolutely, positively didn't want to speak to me. But he was calm, even friendly. "Look," he said, "I last saw her in the sixties. Since then, I've only seen her in the newspapers and on television. When my mum saw her in 2000, she didn't even realize Sandra was her child. She at that stage had Alzheimer's. The *Sunday Times* said she was happy at seeing Sandra's children. The nurse said that she was completely confused with Alzheimer's." Sandra agrees that her mother was forgetful and confused, but says she definitely recognized her daughter. Tony Fabian and Karien van der Merwe agree.

"Everything that went wrong is blamed on apartheid. I think there's more apartheid in America."

I told him, "Your sister remembers that you taught her to ride a bicycle, that you walked with her to watch the cows."

He sighed. "You don't notice looks when you're a kid," he said. "You don't notice until people start saying things. Then you realize she's much darker than you. It doesn't upset you when you're a child. You don't realize when you're small. When you're kids, you play together, until people start to talk and ignore you. My parents stayed every time at home because they were ignored by the community.

"She went through a tough time, I agree; she couldn't be white and she couldn't be black. It's something in the past—what can you do? I'm protecting my children in the real world. They don't know about her. I know what I went through, and I don't want them to go through that."

"Would they?" I asked.

"I think so. Still there is in every country a way of apartheid. It would affect my children."

"Sandra knows you suffered," I said, "although she doesn't know the details. I asked her, 'What would you say to your brother if you saw him?' And she said, 'I would ask for his forgiveness and tell him I loved him.'" There was silence and another sigh.

"So," I said, "you feel that your family worked very hard to give Sandra what they believed was best for her—a life as a white person. When she turned her back on it, they felt it was a betrayal. It was a triple pain to them, in fact: a betrayal, the loss of a child, and the humiliation and cruelty by the community."

Leon confirmed my assessment of his position. "When I was in Windhoek dating my now wife, some people in town went to my girlfriend's father and said, 'Why would you want your daughter to go out with that bloke? His sister's a *kaffir*.' It's been hell to go through. It's a scandal. My mother talked of taking her own life."

"Elize feels that there's a generation in Piet Retief coming to the end of life and thinking, 'We wronged that family,'" I said.

"I hope so," Leon said.

"You asked me the other day why people are so interested in Sandra's story." I said, "I think people are looking at the past in order to understand how to be with each other now. White people are interested because of their own guilt, and everyone is interested because Sandra's story illustrates the arbitrariness of race. What can race mean if you're white one day and coloured the next, and then two years later white again?"

"Yes," he said, "she had a hard time." But he returned instantly to his chief theme. "I have to worry all the time. What if my children answer my cell phone and it's some press person asking about this? When will the hell end?"

Leon said that he doesn't want his name mentioned in the book. I told him that his name is a matter of public record, but assured him that I was trying to put Sandra's story in a historical, political, and sociological context, and I'd like his help. I told him that what he's said to me so far does precisely what he wants—sets the record straight, as he sees it. "I want a copy of that book," he said.

"I appreciate that it costs you a lot of pain to talk to me," I said. "So thank you, Leon."

"Pleasure," he said.

32

THE RAINBOW TUCK SHOP

THE THIRD TIME SANDRA'S TELEPHONE AND ELECTRIC were turned off, Elize refused to bail her out; "I let her sit in the dark for five days," Elize says. "I said, 'I suggest you and the family decide what you want to do about it.'"

In August 2002, the Laings, including Henry and Elsie, held a family meeting while Johannes was at work, and Sandra decided to open a tuck shop in her home, selling bread, milk, tea, and cigarettes through the front-door burglar bars. She sent Anthony to the squatters camp a mile away, to find out where the only other tuck shop in the area got its bread. "Anthony waited for the bakery truck and talked to the driver," she says, "and from then, they came every day here." Sandra called a dairy and arranged for milk delivery. "People are glad my shop is here, because it's too dangerous to go to the squatters camp at night. Or even in the afternoon."

Neighbors flocked to the front-hall mini-mart. It was such a success that in November 2002, Sandra shifted operations to the garage. Elize contributed toward stocking the shop, and recruited a Piet Retief Primary alum, her friend Carel, to donate a counter that ran across most of the front of the garage. Another friend offered shelves, wallboard, paint, and labor. Sandra chose the name Rainbow Tuck Shop because Nelson Mandela spoke of a rainbow nation in his inaugural address.

"There's no resting," Sandra said happily when I stopped by on a February morning in 2003. She was preparing for the grand opening of the Rainbow Tuck Shop, making a batch of *shubops*, little popsicles that she sold for fifty cents. In a bucket, she brewed pastel sugary syrups diluted with water, then ladled the liquid into baggies, twisted them shut, and popped them in the small freezer, also donated by Elize's friend Carel. Sandra had gorgeously organized the well-stocked shop, adding butter to the inventory, and paraffin, from a 20-liter tin that she decanted into smaller tins. Paraffin was a big seller; the neighbors needed it when their electricity was switched off for nonpayment.

On a run to a wholesaler in Brakpan that afternoon, Sandra grabbed big plastic bags of popcorn and Nik Naks, a nasty-looking but popular snack that resembles Day-Glo packing material; just the right bottles of fish oil; a six-pack of Doom bug spray. We stopped at a municipal office so Sandra could pick up a permit application for the tuck shop. Ultimately she decided not to register the shop because the process was costly, and the municipality, she discovered from asking around, had an unwritten policy of looking the other way and allowing informal unlicensed businesses to flourish in residential areas.

I'd never seen Sandra so content and confident, directing complicated operations with energy and aplomb. But then she exhibited the oddest holdover from her earlier state of emotional and cognitive foreclosure, a textbook example of willed blindess. Elize had asked us for a list of everything sold in the shop because she'd shanghaied yet another friend to print advertising flyers. Standing in the middle of the garage, surrounded by shelves she'd stacked with pleasing arrays of bread, oil, sweets, laundry and face soap, coffee, tea, jelly, cigarettes, matches, popcorn, Sandra began dictating to me the tuck shop's inventory. She closed her eyes to concentrate and struggled to recall what she sold. It didn't occur to her that she could simply open her eyes and look.

The shop cleared R100 (about $10) a day, a good take, and sometimes R130; once she made R180. The three younger boys and Elsie helped at the counter, and Anthony kept the books. Johannes took Sandra to buy goods, borrowing his brother's car. Sandra said she was putting R20 a day aside for savings.

From one of the companies she consulted for, Elize secured a community development grant toward keeping the shop stocked and holding a grand opening celebration. At Elize's suggestion—she didn't want Sandra's progress to slip away—the company's human resources manager also found therapist number three, and rustled up another grant to pay for her services.

Agnes Galant—a pseudonym—is an Afrikaans-speaking coloured woman five years older than Sandra, raised in a suburb of Johannesburg. Her father, too, was a shopkeeper, the owner of a supermarket and café. Like Sandra, she is a single mother and young grandmother. And like Sandra, she grew up in a family riven by race. Agnes's father had a light-skinned sister who passed for white, married a white man, raised their children as whites, and cut off communication with her coloured family. "Because to be white meant a better life, she moved out of the house very early, and got married to a white," Agnes told me when we met for iced coffee at a sidewalk café near her large home in an upscale, mixed-race suburb north of Johannesburg. "If my dad saw his sister in the street and she was with her white family or friends, they would pass each other and she would put her hands behind her and wave from the back, so they wouldn't see."

Agnes taught high-school social studies for eighteen years before switching to corporate work, first designing and running on-site schools, then studying to become a corporate trainer specializing in harmonization, motivation, and gender issues. Her clinical training consisted of a six-week course in Process Therapy, a sort of analysis-lite. "I see myself more as a facilitator than a therapist," said Agnes, who sounds like Bette Davis and looks like a young Aretha Franklin. "I don't believe in long-term things. With Sandra, the issues are very deep, but I want to empower her as quickly as possible. I don't want to interpret, because one could be so wrong."

She was very worried about Sandra's blowing her money, and couldn't get over the Famous Overpriced Dining-Room Table. "Sandra has got a poor girl's mentality," Agnes said. "Whether you give her six hundred rand or a million, it's got to be used, because there won't be tomorrow. I'd like to give Sandra very basic financial skills, so she can make wise decisions in terms of a longer-term sustainability. My concern would be that she's got a sense of guilt that she hasn't been able to provide for her children, and my fear would be that the kids have a sense of entitlement. Yes, they can all benefit from her success, but she needs to be in control of that, not the kids. They need to make a contribution.

"I see Sandra as a survivor. With such a difficult history, it could be a totally different story. There could have been alcoholism, prostitution. I see tremendous strength there. I want to work with that strength."

Agnes finds it impossible to believe that in grade school, Elize and Sandra didn't understand that race was the source of Sandra's persecution by Van Tonder and their classmates. "Children know," she said. "My two boys, for example: One is a bit tannish, and one's really white. When I took them to the park, white children said to me, 'Tannie, Tannie, why is the one child white and one so tan? Is the pa a *kaffir*?' That at age three or four.

"Over the years, as a non-white girl, I've had to go through a lot of soul-searching, looking at my own racism, my own not being accepting of people. Even as an educated, enlightened woman, it's deep."

"In which direction does your racism go?" I asked. "Toward which groups?"

"Both, to be quite honest. Because we were always in the middle. But I also know that we're an extremely forgiving community. I can see people for who they are now. I can now see another human being without color, and it's taken me fifty-three years.

"But my skepticism is very real. Up till today, people must not fool themselves. There's no such thing as people hugging each other and getting on with their lives. There is such segregation that you would not believe. There's a different kind of transformation that needs to happen. A law's not going to make people accept each other. For example," Agnes said, "Sandra doesn't trust Elize."

"Really? Why do you say that?"

"She wants Elize in her life, because she knows Elize is doing a lot to support her. She really does a lot for Sandra. But Sandra's also saying, 'So what's in this for Elize?' Not in so many words; I'm interpreting that now. Because of the way Sandra said, 'I can't remember her.'"

"Did Sandra actually say, 'What's in this for Elize'?"

"No. It was her body language, when she said to me, 'Elize has come into my life; but I don't remember her at all from school.' It was the way she said that to me." In her six weeks of therapeutic training, Agnes had apparently missed the class on projection.

"Here's Elize: In a manipulative way, it's what she can get out of—I think Elize is also going through her own struggles. I think she wants to say, 'I embrace change and I'm different.' But she hasn't dealt with any of the issues herself, in terms of her own racism. Having been married to an Indian, she can probably accept and go against the tide, but I think there's a long way for her to go. *Ja,* to me, it's about another white woman having to bail out another black person. That's my own reading of it. It's about coming in like the white fairy godmother.

"She's got her heart in the right place with this project. I mean the hours, the time. I wish I could articulate this better. I need to really just work through this myself. I need to be honest: Is it my own issues again, about another white person? This is about me, not about Elize, really; it probably takes me back to very deep issues. But I'm aware of it, and once I've overcome that, we can just get on with it. Because Elize and I are really working well together; you can't help but like her. She's really a fantastic person.

"Probably where this comes from is when Elize just brought all the stock for the shop without asking Sandra what she needed. Elize got this donation and went buying stuff, what she thought was right. It was the wrong things totally."

"Are you sure she bought stock without asking Sandra what she needed?"

Agnes was positive. But she was wrong. I asked Sandra and Elize separately, and they both told the same story: Sandra made a list, and Elize bought everything on it. She made one small cultural blunder: the list said "tea," and she bought *rooibos,* an herbal brew she likes, instead of Joko, the brand of black tea that Sandra's neighbors favor.

The weight of an unhappy history sometimes threatens to crush Agnes's commitment to forgiveness and nonracialism, but she struggles to maintain it with consciousness and an open heart. Sometimes she is successful, and sometimes not.

One day Agnes, Sandra and I were sitting in Sandra's garage and Agnes spoke to me with passion about how upset she is at the way young women of color are internalizing European standards of attractiveness—and waify and pale. How they should celebrate their skin, their hair, their amplitude. And then one of Sandra's neighbors, who is coloured, came to visit with a little blond, blue-eyed boy of four or so. The woman went into the backyard for a moment with the toddler and Sandra's grandson Naijan. "Are both the parents coloured?" Agnes asked Sandra.

"That's not her child," Sandra said. "This lady looks after the little boy for a white family."

"Ah, I see," Agnes said. "I wondered how he came out so beautiful."

A *kraal* organized itself around Sandra, friends and neighbors who enjoyed hanging out in the shop every day, chatting and laughing. One Saturday morning before the big launch, Elize's sister, brother-in-law, and niece came to paint a sign for the shop on Sandra's front yard wall. A crowd of kids—Sandra noticed that they were black, coloured, Indian, and white—shared *shubops* and added to the noise of the TV and stereo Sandra had moved to the garage. Amid the cheerful din, Sandra practiced her thank-you speech for the grand opening ceremonies. "I want to say to the people who helped me with the tuck shop thank you very much. And I'd like to thank my family for standing by me all these years.

"Since I was in Tsakane I dreamed that I would have a shop and my whole family would work in the shop. I'm happy it's happening now. My life is better now. I don't struggle, I have money to buy bread."

The racially mixed group of seventy-five people—family, friends, neighbors, and dignitaries—found the launch of Sandra's Rainbow Tuck Shop entertaining and moving.

Elize had organized refreshments, invited a brace of pastors to bless the food and the endeavor, and gathered an odd but affecting array of performers—a chorus of developmentally disabled children who sweetly sang the national anthem, a children's violin ensemble, a Zulu dance troop.

Sandra was nervous but beaming. Though she'd talked about wanting to lose weight before the launch, she'd hit her highest weight ever, achieving a planetary roundness. She'd gotten a fashionable buzz cut, but the stylist had taken off a little more than she wanted and Sandra looked like a plump, punk, novice nun. When the time came for her speech, Sandra forgot to thank her family, and they noticed. She was distracted, she says, by wishing that her brothers were there to see that she's made something of herself.

Agnes spoke and called Sandra a gift to the world. Cheryl Carolus, the former High Commissioner to England and at the time CEO of South Africa Tourism, said that Sandra's story of painful exclusion and determined endurance was one to which many South Africans could relate, and that the shop was a symbol of a hopeful future. She'd arranged press coverage of the event; reporters from three newspapers attended. Tony organized a camera crew to document the festivities. The mother of one of the young violinists, a white woman, mentioned to a woman sitting next to her that she'd never been in a "township" before. Overhearing her, one of the black guests whispered to another, "She thinks this is a township?"

Karien wept to see her friend so happy and successful. Another white guest, a teacher of kosher Indian cooking, wept and said that Sandra had helped her feel for the first time a part of the new South African community. Anco Steyn wept because his old schoolmate had pulled herself right after years of trouble. Everyone at the launch had a wonderful time, but the white guests were the ones who responded with visible emotion.

"All that crying that was happening," Agnes said, "for me, that's really transformation. Because people are putting themselves for the first time in Sandra's place, and feeling her pain. They're identifying with her pain. They're realizing, look at what our behavior did to somebody. That's the shift: when they see the pain, and they're confronted with their own prejudice and racism. And Sandra acts as the catalyst."

Three months after the big launch, Sandra's Rainbow Tuck Shop was going strong. The month after that, Sandra was struggling to keep it open.

By the end of June 2003, the shelves were almost empty. Sandra couldn't afford to buy more stock, and the wholesalers had cut off her credit. She sold just enough milk, bread, soft drinks, and sweets to replenish those items, but the shop was dangerously close to closing its doors. Tony Fabian arrived from England for a visit and was startled to encounter a crisis so soon after such a propitious beginning. He and Elize suggested a family meeting.

Henry said the shop was in trouble because Sandra was using it as a personal pantry. Elsie and Jafta, who had moved in with Sandra and Johannes so they could save up for a house of their own, pointed out that Sandra let people give her IOUs that they never paid. Anthony agreed and added that his mother gave away too many things to friends and neighbors. He neglected to mention that he and Prins regularly helped themselves to money from the till. Sandra said very little as the people she was feeding scolded her for using too much food. Johannes said nothing. Sandra told Elize later that day she suspected that the boys were skimming from the till, but she was reluctant to confront them. She also said that she'd given Jafta and Elsie a R25,000 loan, paid for Elsie to go to a weight-loss clinic, and bought each of her kids a cell phone.

Tony said that if the family could come up with the money to open the shop properly, he'd match that, with an advance on Sandra's next film option payment, up to about $500. When Elize called Sandra the next morning to find out how the family intended to raise its share of the funds, Sandra was disappointed. She was hoping that Tony and Elize would bail her out, and asked why the same corporate and individual donors who'd helped launch the shop couldn't pitch in again to get her out of a jam. "I told Sandra that she chose to waste what she got and she will now herself have to find a way to fix the problem," Elize says.

Sandra became furious—the first time she'd ever gotten angry at Elize. "Sandra said she thought that I was her friend, but now she sees another side. I said, 'So, Sandra when I give money I am a friend?' She said yes. 'What am I when I don't give money?' She said, 'Then you don't care about me.' She said she'd phone Leon for money, because he's family and he'll help her. Then she slammed the phone down." Sandra did call Leon asking for money, and damaged their slowly mending relationship. He was terribly upset and turned her down. She wouldn't hear from him for a very long time.

Elize didn't take Sandra's tantrum personally. "I could look beyond it all and see she felt lost and hurt and panicked." Indeed, Sandra soon offered a heartfelt apology. "She said she was sorry for being ugly with me. She felt very frustrated, she said, and she was stressed because her children were manipulating her over money, and she didn't know what to do. She hugged me and said she felt we were closer. In a way, the anger was a step further for her, toward asserting herself, even if it was small and clumsy. She tried to be stronger with the children."

Anthony got a new job, selling burial plots, and pledged to give his mother R1,000 at the end of the month. He didn't. But he did aquire a new TV, a computer, and a DVD player. The family never came up with any funds to match, but a frustrated Tony sent Sandra R5,000 anyway, because he didn't see how else she could earn a sustainable living. Sandra paid the phone bill and Steve's school fees, and bought new stock. Soon the shop was back up to speed.

The population of the house waxed and waned; kids in, kids out. Anthony and Prins got jobs and moved away, lost jobs and moved back. Elsie and Jafta moved out; Johannes's sixteen-year-old grandson Rorisang moved in. Following the African tradition, Sandra fed everyone who visited or bunked with her. A burglar broke into the garage and stole much of the stock. Sandra transferred what was left back into the front hallway of the house and the tuck shop limped along. Then Sandra bounced back, bought burglar bars for the garage, and had the terrific idea of renting video games, which were a huge hit with the neighborhood kids. The front-door tuck shop and garage games room were thriving. Anthony and Prins found good jobs unloading boxes at a warehouse and moved out. Then they were laid off, moved back home, and started drinking.

Twice Sandra caught Prins breaking into the video-game coin boxes. After the second incident, the owner of the video games took them away in a truck, and the family lost R2,000 a month in income, and Sandra chased Prins out of the house. The tuck shop almost closed. Sandra and Johannes told Elize they wished they were back in Tsakane. "The family has gone wrong since coming to this house," Sandra said in despair. "Family togetherness is gone, *ubuntu* [the spirit of the extended community] is gone."

Prins apologized to Sandra and vowed to behave. Then both he and Anthony got their girlfriends pregnant. Johannes's work hours were cut to two days a week. Prins's girlfriend gave birth to a son, Eathen, and the three of them came to live with Sandra. Anthony's girlfriend gave birth to daughter, Vaneshree, and the three of them moved in, too. The boys ran the shop. Sandra adored the babies, but worried so much about money that she told Johannes she wanted to sell the house. Johannes said that the thing would happen again and again until she took control of the shop and stopped allowing the boys to manage her money. The shop was on the verge of closing again.

Sandra and Elize kept me posted on the tuck-shop soap opera by telephone and e-mail. When the cycle of near-disaster and recovery repeated itself for the third time, I told Elize that I just didn't get it. Johannes works, Jafta works, Henry works; Anthony and Prins work off and on—and never lack for electronics—and Sandra gets movie-option money every year. Why did they keep running out of cash? Sandra sighed and said she didn't know, which means she didn't want to talk about it just then.

"The shop goes bust for many reasons," Elize told me. "There's an African tradition of feeding whoever shows up at your house and supporting the extended family, and her kids take advantage of that.

She has a hard time saying no to them; she feels guilty because times were hard when the kids were young, and they take advantage of that, too. And the boys were taking money from the shop. Henry gave her money at first, but then got tired of watching it disappear." Elize also sees an element of keeping up with the Joneses—and the Oliphants, the Ndlovus, the Naidoos, and the Malans—in Sandra's new upscale neighborhood. "Also there is the idea of the film money." Sandra knew that if the movie about her life got made—and Tony was working to secure the last of the funding—she could receive a windfall, and she sometimes spent as if that fortune were right around the corner, no matter how many times Tony explained the vicissitudes of the film business. "There is also," Elize said, "Sandra's great joy in finally being the one who is able to give things to her friends." There is generosity, and also love, guilt, pride, fear, poor impulse control, cultural norms, post-traumatic stress disorder, end-stage capitalism. There is Sandra's needing to be broke so someone can rescue her and prove they love her.

"I look at each up and down in a positive way," Elize said. "Each time so far she's made the comeback herself, and each time I see that she's learned new skills to do so. Each time, she learns the lessons of how not to do it next time."

Elize was right. Things got better, and then they got good. By the time the multi-celled organism that is Sandra's family gathered to celebrate her fiftieth birthday in November 2005, the tuck shop was going strong. Sandra kept the key to the cash box on a string around her neck, tucked into her bra. Johannes was working full-time again, and sometimes even overtime. They'd made a down payment on a used car. Sandra talked the owner of the video games into bringing them back to her garage, and she seemed to have a successful, sustainable, self-destruction–proof business at last.

A remarkable change came over Prins. He married his girlfriend Anita, an Indian woman whose parents kicked her out when she fell pregnant, and they had another son, Micalon, almost immediately. They moved into a flat with Anthony, who'd broken up with his girlfriend but supports his daughter financially; Sandra is proud of that. Anthony got an excellent job as a warehouse manager, and this one stuck. Prins became a househusband, staying home with his two little boys while his wife works, and he loves it. He turns out to have a gift for fatherhood, and when Elize told him so, he beamed. "You're like a different person," she said to Prins recently. "Your face is different." The perpetual scowl has been replaced by a calm grin. "Elize," Prins said, "I feel like a different person. Before, I didn't care about myself or anyone else. I had nothing to live for. Now I do." Everyone was settled but Steve, who was kicked out of school when a teacher hit him for not paying attention, and he hit back.

Then Sandra learned that a huge shopping mall was being built about a mile away from her house, just off the highway. In November 2005, neighbors told her that the town council was sending officers into the area to close all home businesses like tuck shops, auto-body shops, and hair salons. A couple of weeks after that warning, two inspectors came by with a letter saying the tuck shop had to close because it wasn't legal. But Sandra stayed open, keeping watch for inspectors; the municipality had closed its eyes to unlicensed shops and allowed an informal economy to flourish.

Elize moved to Hong Kong with her boyfriend in January 2006. Sandra worried about the separation from one of many surrogate mothers she had gathered to her over the years. Elize promised to call regularly from abroad.

In May 2006, Sandra received a second letter from the municipality saying that the tuck shop must close because the area had been rezoned residential only; if an inspector came back and found the shop open, she'd be subject to a fine of R10,000. Panicked, Sandra called Elize in Hong Kong and begged her to contact the city official in charge of rezoning. Elize gently pointed out that it made more sense for Sandra to handle the matter than for her to intervene from Hong Kong.

Sandra and Johannes went to see the official who'd sent the letter. Mr. van Rooyen of the Boksburg town council appreciated her predicament, but there was nothing he could do. He suggested Sandra rent a shop in the mall, but she couldn't afford it. Meanwhile, the tuck shop did a brisk clandestine business. Karien van der

Merwe made some inquiries and thought Sandra ought to try talk-ing to someone higher up. The two women met with a Mr. Pretorius, who suggested that Sandra sell her house and move to a "red zone," an area both residential and commercial. After the meeting, Sandra felt that staying open was too dangerous, and she closed the Rain-bow Tuck Shop for good.

33

YESTERDAY, TODAY, TOMORROW

HOW ODD, CONSIDERING SANDRA'S HISTORY OF FORCED removals from spaces officially declared off limits to her, that the demise of the Rainbow Tuck Shop hinged on an act of governmental rezoning. Sandra summoned resilience after its loss. The fact that she'd made a success of the shop after overcoming many obstacles is important to her. She's been managing her money well, she told me over the phone not long after she got the final word from the municipality, so Johannes salary will get them through. "I won't sell the house," she said. "It's the only thing that's ever been all mine, that I owned. It's my place." It's a place her family can always come. The most important thing in the world, she says, is to have a happy, healthy family and she has that, though Steve is still not back at school, and that worries her. Her relationship with her brothers worries her, too. She's going to try opening a laundry in the new mall, she said, and Elize, Tony, Karien, and her family are going to help.

Sandra has accomplished a great deal against lousy odds. She's engineered two escapes, boldly and beautifully renouncing privilege in order to insist on being seen the way she saw herself, and then fleeing with her children into the unknown when she felt her life was in danger. She kept her children safe, gave them up when she had to, and got them back, though not easily or quickly. She's run a shop, run a shop into the ground, and run it successfully across the finish line.

She's found a kindhearted mate and created a substitute family of friends and in-laws to supply the affection, approval, and companionship she lost when she left her parents' home. She has shepherded four children into happy, productive adulthood, and maintains close, complicated, contentious, and fiercely loving relationships with them. She's still working on Steve.

Because of her trips back and forth across apartheid's color line—journeys she'd have preferred not to make—Sandra has played a vital role in the history of South Africa: She is the "boundary crosser" who "works in the joints of racist culture like an attack of arthritis." The cultural critic Lewis Hyde was talking about the nineteenth-century former African-American former slave and abolitionist Frederick Douglass when he wrote those words in his extraordinary book *Trickster Makes This World,* but they work for Sandra, too. She's the symbol—the "lethal anomaly," as Hyde puts it—whose existence illuminates the flaws in the system. Her existence also provokes discomfort and embarrassment, anger, and, ultimately, change because it forces people to know what they know, instead of denying it. (In the case of her community in Piet Retief, that knowledge was: We are not pure. Our domination is not rightful or righteous. We have dehumanized the majority of the people in our land for our own benefit. We have justified our bad behavior with bogus science and misused scripture. In the case of her brothers, that knowledge was: we have the same genes she does; they just don't show. We are privileged, she is punished; it could just as easily be the other way around. We will be punished by our connection to her. It's not nice, it's not just, but I have to save my children. I have to save myself.)

And because of this threat, and the change she creates, Sandra is in the poignant position of inspiring more transformation in others than she is able to manage for herself, although she makes more progress all the time. She has served her nation—a conscript, not a volunteer—as a symbol, of different things at different times to different people: of the evils of apartheid, of the evils of race mixing, of reconciliation, of failure, of success.

It's okay work, being a symbol. In Sandra's case, it sometimes pays the bills, occasionally confers confidence and self-esteem, often attracts people who offer help or companionship. But symbolhood hasn't given Sandra what's she's still missing—her remaining white family's acceptance. And it leaves her fair game for self-appointed pundits; the people in Sandra's life, past and present, have expressed strong feelings about who's responsible for her troubles, then and now.

"I blame the Department of Education for pushing her out of school in the first place and the Department of the Interior for classifying her as colored," Abraham Laing said in 1968.

"I blame the father for her situation," said Willy Meyer of the Piet Retief School Committee. "If he had allowed her to go to that diplomatic school, she would have got mixed up with other nations and had a very good education. She wouldn't have married a black man; she'd have married a fellow coloured, an educated man." My Afrikaaner friend thinks Sannie's complicity in Sandra's estrangement from her family is underestimated. Meyer's son Kobus, unaware of the role his father played in Sandra's expulsion, thinks Van Tonder was at fault. "It was 90 percent him. I still say if Van Tonder was a different person, the kicking out would never have happened, never," said Kobus Meyer, now a mechanic in Pongola. "If he had a different attitude he could have explained to the community the situation, and I'm sure everybody would have understood. The same like Adriaan. When Adriaan came, also the children said, '*Ag*, you're not white, you're coloured, what are you doing here?' But with Adriaan it wasn't long that everybody accepted it and there was no hassles."

Mr. Van Tonder is very clear about who's not to blame. Elize Lötter decided to call him, with Sandra's blessing, to ask, among other things, whether it was he or two policemen who drove Sandra home. She got his number from another teacher who'd retired from Piet Retief Primary. "I told him I am Willie Lötter's daughter, and he remembered me. He said, 'Are you the one with the kroessy hair?'" Elize's blonde curls frizz slightly in damp air. "I laughed and said yes I am." He was pleased to hear from her, and had fond memories of her parents. "I said I'm phoning in connection with Sandra. He said, 'Before you carry on: I am at peace with myself. I have nothing to feel guilty about. I did my Christian duty! The past is the past.'" Elize explained that she hadn't called to blame him, but to see if somehow he could help Sandra heal the past. "I shared about Sandra's shop; he had read a story in the *Beeld*, the Afrikaner paper. I said that he could play a role in helping her to find closure with certain things. We chatted some more, and he said it was all right for Sandra to phone him, if it would help her. Then he said,'Tell Sandra I am not angry with her. I felt sorry for her those years and that is still how I feel about her today.'" Elize was so disconcerted she forgot to ask whether he or two policemen drove Sandra home. Sandra has Mr. Van Tonder's number, but she has yet to call.

Some elderly residents of Piet Retief think the Laings' problems were the consequence of Sannie's having slept with a kaffir. Former classmate Isabeau Coetze says, "Sandra was such a quiet little thing. Maybe if she'd had a better personality this wouldn't have happened to her." Sandra's brother Leon believes that her problems are all self-inflicted, not state-inflicted. He said so again when he called Elize Lötter a few weeks after the tuck shop launch, in March of 2003, to thank her for keeping his name out of the story in the *Beeld*. "It was her decision to leave," he said to Elize. "No one told her to run off with a black man. She had all the same opportunities as I did." Elize assured him that she did not, and asked, "Why would she walk away from a loving home?"

Leon paused. "I have to admit my father didn't speak to her as he should have. He was very hard on her."

When I talked to Sandra after the tuck shop closed, she was trying to be optimistic. The best thing that had happened recently, she said, was that Leon called her spontaneously in July 2006, just to see how she and her family were doing. "It was nice," Sandra said. "We just talked like brother and sister." She sighed, and then said with uncharacteristic passion, "If I could just see my brother for ten minutes!" I ask her what she'd say to him. "I'd ask him to forgive me," she said. The old refrain. "Adriaan, too. I left Adriaan when he was only five."

"Are you the only one who needs forgiveness?" I asked. "There's nothing you'd like your brothers to apologize for? Or your parents, if they were here?"

"No," she said, "they're cross with me because I left."

"[So] You think everything is your fault?"

"I think it's my fault. I do."

This conviction has eclipsed even her own conscious belief that apartheid is responsible for her hardships. She seems to be stuck in a process, begun in childhood, of reflexively revising her family history, casting herself as the villain. "In order to cope with abuse," Judith Herman explains in *Trauma and Recovery*, "a child constructs some system of meaning that justifies it. Inevitably the child concludes that her badness is the cause. The child seizes upon this explanation early and clings to it tenaciously, for it enables her to preserve a sense of meaning, hope and power. If she is bad, then her parents are good. If she is bad, then she can try to be good. If, somehow, she has brought this fate upon herself, then somehow she has the power to change it. . . . The profound sense of inner badness becomes the core around which the abused child's identity is formed, and it persists into adult life."

So Sandra and Leon agree on one thing at least. Though in a recent conversation with Elize he revealed a newly compassionate and nuanced understanding of Sandra's history—"I know now why she went with Petrus; he held out the feather of love and acceptance, and she grasped it."—to me, he stressed, as he had several times before, that he believed Sandra to be the architect of her own troubles. He also said that under apartheid, black people had everything he did.

"You're saying black South Africans had the same rights and privileges as white South Africans?"

"That's right."

"Well, Leon, for one thing they couldn't vote."

"Except for that black people had everything that I had." There was no point in summarizing for him the 3,000 pages of apartheid statutes that had restricted every aspect of the lives of nonwhites beyond reason. Leon's form of amnesia seems more profound and intractable than his sister's.

"This is the new South Africa," he said. "That was the old South Africa. Why can't the story stay there?" Apparently some of the old South Africa lingers in Leon's *verkrampte*, conservative, Afrikaner community. He told me that someone recently said to his daughter, "I saw this Sandra Laing in the paper. Isn't she part of your family? She looks like a *kaffir*."

Funny place, this new South Africa. It's a miracle and a mess. Wonderful things have happened. Ten thousand squatters who lived in cardboard shacks now have small permanent homes, Mandela houses, they're called. Forty-five percent more people have safe, clean water compared to a decade ago. In the newspapers that were once forbidden to criticize apartheid, the popular comic strip *Madam and Eve* (now a sitcom, too) makes satirical hay of the relationship between white women and their black maids. On television, the *Big Brother* house was racially mixed. When the Fédération Internationale de Football Association (FIFA) announced that the 2010 World Cup would be held in South Africa, black and white fans jubilantly danced in the streets, blasting their vuvuzelas, long plastic trumpets modeled on a traditional instrument once made of kudu horn.

But crime is such a problem—South Africa has the second highest murder rate in the world, after Colombia—that FIFA has a contingency plan to move the World Cup if necessary. In the new South Africa, four members of the ANC cabinet have been indicted for corruption and one has begun serving a jail sentence. President Thabo Mbeki has been accused by many of mishandling the nation's AIDS crisis—first publicly doubting that the disease is caused by a virus, then delaying the general distribution of antiretroviral drugs. An estimated 5.4 million South Africans out of nearly 48 million are infected with the AIDS virus, according to the Actuarial Society of South Africa; in 2006, an estimated 950 people a day died from AIDS-related diseases.

The South African novelist and Nobel laureate Nadine Gordimer wrote in a 1999 newspaper essay on the occasion of the fifth anniversary of democratic elections, "We have lived five years of free-

dom. Whatever the frustrations as well as the triumphs we've tack-
led, it is an achievement placed toweringly beside the years of
apartheid racism and before them the years of colonial racism—five
years against three centuries."

On the tenth anniversary of democratic elections, she told
those who are impatient with the new regime, in a radio interview,
"We're supposed to have provided perfect housing for everybody,
we're supposed to have completely equalized educational opportunities, we're supposed to have provided work for everybody, and
we're supposed to have done away completely with any inherent
lingering racial prejudice. Well, I look at the big European democ-
racies; they've had several hundred years and they're still not perfect—but we're supposed to have done it in a decade."

Now the new South Africa is turning thirteen. However overwhelming its problems, as Gordimer points out, the nation has, for
the first time, the legal means to solve them, enshrined in a nonracial constitution that insists on equality in principle, even if the
practice lags. And the seven volumes of TRC testimony serve as another moral touchstone.

The same week that I spoke to Sandra and Leon Laing, the
subject of reconciliation made headlines in the new South Africa.
On the last Sunday in August 2006, Adriaan Vlok, the Minister of
Law and Order at a particularly intense period in the covert war
against apartheid's opponents, appeared at the Pretoria office of
Reverend Steve Chikane, a black minister, now Mbeki's chief of
staff, and the survivor of an assassination attempt carried out by
Vlok's minions. The former Minister of Law and Order carried a
bowl and a Bible. He presented the bemused reverend with the
Bible, and requested a glass of water. Vlok poured the water into
the bowl, knelt, and asked to wash the minister's feet as penance
for his past misdeeds. A discomfited Chikane considered the propo-
sition and, though he had misgivings, agreed. Later, the two men
decided to make the gesture public.

The South African media and blogosphere reacted in three basic ways: presenting the facts neutrally; hailing the act as the acme
of reconciliation, and calling it a load of crap. (Or poking gentle fun;

the *Madam and Eve* strip that week showed the white madam and her husband washing the feet of their maid, Eve, who's surveying the proceedings with a satisfied smirk. The husband is saying, "Couldn't we just send chocolates and flowers?")

Several follow-up articles, including a commentary from the man who served as Vlok's deputy Minister of Law and Order. Leon Wessels, now a human rights commissioner, had appeared before the Truth and Reconciliation Commission in 1996, publicly admitting his deeds along with Vlok. Commenting on the foot-washing incident, he wrote, "Reconciliation isn't a one-time thing. It takes a lifetime." Wessels added, "I revisit the statement I made to the Truth and Reconciliation Commission, where I said the excuse 'we didn't know' was simply not available to us. We didn't want to know."

Sandra is struggling to know. She wants to know that her brother forgives her. She wants to know that her children are going to be happier than she was. She wants to know how she's going to survive without the tuck shop. She wants to know how her parents really felt about her. She wants to know everything she's forgotten. It's hard, knowing what you know. Some days she does better than others. Sandra is a faithful reader of *TV Plus*, a magazine that gives detailed daily plot summaries of television serials. Sandra likes to know exactly what's going to happen on each of her soapies at least a month in advance. "I don't like surprises," she says.

BIBLIOGRAPHY

Books:

Appiah, K. Anthony, and Amy Gutmann. *Color Conscious: The Political Morality of Race*. Princeton: Princeton University Press, 1996.

Ashforth, Adam. *Witchcraft, Violence, and Democracy in South Africa*. Chicago and London: University of Chicago Press, 2005.

Bernstein, Hilda. *For Their Triumphs and For Their Tears: Women in Apartheid South Africa*. London: International Defence and Aid Fund, 1985.

Bowker, Geoffrey C., and Susan Leigh Star. *Sorting Things Out: Classification and Its Consequences*. Cambridge, MA: The MIT Press, 2000.

Bunting, Brian. *Rise of the South African Reich*. New York: Penguin, 1969.

Burman, Sandra and Pamela Reynolds, eds. *Growing Up in a Divided Society*. Evanston, IL: Northwestern University Press, 1986.

Cavalli-Sforza, Luigi Luca. *Genes, Peoples, and Languages*. Berkeley and Los Angeles: University of California Press, 2000.

Cock, Jacklyn. *Maids and Madams*. Cape Town: Ravan Press, 1980.

Davis, F. James. *Who is Black?: One Nation's Definition*. University Park, PA: The Pennsylvania State University Press, 1993.

Daymond, M.J. et al., eds. *Women Writing Africa: The Southern Region*. New York: The Feminist Press, 2003.

de Montaigne, Michel. "On the Cannibals." *The Complete Essays.* Penguin Classics, 1993.

De Villiers, Marq. *White Tribe Dreaming.* New York: Viking Penguin, Inc., 1988.

Dubow, Saul. *Scientific Racism in Modern South Africa.* Cambridge: Cambridge University Press, 1995.

Elphick, Richard, and Hermann Giliomee, eds. *The Shaping of South African Society, 1652–1840 (Rev. ed.),* Middletown, CT: Wesleyan University Press, 1988.

Erasmus, Zimitri, ed. *Coloured by History, Shaped by Place: New Perspectives on Coloured Identity.* Cape Town: Kwela, 2001.

Erikson, Erik. *Identity, Youth, and Crisis.* New York: Norton, 1968.

Esman, Aaron, ed. *The Psychology of Adolescence: Essential Readings.* New York: International Universities Press, 1975.

Evans, Ivan. Bureaucracy and Race: *Native Administration in South Africa.* Berkeley: University of California Press, 1997.

Fanon, Frantz. *Black Skin, White Masks.* New York: Grove Weidenfeld, 1967.

Felman, Shoshana, and Dori Laub. *Testimony.* New York: Routledge, 1991.

Finnegan, William. *Crossing the Line: A Year in the Land of Apartheid.* Berkeley: University of California Press, 1994.

———, *Dateline Soweto.* Berkeley: University of California Press, 1995.

Frankel, Glenn. *Rivonia's Children.* New York: Farrar, Straus and Giroux, 1999.

Gobodo-Madikizela, Pumla. *A Human Being Died That Night.* New York: Houghton Mifflin, 2003.

Goodwin, June and Ben Schiff. *Heart of Whiteness: Afrikaners Face Black Rule in the New South Africa.* New York: Scribner, 1995.

Gregory, Steven and Roger Sanjek, eds. *Race.* New Brunswick: Rutgers University Press, 1996.

Harrison, David. *The White Tribe of Africa.* Berkeley: University of California Press, 1982.

Head, Bessie. *A Question of Power.* Oxford: Heinemann, 1974.

Herman, Judith Lewis. *Trauma and Recovery.* New York: Basic Books, 1997.

Horrell, Muriel, et al. *A Survey of Race Relations.* Johannesburg: South African Institute of Race Relations, 1958–2002.

Hyde, Lewis. *Trickster Makes This World: Mischief Myth and Art.* New York: Farrar, Straus and Giroux, 1998.

Janeway, Elizabeth. *The Powers of the Weak.* New York: Morrow Quill Paperbacks, 1981.

Keegan, Tim. *Facing the Storm: Portraits of Black Lives in Rural South Africa.* Cape Town: David Philip, 1988.

Kennedy, Randall. *Interracial Intimacies: Sex, Marriages, Identity and Adoption.* New York: Pantheon Books, 2003.

Krog, Antjie. *Country of My Skull: Guilt, Sorrow, and the Limits of Forgiveness in the New South Africa.* New York: Three Rivers Press, 1998.

Kuzwayo, Ellen. *Call Me Woman.* San Francisco: Spinster/Aunt Lute, 1985.

Lelyveld, Joseph. *Move Your Shadow.* New York: Times Books, 1985.

Leroi, Armand Marie. *Mutants: On Genetic Variety and the Human Body.* New York: Viking, 2003.

Maclennan, Ben, ed. *Apartheid: The Lighter Side.* Cape Town: Chameleon Press and Carrefour Press, 1990.

Mandela, Nelson. *Long Walk to Freedom.* Boston: Little, Brown and Co., 1994.

Marx, Anthony W. *Making Race and Nation: A Comparison of the United States, South Africa and Brazil.* Cambridge and New York: Cambridge University Press, 1998.

McClintock, Ann. *Imperial Leather: Race, Gender and Sexuality in the Colonial Contest.* New York: Routledge, 1995.

Miller, Alice. *Banished Knowledge: Facing Childhood Injuries.* New York: Doubleday, 1991.

Neisser, Ulrich, and Robyn Fivush, eds. *The Remembering Self: Construction and Accuracy in the Self-Narrative.* New York: Cambridge University Press, 1994.

Nixon, Rob. *Homelands, Harlem and Hollywood*. New York and London: Routledge, 1994.

Ntanlala, Phyllis. *A Life's Mosaic*. Berkeley: University of California Press, 1993.

Nuttall, Sarah, and Carli Coetzee, eds. *Negotiating the Past: The Making of Memory in South Africa*. Oxford: Oxford University Press, 1998.

Paton, Alan. *Too Late the Phalarope*. New York: Scribner's, 1953/1981.

Piaget, Jean. *The Child and Reality: Problems of Genetic Psychology*. Harmondsworth: Penguin, 1976.

Platzky, Laurine. *The Surplus People: Forced Removals in South Africa*. Cape Town: Ravan, 1985.

Sparks, Allister. *Tomorrow is Another Country*. Chicago: University of Chicago Press, 1995.

Stoler, Ann Laura. *Carnal Knowledge and Imperial Power: Race and the Intimate in Colonial Rule*. Berkeley and Los Angeles: University of California Press, 2002.

Suzman, Helen. *In No Uncertain Terms: A South African Memoir*. New York: Alfred A. Knopf, 1993.

Tatum, Beverly Daniel. *"Why Are All the Black Kids Sitting Together in the Cafeteria?": A Psychologist Explains the Development of Racial Identity*. New York: Basic Books, 2003.

Thompson, Leonard. *A History of South Africa* (Rev. ed.). New Haven: Yale University Press, 1995.

Van den Berghe, Pierre L. *South Africa: A Study in Conflict*. Berkeley: University of California Press, 1965.

———. *Race and Racism: A Comparative Perpective*. New York, John Wiley and Sons, 1967.

Van Woerden, Henk. *A Mouthful of Glass: The Man Who Killed the Father of Apartheid*. Johannesburg: Jonathan Ball, 1998.

Waldman, Michael, *Planet Ustinov*. London: Simon and Schuster, Ltd., 1998

Welty, Eudora. *One Writer's Beginning (The William E. Massey Sr. Lectures in the History of American Civilization)*. Cambridge, MA: Harvard University Press, 1998.

Zimmer, Carl. *Smithsonian Intimate Guide to Human Origins*. New York: Smithsonian Books/Collins, 2005.

Newspaper and Magazine Articles

Ananthaswamy, Anil. "Under the Skin." *New Scientist*, April 20, 2002. p. 36.

Angier, Natalie. "Do races differ? Not really, genes show." *New York Times,* August 22, 2000.

Armstrong, Sue. "Watching the 'race' detectives—The results of South Africa's race classification laws." *New Scientist*, April 20, 1991, 61ff.

Bikitsha, Doc. "Sandra finds home in a homeland . . ."*Rand Daily Mail,* October 11, 1978, 2.

Bosch, David J. "The Afrikaner and South Africa." *Theology Today,* July 1986 [vol 43-2] 210.

Breier, David. "I now pronounce you white, you black, you . . .", *Sunday Star*, April 24, 1988.

Bridgland, Fred. "Crime hurts South Africa's plan to host World Cup." *The Scotsman*, August 9, 2006.

Cape Times. "Sandra Laing at White Convent." Feb. 7, 1968.

Cape Times. "White Girl Race Victim Plans to Marry Black." March 5, 1974.

Cape Times. "White girl 'too dark,' no classes for 17 months," Aug. 8, 1967.

Die Beeld. "Sandra Weer Wit Na Lang Stryd" [Sandra White Again After Long Battle]. July 30, 1967.

Die Transvaler, "Sandra Se Bantoe Laaste Strooi." [Sandra's Bantu is the Last Straw]. March 6, 1974.

Gordimer, Nadine. "Five Years into Freedom." Johannesburg *Sunday Times*, June 27, 1999.

Jacobs, Craig. "Storm blows up as mine closes and dumps dry up." Johannesburg *Sunday Times*, October 24, 1999.

Johannesburg *Sunday Times.* "Vlok kneels at feet of Chikane." August 27, 2006.

Johannesburg *Sunday Times.* "Why Vlok's act just won't wash," [editorial] Sept. 3, 2006.

Katz, Marcelle. "Relative Values." London *Sunday Times* magazine, August 13, 2000, 1.

Lee, Felicia. "From Noah's Curse to Slavery's Rationale." *New York Times*, November 1, 2003.

le Roux, Karen. "'Who Brought My Daughter to Me? Tell them thank you.'" Johannesburg *Sunday Times*, Jan. 23, 2000.

Lillah, Ruwaydah. "Sandra's Long Road to Serenity." *Drum*, February 6, 2003.

Mail & Guardian. "ANC's Year of Shame." Nov. 21, 2006 national sec.

Maxwell, Kate. "Sandra Laing: The girl nobody wanted." *Express*, February 10, 1985.

McGreal, Chris. "Stuck in the past." London *Guardian*, March 16, 2001.

News/Check. "Races: Declassified." December 1, 1967, p. 5.

New York Times. "South Africa Girl Center of Dispute." Oct. 2, 1967.

New York Times. "The Durban Mailman." May 2, 1960.

New York Times. "Violence in black townships continues." July 24, 1976.

Noble, Kenneth B. "Kwathema Journal: As Apartheid Crumbles, Victim Finds Little Solace." *New York Times,* September 20, 1991, A4.

Olson, Steve. "The Genetic Archaeology of Race," *The Atlantic Monthly*, April 2001, 69–80.

Paton, Carol. "South Africa: the truth in black and white." Johannesburg *Sunday Times*, September 3, 2000.

Rand Daily Mail. "She has rejected us, says mother." March 8, 1974.

Rapport. "Blas Sandra wil nou swart word" [Sallow Sandra now wants to be white]. March 8, 1974.

Smith, Margaret. "'Coloured' Sandra May Get Reprieve." *Rand Daily Mail*, July, 1967.

Smith, Margaret. "Sandra Can't Quite Understand; White, then Coloured, then White Again." *Rand Daily Mail*, July, 1967.

Swarns, Rachel. "Tsakane Journal: Apartheid Still Burdens a Girl Who Didn't Fit." *New York Times*, June 10, 2000, A4.

Taylor, Frank. "The Court That Judges Colour." London *Daily Telegraph*, c.1966.

Thatcher, Gary. "South Africa's Archipelago: Strangers in their own land." *Christian Science Monitor*, September 16, 1981, 12.

Thornycroft, Peter. "Confessions of a human classifier." *Sunday Star*, Feb. 17, 1991.

Van der Merwe, Jan. "Black Is Beautiful Now for White Sandra." Johannesburg *Sunday Times*, June 27, 1976.

Vos, Suzanne. "Two die in race tangle 'suicide pact.'" Johannesburg *Sunday Times,* July 10, 1977.

Wade, Nicholas. "Gene Study Identifies 5 Main Human Populations, Linking Them to Geography." *New York Times*, Dec. 20, 2002.

Wines, Michael. "Shantytown Dwellers in South Africa Protest the Sluggish Pace of Change." *New York Times*, Dec. 25, 2005, 10.

Other Articles

Coetzee, J. M. "Blood, Taint, Flaw, Degeneration: The Case of Sarah Gertrude Millin," *English Studies in Africa* 23, no. 1 (1980), 41–58.

Corson, David J. "Social Justice and Minority Language Policy," *Educational Theory* (spring 1992) Volume 42:2, 181–200.

Harrison, Faye V., ed., "Contemporary Issues Forum: Race and Racism," *American Anthropologist*, 100, no. 3 (September 1998).

Lund, Giuliana. "Healing the Nation: Medicolonial Discourse and the State of Emergency from Apartheid to Truth and Reconciliation." *Cultural Critique* 54 (spring 2003): 88–119 [University of Minnesota Press].

Posel, Deborah. "What's In a Name? Racial Categorizations Under Apartheid and Their Afterlife." *Transformation: Critical Perspectives on South Africa* 47 (2001): 55.

Rosenberg, et al. "Genetic Structure of Human Populations." *Science* 298 (5602), (Dec. 20, 2002): 2381.

Schwerin, Alan. "Victory is Ours: Some Thoughts on Apartheid and Christianity." *Janus Head*, summer 1999, (*http://www.janushead.org*).

Doctoral Dissertations, Papers, Reports, Online Material:

AFRA [Association For Rural Advancement]: "Reprieves in Transvaal: Driefontein and Kwangema." Report Sheet No. 28, Jan. 1986, *http://www.disa.nu.ac.za.*

———. "Who got there first: Blacks in S.A." Factsheet, July 1980, *http://www.disa.nu.ac.za.*

Aliber, Michael, et al. "Synthesis Report of the 2005 Development Report: Overcoming Underdevelopment in South Africa's Second Economy." Capetown: Human Sciences Research Council, July 2005, *http://www.hsrc.ac.za*.

Armstrong, W. P. "Polygenic Inheritance." *Wayne's Word, http://waynesword.palomar.educ.lmeter5.htm*.

Du Plessis, Irma. "The Body in Fiction: Afrikaner Nationalism and Popular Children's Literature in the 1940s." Wits Instiute for Social and Economic Research. (WISER) *On the Subject of Sex and the Body* seminar series, Oct. 15, 2002, *http://www.wiserweb.wits.ac.za/PDF%2-Files/events%20-62009-2000compiled.PDF*.

Ekurhuleni Metropolitan Municipality. "Executive Summary: Ekurhuleni Growth and Development Strategy 2025." Germiston 2003.

Goldman, Sarron. "White Boyhood Under Apartheid: The Experience of Being Looked After by a Black Nanny." Doctoral thesis, ETD (Electronic Theses and Dissertations) no. 06032004-144915, University of Pretoria, Oct. 10, 2003.

Hirsch, Lee. *Amandla! A Revolution in Four Part Harmony.* 2000 (Documentary film).

iafrica.com. "Why do family murders occur?," May 30, 2000.

Madam and Eve. Cartoon number 003278, August 30, 2006, (*www.madamandeve.co.za./archive*).

Mail and Guardian Online. "Former deputy says Vlok apology a watershed moment," *http://www.mg.co.za*, August 27, 2006.

Mbuli, Cecil. "Folklore: The Tale of the Tail." At *http://www.visitswazi.com*.

Raditlhalo, Samuel. *"Who am I?": The Construction of Identity in Twentieth-Century South African Autobiographical Writings in English.* [Doctoral Dissertation, University Library Groningen, 2003].

Rassool, Ciraj. "Townships in South Africa: A Brief History." *http://www.colophon.be/pages/township_en.html*.

Scheper-Hughes, Nancy. "Mixed Feelings: The Recovery of Spoiled Identities in the New South Africa." Delivered at the Conference on Identity: Personal, Cultural and National, June 2–4, 1994, the Chinese University of Hong Kong. Available online through the National Humanities Center, *http://www.nhc. rtp.nc.us/publication/hongkong/scheper.htm.*

Simpson, Graeme. "Jackasses and Jackrollers: Rediscovering Gender in Understanding Violence." Research paper written for the Centre for the Study of Violence and Reconciliation, 1992, 7 *http://www.csvr.org.za/papers/papjack.htm.*

South Africa: The Good News. "Many Feet to Wash," Sept. 8, 2006 *http://www.sagoodnews.co.za.*

"South African Weather Service Lightning Detection Network," Jan. 13, 2006. (*www.weathersa.co.za/pressroom*)

Statistic South Africa. *Census 2001: Census in Brief/Statistics South Africa.* Pretoria: Statistics South Africa, 2003, *http://www.statssa.gov.za.*

The Black Sash. "The Tragedy of Sandra Laing," Nov. 1967 (*www. disa.nu.ac.za.*)

The Black Sash. "Sandra Laing: A Statement Issued by National Conference." Nov. 1967, *http://www.disa.nu.ac.za.*

The Joint United Nations Programme on HIV/AIDS., "2006 Report on the Global AIDS epidemic: Executive summary, *http://www.unaids.org/en/HIV_data/2006GlobalReport/default.asp.*

Transcripts

Big Idea (Radio National, Australian Broadcasting Company) "Beyond the Miracle: Ten Years After Apartheid," April 4, 2004, *http://www.abc.net.au/rn/bigidea/stories/s1077245.htm.*

van der Merwe, Karien, producer. *Special Assignment* (SABC), Dec. 7, 1999.

White, Peter, host. *No Triumph, No Tragedy* interview with Sandra Laing (BBC Radio 4 Series) July 27, 2000.

NOTES

1. Removed

The account of Sandra's removal from school is based on her recollections and on documents in her Department of Home Affairs file, obtained through South Africa's Promotion of Access to Information Act. Contemporary newspaper accounts occasionally offer conflicting details; a discussion of those discrepancies can be found in Chapter 30, "Unreliable Narrators."

Page

6   *Population Registration Act*: For an annotated list of all race laws passed in South Africa from 1948 to 1968, see Bunting, Brian, "South Africa's Nuremburg Laws," *The Rise of the South African Reich*. New York: Penguin, 1969; online at www.anc.org.za/ books/reich.html. See also Horrell, Muriel, *Laws Affecting Race Relations in South Africa, 1948–1976.* Johannesburg: South African Institute on Race Relations (SAIRR), 1978

three racial categories: Bowker, Geoffrey C. and Star, Susan Leigh, "The Case of Race Classification and Reclassification Under Apartheid," *Sorting Things Out: Classification and Its Consequences.*(Cambridge, MA: The MIT Press, 2000, p. 197. This thought-provoking book deals with, among other matters, the not-immediately-obvious ways in which classification changes human interaction; it includes a brief discussion of "The Case of Sandra Laing," pp. 220–221

Segregation and white supremacy, the explicit goals: "In a policy statement made in the Assembly on 5 February [1965], [Prime Minister] Verwoerd reiterated his opinion that peace could be ensured in South Africa only by separating Whites and Africans to the maximum extent possible." Horrell, Muriel, *A Survey of Race Relations: 1965*. Johannesburg: SAIRR, p. 1. Verwoerd concurred with Boer war hero and Afrikaner nationalist J.B.M. Hertzog, who'd said, four decades earlier, "Whatever the rights of the native may be, they have no right to call on us to do anything that might jeopardize our supremacy." Lelyveld, Joseph, *Move Your Shadow: South Africa, Black and White*. New York: Elisabeth Sifton Books/Penguin Books, 1986, p. 54. A brilliantly reported book that greatly enlarged my understanding of the apartheid culture in which Sandra was raised.

about *3.5 million citizens in 1966*: Horrell, Muriel, *A Survey of Race Relations, 1967*. Johannesburg: SAIRR, 1967. p. 19

determining where they lived and worked: Bowker, p. 197

7 according to the letter of the law: The Group Areas Act of 1950 restricted every residential area in South Africa to a specific racial group. A black or coloured person could live in a white area like Brereton Park only with a pass identifying them as a domestic employee. Bunting, Chapter 9

2. Goggas

Page

9   *nearly 200 of them:* As reported by seven people who boarded in the hostel from 1962–1966, and their parents. The portrait of daily life in the hostel is drawn from interviews with these former students.

10   *has never forgotten her first glimpse:* from an interview with eyewitness Anna Marsili, the mother of a classmate.

Confidential letter: From Sandra's Department of Home Affairs file. The letter was translated by Karien van der Merwe, who also translated all other documents and articles written in Afrikaans, except for Sandra's 1989 letter from Sannie, which Sandra translated.

3. Hidden History

Page

13   *Afrikaans, the language that evolved:* Daymond, M.J., *et. al.,* eds., *Women Writing Africa: The Southern Region*. New York: The Feminist Press, 2003, p. 58

Used disparagingly by nineteenth century British: Thompson, Leonard, *A History of South Africa* (Revised Edition). New Haven: Yale University Press, 1995, p. 56

15 an average of 174 armed robberies a day: South African Police Service, Crime Statistics/Gauteng *www.saps.gov.za/statistics/ reports/crimestats/2006/gauteng*

16 *patches of poisoned soil:* Jacobs, Craig, "Storm blows up as mine closes and dumps dry up," Johannesburg *Sunday Times*, October 24, 1999

40 percent unemployment . . . more than nearly a million people of color: "Executive Summary: Ekurhuleni Growth and Development Strategy 2025." (Germiston: Ekurhuleni Metropolitan Municipality, 2003). In year 2003, the cities and townships of the East Rand became Ekurhweleni ["Place of Peace" in Zulu] Metropolitan Municipality

17 *most of the wealth is still in the hands of whites::* Aliber, Michael, et. al. "Synthesis Report of the 2005 Development Report: Overcoming Underdevelopment in South Africa's Second Economy." Capetown: Human Sciences Research Council, July 2005 [*www.hsrc.ac.za*], p. 5

21 *some postcolonial theorists:* See McClintock, Anne, *Imperial Leather: Race, Gender and Sexuality in the Colonial Contest.* (New York and London: Routledge, 1995), p.305 on the politics of interpretation. The issue of cultural mediation is also addressed in the superb introduction to Daymond, *et. al.* p. 10: "It is in the nature of reproducing and translating [oral accounts] that intervening presences—interviewer, transcriber, translator—shape, and misshape, the text that we read." Gayatri Spivak, among others, warns of the appropriation by academic "first-world" women of the voices of "third-world" women. Spivak, Gayatri Chakravorty. "Three Women's Texts and a Critique of Imperialism," Critical Inquiry 12 (1), 1985, pp. 243–246, cited in Daymond, p. 6

most scientists agree: see, for example, Harrison, Faye V., ed., "Contemporary Issues Forum: Race and Racism," *American Anthropologist*, Volume 100, Number 3, September 1998. Among those who disagree are Neil Risch of Stanford University, who argues "that race [is] a valid area of medical research," since geographical roots established after the dispersal of humankind's African ancestors, about 50,000 years ago, reveal something about a person's genetic makeup. Wade, Nicholas, "Gene Study Identifies

5 Main Human Populations, Linking Them to Geography," *New York Times*, Dec. 20, 2002

of the 25,000 or so genes : Ananthaswamy, Anil, "Under the Skin," *New Scientist*, April 20, 2002. p. 36. See also Rosenberg, et.al., "Genetic Structure of Human Populations, *Science* [vol. 298, issue 5602], Dec. 20, 2002, p. 2381; and Olson, Steve, "The Genetic Archaeology of Race," *The Atlantic Monthly*, April 2001, pp 69–80: "The genetic variants affecting skin color and facial features are essentially meaningless—they probably involve a few hundred of the billions of nucleotides in a person's DNA. Yet societies have built elaborate systems of privilege and control on these insignificant genetic differences."

To put it another way: Cavalli-Sforza, Luigi Luca, *Genes, Peoples, and Languages*. Berkeley and Los Angeles: University of California Press, 2000. p. 29 ff. See also Angier, Natalie, "Race is an unscientific concept, experts say," *New York Times*, August 30, 2000: "Through transglobal sampling of neutral genetic markers—stretches of genetic material that do not help create the body's functioning proteins but instead are composed of so-called junk DNA—researchers have found that, on average, 88 to 90 percent of the differences between people occur within their local populations, while only about 10 to 12 percent of the differences distinguish one population, or race, from another."

22 *a group that is socially defined*: van den Berghe, Pierre L., *Race and Racism: A Comparative Perspective*. New York, John Wiley and Sons, 1967, p. 9ff. Van den Berghe also offers a helpful and succinct definition of racism: The "association of genetically caused differences in physical appearance with characteristics to which they are wholly unrelated."

47.4 million citizens: Statistics South Africa 2006 estimate, Statistical Release P0302 (www.statssa.gov.za.publications/P0302)

"historically coloured, politically black": Erasmus, Zimitri, "Introduction: Reimagining Coloured Identities in Post-Apartheid South Africa," in Erasmus, Zimitri, ed., *Coloured by History, Shaped by Place: New Perspectives on Coloured Identity*. Cape Town: Kwela, 2001, pp. 13–28

To the first European settlers: Armstrong, James C. and Worden, Nigel A., "The Slaves, 1652–1834," in Elphick, Richard and Giliomee, Hermann, eds., *The Shaping of South African Society, 1652–1840*. Middletown, CT: Wesleyan University Press, 1989. p. 122

23 *only Afrikaners to bear a name suggesting entitlement*: Bowker, p. 197

the terms white, colored, *and* black *for contemporary individuals:* Statistics South Africa, the official government data bank, continues to classify people by population group, it explains, "in order to monitor progress in moving away from the apartheid-based discrimination of the past. However membership of a population group is now based on self-perception and self-classification, not on a legal definition." *Census 2001: Census in Brief/Statistics South Africa.* Pretoria: Statistics South Africa 2003. (*www.statssa. gov.za*).

Linda James Myers: Tatum, Beverly Daniel, *"Why Are All the Black Kids Sitting Together?"* New York: Basic Books, 2003, p. 15.

4. Glad as a Bird

Page

24   *I immediately noticed:* Katz, Marcelle, "Relative Values," London *Sunday Times Magazine*, August 13, 2000, p.1

25   *born in Memel.* Formerly part of Germany, Memel is now Klaipeda, Lithuania. Alfred's birthplace and date of arrival are noted on his identity card, a copy of which is part of Sandra's government file.

attracted a community of Germans: www.pietretief.co.za

Dutch reformed church, similar to the Lutheran faith: Van den Berghe, p. 13

26   *Sannie and Abraham married:* Sandra and I found this information, previously unknown to her, in her government file.

31   *Pixley ka Isaka Seme . . . Land Act of 1913:* Thompson, p. 174. See also "Reprieves in Transvaal: Driefontein and Kwangema, " AFRA (Association for Rural Advancement) Report Sheet No. 28, January 1986. The archive of AFRA, non-governmental organization (NGO) involved in land rights, is available through the extraordinary Digital Imaging Project of South Africa (DISA), *www.disa.nu.ac.za.* a nonprofit initiative that makes available the holdings of South African research libraries and archives.

34   *made a point of being absent:* According to the recollections of Willy Meyer, a member of the Piet Retief School Committee in 1966. As an elder in the town's Dutch Reform Church, he made such visits to the Laings.

35   *endures more annual lightning:* "South African Weather Service Lightning Detection Network," Jan. 13, 2006. (*www.weathersa. co.za/pressroom*)

5. Prickly Pear

The details of daily life at Piet Retief Primary come from the accounts of students, parents, and teachers affiliated with the school in the 1960s.

Page

40 *They learned that . . . Noah cursed his son:* From the recollections of Karien van der Merwe and others who attended Afrikaner boarding schools. See also Lee, Felicia, "From Noah's Curse to Slavery's Rationale," *New York Times*, November 1, 2003

43 *Wollie vigorously and vocally disapproved:* For more about the instilling of anti-English bias in Afrikaners, see le Roux, Pieter, "Growing Up Afrikaner," in Burman, Sandra and Reynolds, Pamela, eds., *Growing Up in a Divided Society*. Evanston, IL: Northwestern University Press, 1986, pp. 196–197

44 *concentration camps:* van den Berghe, p. 33. The term was used first in the 19th century to describe Spanish prison camps in Cuba and American prison camps in the Philippines, but didn't become widely known until the Boer War.

Kaffir, originally Arabic for infidel: Van den Berghe, p. 10

45 *two divergent systems of schooling.* An astute and succinct overview of Christian National Education and Bantu Education can be found in Finnegan, William, *Crossing the Line: A Year in the Land of Apartheid*. Berkeley: University of California Press, 1994, pp. 121–124. For a moving account of the dire effects of The Bantu Education Act on a black community see Ntanlala, Phyllis, *A Life's Mosaic: the Autobiography of Phyllis Ntantala*. Berkeley: University of California Press, 1992), pp. 162–63

What is the use of teaching the Bantu: in a speech before the South African Senate, June 1954, quoted in Bunting, Chapter 11

If the native is being taught: Bunting, Chapter 11

46 *the government spent ten times more:* Thompson, p. 196

6. Dancing in her Chair

Page

51 *the wee would run down her leg:* "Traumatic events violate the autonomy of the person at the level of basic bodily integrity . . . Control over bodily functions is often lost . . ." Herman, Judith Lewis, *Trauma and Recovery*. New York: Basic Books, 1997, pp.

52–53. Hermans's book was indispensable to my understanding of Sandra's psychological predicament in childhood, and the survival strategies she depended upon.

54 *several studies by psychologists*: Foster, Don, "The Development of Racial Orientation in Children: A Review of South African Research," in Burman, pp. 164–168

55 *children in crisis sometimes accept*: Herman, pp.101–106

56 Christian National Education in action: On political indoctrination in the schools, see also le Roux in Burman, pp. 188–195: "There is no doubt that the Christian National Education to which the Nationalist government committed itself was designed to inculcate specific values. There was no pretence, to the horror of liberal educations, that education should be neutral." p. 187

57 *explaining his view of racial differences*: Private correspondence

7. Scandal-tongues
Skindertong is variously translated from Afrikaans into English as "scandaltongue," "slandertongue," or "gossip."

Page

58 *"Mrs. Laing said she was aware"*: Smith, Margaret, "'Coloured' Sandra May Get Reprieve," *Rand Daily Mail*, July, 1967

60 discrepancies between hard-line prescriptions: Stoler, Ann Laura, *Carnal Knowledge and Imperial Power: Race and the Intimate in Colonial Rule*. Berkeley and Los Angeles: University of California Press, 2002, p. 8

61 *a white man was acquitted:* MacLennan, Ben, ed., Apartheid: The Lighter Side. Cape Town: Carrefour Press and Chameleon Press, 1990. p. 18. An anthology of press clippings and government documents so horrifying in their insanity that they're funny. Sandra earned an entry in the book: "'Eleven-year-old Sandra Laing, who was White, then declared Coloured and has now been classified White again, does not quite understand what happened to her.' *Sunday Times*, August 6, 1967.'"

the indoctrination that began at birth: le Roux, in Burman, p. 187: "Unashamedly the educational system, the news media, and cultural organizations were given the task of promoting a particular perception of reality."

62 *"If her appearance is due . . .'"* Smith, *Rand Daily Mail*, July 1967.

the research of South African geneticist J.A. Heese: Elphick, Richard, and Shell, Robert, "Intergroup Relations: Khoikhoi, settlers, slaves and free blacks, 1652–1795," in Elphick, p. 202

The races have been mixing for so long: "White-black and white-coloured sexual contacts were frequent for a century or more after the Boers first settled in Cape Province, and then firm steps were taken to limit interracial liaisons and intermarriage." Davis, F. James, *Who is Black?* University Park, PA: The Pennsylvania State University Press, 1993, p. 95. "The willingness of European men to have sexual relations outside their group was no sign of the fluidity of social boundaries. Only the willingness to allow the offspring of such unions to inherit one's name, fortune, and community status [would be such a sign]." Elphick, Richard, and Giliomee, Hermann, "The origins and entrenchment of European dominance at the Cape, 1652–c.1840," in Elphick, p. 538

63   *the lands the whites claimed*: Thompson, pp. 6, 11 and 15

      As a result of this moral loophole: Elphick and Shell, in Elphick, p. 188–189. Furthermore, they note, only a small number of baptized slaves were subsequently freed. p. 189

64   *The company slave lodge served*: Armstrong, James C. and Worden, Nigel A., "The slaves, 1652–1835," in Elphick, p. 124

      But many of the female children: Thompson, p. 45

65   *often explain polygenetic inheritance this way*: Armstrong, W.P., "Polygenic Inheritance," *Wayne's Word* (*http://waynesword.palomar.educ.lmeter5.htm*)

66   *a South African magazine used the term*: Lillah, Ruwaydah, "Sandra's Long Road to Serenity," *Drum*, February 6, 2003

      known only to the press as Basil E.: Armstrong, Sue, "Watching the 'race' detectives—The results of South Africa's race classification laws," *New Scientist*, April 20, 1991 [vol 120 issue 1765], p. 61ff.

8. Skin Complaint

The documents cited in this chapter—letters, memos, and official summaries—come from an official file on Sandra kept by the Department of Home Affairs, obtained by Sandra under the Promotion of Access to Information Act of 1998, with the help of Karien van der Merwe, who also patiently photocopied them in Pretoria.

Page

68   *he thought press coverage would help*: Die Beeld notes in a July 30, 1967 article, "Sandra Weer Wit Na Lang Stryd" (Sandra White

Again After Long Battle), that it was the first newspaper to bring Sandra's plight to the attention of the public; "Laing said he thought the story in the *Beeld* was responsible for the reclassification [from coloured to white]."

74 *the downfall of civilizations*: Nixon, Rob, *Homelands, Harlem, and Hollywood*. New York: Routledge, 1994, p. 45. Nixon's chapter on Hertzog and television, "The Devil in the Black Box," is especially enjoyable and enlarging, as is a chapter about racial heritage, "Border Country," which mentions Sandra in a footnote.

Vorster, a Nazi sympathizer: Thompson, p. 189 He was imprisoned for supporting Germany in World War II after South Africa entered the war on the side of the Allies.

75 *a definition of whiteness*: Population Registration Act, no. 30 of 1950, section 1

9. An Affront Against Nature

Page

82 *don't have the same feelings:* In her pioneering book *Maids and Madams*, (Cape Town: Ravan Press, 1980) sociologist Jacklyn Cock interviewed white women and—employing black interviewers to do so—their black servants. Among the comments she collected from the white "madams" about their black housekeepers: "They are very mentally inferior. They don't think like us . . . you only get the odd one with a bit of intelligence, " and "They don't think and feel like we do." Elize Lötter told me in 2002, "Some whites in the [cultural diversity] classes I taught believed that black people don't grieve when their children die."

The preservation of the pure race tradition: Eloff, Gerrie, *Rasse en Rassevermenging (Race and Race Mixing)*, Bloemfontein: 1942, cited in Dubow, Saul, *Scientific Racism in South Africa*. Cambridge: Cambridge University Press, 1995. p. 270. Cited also in Thompson p. 184 1941, p. 104

83 *the defilement of white women by black men*: Dubow, p. 181

declare the vanquished not quite human: Thompson notes (p. 92) that in the Boer Republics, mixed race servants of the *voortrekkers* were referred to as *skepsels*, creatures, rather than *mense*, people. See also Linton, Ralph, *The Study of Man*. East Norwalk, CT: Appleton-Century-Crofts, 1936, pp. 46–47: ". . . it was only with the discovery of the New World and the sea routes to Asia that race assumed a social significance . . . Europeans have not been content merely to accept their present social and political dominance as an established fact. Almost from the first they have attempted to rationalize the situation and to prove to themselves that their subjugation of other racial groups was natural and inevitable." Quoted in Sanjek, Sanjek, Roger, "The Enduring Inequalities of Race," in Gregory, Steven and Sanjek, Roger, eds. *Race.* New Brunswick: Rutgers University Press, 1996, p. 2

Africa and the Americas had become a fantastic: McClintock, p. 22

84   *Ready to be disgusted and fascinated*: Elphick and Giliomee in Elphick, p. 525

show so little of humanity . . . reverse of humankind: quoted in Schwerin, Alan, "Victory is Ours: Some Thoughts on Apartheid and Christianity," *Janus Head*, Summer 1999 (*www.janushead.org*) The khoikhoi were nearly wiped out by smallpox in 1712 (Elphick, p. 22); the descendants of most of the survivors were ultimately subsumed into the colored community.

Scholars began categorizing humankind: Dubow, pp. 25–26

Certainly people fought and conquered: Sanjek, p. 4

85   *most whites in the Cape Colony*: Elphick, p. 82

the system of race relations: Elphick, p. 15, p. 96, and p. 528

the Afrikaners fiercely resented the influx: Thompson, p. 68

the so-called Great Trek: For a balanced and culturally sensitive account of the Trek and the histories of the African people encountered by the trekboers, see Etherington, Norman *The Great Treks*, London: Longman, 2001

not so much [the slaves'] freedom: quoted in Thompson, p. 88

86   *several thousand colored servants*: Thompson, p. 67

the area had been cleared of its tribal inhabitants: Thompson, p. 88 see also the AFRA Factsheet: Who got there first: Blacks in S.A.," July, 1980, (*www.disa.nu.ac.za*): "Following the defeat of [the Zulu king] Dingane in 1839, many of the former occupants of Natal returned to their ancestral lands, only to find them occupied by colonists, for whom they now had to work as laborers."

Battle of Blood River: Thompson, p. 91

the Boer Republics: ibid., p. 102

British annexed the diamond fields: ibid., p. 114

Two conflicts they call the Wars of Independence: van den Berg, pp. 32–33.

87 *Blacks outnumbered whites:* Thompson, p.153. In Natal province, Africans outnumbered whites ten to one. Thompson, p. 148

poor whites, almost all of them Afrikaners: Dubow, p.17

finding common cause: Dubow, p. 171–172

the most oppressed group: McGreal, Chris, "Stuck in the past," London *Guardian*, March 16, 2001. Under Christian National Education, he notes, "For decades, children of all races learned that the Afrikaner was the real victim of South Africa's perpetual strife . . . [apartheid] was not a form of oppression . . . but a survival strategy for people persecuted on all sides."

88 *secret society called the Broederbond:* It was immensely powerful. "Particularly in the Church, the schools, and the media it became very difficult if not impossible to obtain an important post if one did not have the support of the secret Afrikaner Broederbond. Le Roux in Burman, p. 188

"vigorous" and "virile" masses . . . fear of racial mixing: Dubow, p. 180–181

It is afternoon and the Bantu houseboy: Quoted in Nixon, p. 52

Hysteria about the consequences: Dubow, p. 183. In the parliamentary debates before leading the passage of the 1949 Mixed Marriages Act, Dubow notes, National Party members were particularly worried about preserving "race purity." The debate touched directly on the fears that Sandra's presence in the Laing family would kindle in their neighbors: "Mendelian eugenic theory was also reflected in comments about the sudden emergence of atavistic 'throwbacks' in families generally considered to be white." Dubow, p. 182

89 *evoked ambivalence in the Afrikaners:* "The differences between the 'poor white' Afrikaners and the Coloureds, especially, were not all that easy to make out, on either side of the color line. Both groups spoke the same language and felt the same longing for a recognition of the wrongs done to them in the past. But what a child could not understand was this: that the war between the races was always fought most fiercely when the differences between them were least apparent." Van Worden, Henk, *A Mouthful of Glass.* (Johannesburg: Jonathan Ball Publishers, 1998). The book is a fictionalized biography of Demetrios Tsafendas, who assassinated Hendrik Verwoerd in 1966.

the Dutch Reformed Church—a separate branch: Thompson, p. 66. Blacks were barred entirely. The bigotry of the Dutch Reformed Church is highlighted in a joke from the 1960s related by Le Roux:

A white Pretoria policeman spots a black man kneeling in a house of worship and demands to know what he's doing there. "Polishing the floors, baas," the man tells him. "Oh, that's OK then," the policeman says. "I thought you were praying." Burman, p. 192

The coloured community served as a buffer group, Davis, p. 92

"brown Afrikaners": Nixon, p. 105: "Coloureds have been subjected both to white claims on their allegiance—as 'brown Afrikaners'—and to disclaimers—as 'nonwhites' . . . when whites have found it politically expedient to attempt to set 'colored' and the African majority at loggerheads, 'coloreds' have become 'half-brothers' and 'half-sisters, 'almost family.'

This notion was popularized: For a discussion of Fantham and Porter and their views on the degeneracy of mixed race people, see Dubow, pp. 135–136

90   "The coloured race . . ." Millin, Sarah Gertrude, *God's Stepchildren* (London: *Constable,* 1924), quoted in Coetzee, J. M., "Blood, Taint, Flaw, Degeneration: The Case of Sarah Gertrude Millin," *English Studies in Africa* 23, no. 1, 1980, pp. 41–58. See also Nixon, p. 105: . . . the imagery of partial kinship [between coloreds and Afrikaners] has also been used to patronize or ostracize 'coloreds' as prodigal and degenerate, the embodiments of moral dissolution. This view was notoriously advanced by Sarah Gertrude Millin's 1924 novel, *God's Step-children*, a fictional polemic against miscegenation as a biological, familial, and national tragedy."

the flaw in the blood: Coetzee, J. M., ibid.

more than eleven thousand five hundred: Sanjek, Roger, "The Enduring Inequalities of Race,"in Gregory, Steven and Sanjek, Roger, eds. *Race.* New Brunswick: Rutgers University Press, 1996, p. 7

91   *the evidence is that the European:* Cronje, Geoffrey, *A Home for Posterity*, 1945. Furthermore, Cronje "argued that the only way to ensure the long-term survival of the Afrikaner people was to separate the races into completely distinct territories." Thompson, p. 185

"all other Afrikaner mothers..." Bosch, David J., "The Afrikaner and South Africa," *Theology Today,* July 1986 [vol 43–2], p. 210

The popular ideal of the volksmoeder: McClintock, p. 377. As McClintock and others have pointed out, the invention of the Volksmoeder ideal did more than make Afrikaner nationalism and women's sexual purity synonymous. ". . . the Volksmoeder discourse . . . was aimed at moving women out of the workplace and factories where they were building class alliances with black women and to remove them from positions of decision-making. Du Plessis, Irma, "The Body in Fiction: Afrikaner Nationalism and Popular Children's Literature in the 1940s," Wits Instiute for Social and Economic Research (WISER) *On the Subject of Sex and the Body Seminar Series*, October 15, 2002. Available online at *www.wiserweb.wits.ac.za*

whites who weren't Afrikaners: The British ended slavery in the Cape in 1834, but "[n]ever did they contemplate overturning a labour system which was the product of 180 years of Cape history—a system in which brown-skinned workers laboured cheaply and diligently for white-skinned farmers and entrepreneurs." Elphick, p. 50

92   "Mr. Laing said...": Smith, Margaret, " 'Coloured' Sandra May Get Reprieve," *Rand Daily Mail*, July, 1967

10. Pigmentocracy

Lancelot Hogben (1895–1975), a British biologist and critic of eugenics who taught in South Africa, derisively called the country a "pigmentocracy" in his introduction to a 1939 book called *Half-caste*, by Cedric Dover. For more on Hogben's opposition to racist science in South Africa, see Dubow, p. 193. Several other works were extraordinarily helpful in illuminating the mechanisms and effects of race classification: Muriel Horrell's *Race Classification In South Africa*, (Johannesburg: SAIRR, 1958); reports of the SAIRR from 1958 until 1991; Bowker, pp. 193–225; and Lelyveld, pp. 91–93. Descriptions of pseudoscientific race tests may also be found in the article "Concern At Methods of Classifying Coloureds," Johannesburg *Sunday Time*, August 21, 1955

Page

93   *[Sandra Laing] was recently expelled*: Taylor, Frank "The Court That Judges Colour,: London *Daily Telegraph*, c. 1966

94   *the odd case of Mr. David Song:* Horrell, Muriel, "The Song Case," A Survey of Race Relations:1962. Johannesburg: SAIRR, 1962, pp. 69–70

The board granted a classification change: "These miraculous transformations are tabulated and announced on an annual basis. In my first year back in South Africa [1980], 558 coloreds became whites, 15 whites became coloreds, 8 Chinese became whites, 7 whites became Chinese, 40 Indians became colored, 20 coloreds became Indians, 79 Africans became colored, and 8 coloreds became Africans. The spirit of this grotesque self-parody . . . is obviously closer to Grand Guignol than the Nuremberg Laws; in other words, it's a sadistic farce." Lelyveld, p. 85

95   *Johannes Botha, a white mail carrier:* "The Durban Mailman," *New York Times*, May 2, 1960

96   *white miners . . . earned:* The real wages of the Africans were less than they had been in 1911. Thompson, p. 195

97   *"obviously nonwhite in looks":* Horrell, *A Survey of Race Relations,* 1967 (Johannesburg: SAIRR, 1967) p. 22

"A man who looks White . . . ": ibid

most were civil servants: Armstrong, p. 61; Horrell, 1967, p. 19

the case of twin boys: Horrell, 1967, ibid.

the story of Raymond Du Proft: Harrison, David, *The White Tribe of Africa. South Africa in Perspective.* Berkeley: University of California Press, 1982, 173ff. A similar case was reported in the Johannesburg *Sunday Times* of July 10, 1977: Michael Smith, an "unemployed artisan who had applied unsuccessfully to have his race classification changed from Bantu to coloured" shot himself after the Appeal Board and the Supreme Court both turned down his request for a race change. At the time of that decision, he told reporter Suzanne Vos, " 'You whites, you whites, you hurt us so much. How is it going to harm you if I'm classified a coloured? Coloureds get paid more. That's one reason I want to be a coloured.'" Vos, Suzanne, "Two die in race tangle 'suicide pact,' Johannesburg *Sunday Times*, July 10, 1977

98   *the minister of the Interior testified:* Horrell, 1967, p. 19 and p. 27

the arbitrariness of race: In a sardonic 1988 essay on race classification headlined "I now pronounce you white, you black, you . . ." (*Sunday Star*, April 24, 1988) political correspondent David Breier, pointing out how odd it was that in the previous year 438 coloured people became white at the stroke of a pen, mischievously concluded "One suggestion is that if all black were classified white and all whites were classified black, South Africa would have a white majority and its problems would be solved—except for the black minority, of course." Even the original proponents of race classification were aware of how arbitrary the categories were, and how much of a social construct. The Minister of the Interior in 1950 told parliament that since "[race was determined by] the judgment of society—conventions that have grown up during the hundreds of years we have been here . . . the classification of a person should be made according to the views held by the member of that community." Quoted in Posel, Deborah, "What's In a Name? Racial Categorizations Under Apartheid and Their Afterlife," Transformation: Critical Perspectives on South Africa, 47 (2001), p. 55

Japanese were classified: "Classification of Japanese Persons," *A Survey of Race Relations*: 1962. Johannesburg: SAIRR, 1962, p. 68

not much, scientists say: "'Race is a social concept, not a scientific one,' said Dr. J. Craig Venter, head of the Celera Genomics Corp. of Rockville, Maryland [and chief of the human genome project]. Angier, *New York Times*, August 30, 2000

superficial adaptations to geography: Zimmer, Carl, *Smithsonian Intimate Guide to Human Origins*. New York: Smithsonian Books/ Collins, 2005, pp. 152–153

no line in nature: Sanjek, Roger, "The Enduring Inequalities of Race,"in Gregory, Steven and Sanjek, Roger, eds. *Race*. New Brunswick: Rutgers University Press, 1996, p. 7

99   *another South African girl*: *Newsweek*, July 3, 1970, p. 31, cited in Bowker, p. 221

11. Lessons at Home

Page

104   "In March last year, Sandra:" Smith, Rand Daily Mail, 1967.

105   *Justice Galgut issued a ten-page decision:* A copy of the decision, portions of which are quoted in this chapter, as well as copies of Department of Home Affairs memos about the case, and letters to the department from indignant citizens, were all part of Sandra's government file.

12. Declare the Thing a Bastard

Page

108   *sent the Laings a letter*: A copy is in her file

109   *268 objection . . . 88 appeals*: Horrell, 1966 and 1967

150,000 borderline cases: Bunting, Chapter 11: "at the beginning in August 1966 it became compulsory for every South African over the age of sixteen to be in possession of an identity card, yet there were still approximately150,000 'borderline' cases to be settled."

The reason for the introduction of the amending bill: Suzman, Helen, *In No Uncertain Terms*. New York: Alfred A. Knopf, 1993, Horrell, 1967, p. 23

110 *Spirited opposition to the amendment:* The discussion of debate on the amendment involving Minister le Roux and Sir de Villiers Graaf is found in Horrell, 1967, pp. 26–27

to close the gate: the Minister of the Interior spoke on September 15, 1966, before the House of Assembly. Bunting, chapter 11

the bill passed: The Population Registration Amendment Act, No. 64 of 1967 reads in part: ". . . a person shall be classified as White if his natural parents have both been so classified." Horrell, 1967, p. 24

112 *The English language press*: Smith, Margaret, "Sandra Can't Quite Understand; White, then Coloured, then White Again," *Rand Daily Mail*, July, 1967

113 *Agreed to have her reassigned*: "South Africa Girl Center of Dispute," *New York Times*, Oct. 2, 1967

114 *White schools, afraid of the attendant publicity:* "White girl 'too dark,' no classes for 17 months," *Cape Times*, August 8, 1967

115 *The tragedy of Sandra Laing*: "Sandra Laing: A Statement Issued by National Conference," *The Black Sash*, November 1967 (*www.disa.nu.ac.za*)

116 *By classifying and then twice reclassifying:* "Races: Declassified," *News/Check* December 1, 1967, p. 5

13. Memory in Transit

Page

120 *The languages are so similar:* Mkhonza, Sarah, "The Writer as Woman: Experiences in Swaziland," in *Women and Activism: Women Writers Conference, Harare, 29–30 July 1999*. Harare: Zimbabwe International Book Fair and Zimbabwe Women Writers, p. 34. Cited in Daymon, p. 63

121 *It wasn't so unusual:* For a fascinating study of the relationship between white employer and black housekeepers, see Cock, Jacklyn, *Maids and Madams* Cape Town, Ravan Press, 1980

122 *The Institute for Healing of Memories:* This extraordinary organization, dedicated to "remembering the apartheid years and healing the wounds" through inclusive workshops and seminars, was

founded by Father Michael Lapsley, an antiapartheid activist who lost both hands to a letter bomb. (*www.healingofmemories.co.za*)

The memory is a living thing: Welty, Eudora, *One Writer's Beginning (The William E. Massey Sr. Lectures in the History of American Civilization)* Cambridge: Harvard University Press, 1998, p.104

14. The Wronged and Suffering Party

Page

125 *Yesterday her parents received*: "Sandra Laing at White Convent," *Cape Times*, Feb. 7, 1968

127 Abraham Laing's letters to the minister of Home Affairs, the
129 replies he received, and internal memos about the correspondence were found in Sandra's Department of Home Affairs file.

15. Courting Disaster

The information in this chapter comes from conversations with Sandra Laing. A passage from Anne McClintock's *Imperial Leather* was a touchstone for its presentation: "Oral history involves the technological reproduction of people's memories; the unstable life of the unconscious; the deformations, evasions and repressions of memory, desire, projection, trauma, envy, anger, pleasure. These obscure logics cannot be wished away as the irksome impurities of oral history, but should be integrated into oral history, as a central part of the process. No oral history is innocent of selection, bias, evasion and interpretation." p. 311

16. Crossing the Border

Page

139 *The power to disbelieve*: Janeway, Elizabeth, *The Powers of the Weak*. New York, Morrow Quill Paperback, 1981, p. 167

141 Siestog! *It means*: Kromhout, Jan, ed., *Klein Woordeboek/Little Dictionary*. Cape Town: Pharos, 2000, p. 124

The usual catchy definitions: Krog, Antjie, *Country of My Skull*. New York: Three Rivers Press, 1999, p. 342

According to the Centre for the Study of Violence and Reconciliation: Simpson, Graeme, "Jackasses and Jackrollers: Rediscovering Gender in Understanding Violence," research paper written for the Centre for the Study of Violence and Reconciliation, 1992, p. 7 (*www.csvr.org.za/papers/papjack.htm*)

142   *the Afrikaner patriarch depends:* "Why do family murders occur?,"
        iafrica.com, May 30, 2000

17. In the Chokey

The details in this chapter were supplied by Sandra and by Jenny
Zwane. Sandra may have been jailed under the General Law
Amendment Act, the Population Registration Act, or the Immorality Acts. According to a spokeswoman in the office of the magistrate
of Carolina, no records remain from the time of her incarceration.

18. Stronger Inside

Page

148   *a national migrant labor system:* Thompson, pp. 192–193

19. Mother Cries

Department of Home Affairs memos, Abraham's letter, official correspondence and Sandra's affidavit are part of Sandra's government file.

Page

160   *sangomas, indigenous healers*: For a fascinating and detailed account
        of the role of witchcraft in postapartheid South Africa, see Ash-
        forth, Adam, *Witchcraft, Violence, and Democracy in South Africa.*
        Chicago and London: University of Chicago Press, 2005. In it
        he explores "how issues of spiritual insecurity—the dangers,
        doubts and fears arising from the sense of being exposed to in-
        visible evil forces—relate to other dimensions of insecurity in
        everyday life such as those arising from poverty, violence, polit-
        ical oppression, and disease," p. 1

163   *White Girl Race Victim:* "White Girl Race Victim Plans to Marry
        Black," *Cape Times*, March 5, 1974

        Sallow Sandra Now Wants: "Blas Sandra wil nou swart word," *Rap-
        port*, [filed by the Department of Home Affairs on March 8, 1974]

164   *Sandra will have to make her own path through life*: "Sandra Se Ban-
        toe Laaste Strooi,"[Sandra's Bantu is the Last Straw], *Die Trans-
        valer*, March 6, 1974

        Yesterday, [Laing's] mother, a postmistress: "Mother: She has rejected
        us," *Rand Daily Mail*, March 8, 1974

165   *For the Laings to have chosen:* Private correspondence

20. Black Spot

Page

167   *After the shooting:* "Violence in black townships continues," *New York Times,* July 24, 1976

168   *Sandra Laing, 20, said this week:* "Black Is Beautiful Now for White Sandra, Van der Merwe, Jan, Johannesburg *Sunday Times,* June 27, 1976

169   *The Surplus People's Project:* Thompson, p. 194. A comprehensive study of forced removals and their effects can be found in Platzky, Laurine, *The Surplus People: Forced Removals in South Africa.* Cape Town: Ravan, 1985

one of ten so-called homelands: Thompson, pp. 91–94

to remove all black people from South Africa: Lelyveld, p. 88

rendered tribal affiliation meaningless: Raditlhalo, Samuel, "Who am I?": The Construction of Identity in Twentieth-Century South African Autobiographical Writings in English. [Doctoral Dissertation, University Library Groningen, 2003] pp. 85–86: ". . . in order to protect themselves, the Afrikaners embarked on enforcing 'identities' that the recipients did not want . . . the ethnic variety of whites was not a barrier to all white people being regarded as 'one race' which could conceivably be viewed as 'one nation', [but] . . . since black South Africans spoke various languages, they were 'different nations'."

It is accepted Government policy: Thompson, p. 193. Similarly, "Mr. G. F. L. Froneman (a prominent Nationalist M.P.) said that the Bantu 'are only supplying a commodity, the commodity of labour . . . It is labour we are importing and not labourers as individuals . . .'" Horrell, Muriel, *A Survey of Race Relations: 1965.* Johannesburg: SAIRR, pp. 1–2

172   *responded to the pressure and poverty:* Thatcher, Gary, "South Africa's Archipelago; Strangers in their own land," *Christian Science Monitor,* September 16, 1981, p. 12. See also: Thompson, p. 202: "Wilson and Ramphele also emphasized the 'widespread disorganization of family life due to the migratory labor system' and the political economic, and social powerlessness experienced by a large proportion of black South African men, which engenders a frustrated rage that all too often manifests itself in domestic violence, particularly against women." [Quote from

Wilson, Francis and Ramphele, Mamphela, "Children in South Africa," in Children on the Front Line (New York, 1987) p. 52]

174   *Sandra Finds Home in a Homeland*: Bikitsha, Doc, "Sandra finds home in a homeland . . ." *Rand Daily Mail,* October 11, 1978, p. 2

South Africa's harsh racial laws: The reporter is referring to the Population Registration Act and the Group Areas act, but he might also have noted that in 1978 the government spent ten times as much per capita on white students as on African students (Thompson p. 196) and that mortality rates for both African and colored children aged one to four years old were thirteen times as high as for whites. (Thompson, p. 203)

177   *a famous Swazi saying*: Mbuli, Cecil, "Folklore: The Tale of the Tail," at *www.visitswazi.com*

21. The Next Escape

Page

179   KwaThema was built in 1952: "KwaThema History," *www. Ekuhurleni.com*

The townships were an experiment: Ciraj Rassool, "Townships in South Africa: A Brief History." Rassool, a history professor at University of the Western Cape, wrote this excellent piece to accompany a CD collection of township music released by Colophon records. (*www.colophon.be/pages/township_en.html*) See also Evans, Ivan, "The 'Properly Planned Location,'" in *Bureaucracy and Race: Native Administration in South Africa*. Berkeley: University of California Press, 1997.

181   *yet another affidavit*: government file

182   *Sandra had never encountered coloured culture:* For more about customs and attitude in a coloured community near Cape Town, see Scheper-Hughes, Nancy, "Mixed Feelings: The Recovery of Spoiled Identities in the New South Africa," delivered at the Conference on Identity: Personal, Cultural and National June 2–4, 1994, The Chinese University of Hong Kong. Available online through the National Humanities Center, *www.nhc.rtp.nc.us/publication/hongkong/scheper.htm*. Coloured culture isn't monolithic, of course, any more than are black and white cultures. "[Sociologist] Zimitri Erasmus has said, '. . . we need to move beyond the notion that coloured identities are "mixed race" identities. Rather, we need to see them as cultural identities comprising de-

tailed bodies of knowledge, specific cultural practices, memories, rituals and modes of being.' " Daymond, p. 61

22. Lipstick Soup

Page

189 *Sandra was officially declared*: government file

194 *complex posttraumatic stress disorder*: Herman, p. 119: "The responses to trauma are best understood as a spectrum of conditions rather than a single disorder." A list of symptoms (p. 121) includes "A history of subjection to totalitarian control over a prolonged period (months to years) . . . explosive or inhibited anger . . . amnesia . . . transient dissociative episodes . . . paralysis of initiative . . . guilt and self-blame . . . repeated search for rescuer."

emotional detachment and profound passivity: Herman, p. 43

They lose their trust in themselves: Herman, p. 56

195 *One of nature's small mercies:* Herman, p. 43

paralysis of initiative: Herman p. 121

the disappearance of activists: Thompson, p. 235

a symbol in the public imagination: Maxwell, Kate, "Sandra Laing: The girl nobody wanted," *Express*, February 10, 1985

196 *the Dutch-Reformed Church issued a statement:* "The Immorality and Prohibition of Mixed Marriages Act," *Race Relations Survey, 1985.* Johannesburg: SAIRR, 1985, p. 9

P. W. Botha jailed unprecedented numbers: Thompson, p. 235

23. We All Got the Same
The information in this chapter comes from conversations with Sandra Laing.

24. The Perils of Harmonization

Page

204 *releasing Mandela from prison:* Mandela was freed nine days after the announcement. For an extraordinary account of the events leading up to his release, see Nelson Mandela's autobiography *Long Walk to Freedom* (Boston: Back Bay Books, 1994).

205 *If, to survive, a child is required:* Miller, Alice, Banished Knowledge: Facing Childhood Injuries. New York: Anchor, 1991, p. 39

206 *She told the* New York Times: Noble, Kenneth B., "Kwathema Journal: As Apartheid Crumbles, Victim Finds Little Solace. *New York Times,* September 20, 1991, p. A4

   I don't tell my friends at the bowling club: Thornycroft, Peter, "Confessions of a human classifier," *Sunday Star,* Feb. 17, 1991

207 *peaceful transfer of power:* for a fascinating account of that process, see Sparks, Allister, Tomorrow is Another Country. Chicago, University of Chicago Press, 1995. Mandela was inaugurated as president on May 10, 1995.

   nearly 4 million whites: South Africa Survey. 1994 Report, Statistics South Africa (*www.statssa.gov.za*)

25. Screening

Page

212 *television program about South Africa: The footage didn't make it into the series, "In the Footsteps of Mark Twain," but the interview and screening are mentioned in a book by the producer/director:* Waldman, Michael, *Planet Ustinov.* London: Simon and Schuster Ltd., 1998, p. 226–228

26. Bold is to Beautiful as Truth is to Reconciliation

Page

216 *300 million viewers in 100 countries: www.boldandbeautiful.com*

   a real life apartheid drama: For an unforgettable account of the TRC by poet and journalist and journalist who covered the hearings, see Antjie Krog's *Country of My Skull.* New York: Three Rivers Press, 2000. Also rewarding is *No Future Without Forgiveness,* Bishop Desmond Tutu's memoir of his experiences as head of TRC. (New York: Doubleday, 1999).

   there is not a single person: quoted in Lund, Giuliana, "Healing the Nation: Medicolonial Discourse and the State of Emergency from Apartheid to Truth and Reconciliation," *Cultural Critique* 54, Spring 2003, pp. 88–119 [University of Minnesota Press].

217 *one woman whose child had disappeared:* For more testimony from and superb commentary on the TRC hearings, see Kroeg, pp. 39–43, and Gobodo-Madikizela, Pumla, *A Human Being Died That Night.* Boston and New York: Houghton-Mifflin, 2003. The seven-volume final report of the TRC is available at *www.doj.gov.za/trc/report/index.htm*

This lends some small degree: Gobodo-Madikizela, p. 26

killing apartheid's opponents: Gobodo-Madikizela, p. 66

there were two South Africas: Gobodo-Madikizela, pp. 108–109

218 *never mind Kant's categorical imperative*: In an article about social justice, David Corson defined Kant's categorical imperative thusly: what each person can will for all, without contradiction, becomes a just and binding universal law. "Conversely," he continued, "where such laws cannot be generalized, they are not just. For example: Afrikaner South Africans, who support apartheid would have to argue that they would still support these laws even if they were counted among the victims of apartheid instead of among the beneficiaries." Corson, David J., "Social Justice and Minority Language Policy," *Educational Theory*, Spring 1992, Volume 42:2, pp. 181–200

A policy of good-neighborliness: In Lee Hirsch's 2003 documentary *Amandla! A Revolution in Four Part Harmony*, archival newsreel footage shows Prime Minister Hendrik Verwoerd explaining apartheid as "really a policy of good neighborliness."

whites blamed the poverty of blacks: Dubow, p. 158

27. "A Decent White"

Page

220 *half-hour segment*: it aired December 7, 1999

222 *I gave the most naïve interview:* from Karien van der Merwe's personal files

still fought amongst themselves: See Thompson p. 201: "In the urban ghettos, Africans mingled, regardless of ethnicity. For example, they ignored the government's attempt to carve up the townships into ethnic divisions; they married across ethnic lines; and members of the younger generation identified themselves as Africans (or even, comprehensively, as Blacks, thus including Coloureds and Indians) rather than as Xhosa, Zulu, Sotho, Pedi or Tswana."

clashed with the Zulu-led Inkatha Party: Thompson, p. 230

224 *When you came to live*: I'm grateful to Karien van der Merwe for the transcripts of outtakes from her *Special Assignment* segment.

229 *a friend who is an ex-police officer*: Le Roux, Karen, "'Who Brought My Daughter to Me? Tell them thank you'" Johannesburg *Sunday Times*, Jan. 23, 2000

28. Reunion

231   *The moment she has been aching for*: Le Roux, *ibid*

234   *Leon Laing says he is sorry*: Swarns, Rachel "Tsakane Journal: Apartheid Still Burdens A Girl Who Didn't Fit, " *New York Times*, June 10, 2000, p. A4

       My two brothers: White, Peter, *No Triumph, No Tragedy* (BBC Radio 4 Series). From transcript of interview with Sandra Laing, July 27, 2000

       In those early years: Katz, Marcelle, Relative Values, London *Sunday Times Magazine*, August 13, 2000, p.1

235   *My first response was tears*: private conversation

236   *she doesn't like black people*: Karien also reports that the nurse said that when the *Special Assignment* segment aired in 1999, Sannie denied having a daughter, but she was happy when Sandra came.

29. Durable Goods

Page

244   *free textbooks*: "In her book *A Decade of Bantu Education,* Muriel Horrell [of the SAIRR] calculated that, in direct taxation and voluntary contributions, African parents contributed proportionately more to the education of their children than did any other section of the population . . . African children pay for items which are supplied free to white children." Bunting, Chapter 11

       many years have passed: personal correspondence, used by permission of Elize Lötter

247   *A possible outward sign of God's grace*: van den Berghe, pp. 14–15

248   *In these ads*: Bertelsen, Eve, "Ads and amnesia: black advertising in the new South Africa," in Nuttall, Sarah and Coetzee, Carli, *Negotiating the Past: The Making of Memories in South Africa*. Cape Town: Oxford University Press, 2000, p. 233

       Distinction is increasingly conferred by possessions: Bertelsen in Nuttall, pp. 223–224

30. Unreliable Narrators

Page

254   *in a well known 1993 experiment*: described in Neisser, Ulric, "Self-Narratives: True and false," in Neisser, Ulric and Fivush,

Robin, eds. *The Remembering Self: Construction and accuracy in the self-narrative.* New York: Cambridge University Press, 1994, p. 5

255 *these studies show a good deal of forgetting:* Neisser, p. 7

257 *narrative memory consists:* Neisser, p. 2. Notes Neisser, "Even when people strive for accuracy, what they remember may not be just what happened."

258 *There cannot be a final and complete reconstruction:* Gobodo-Madikizela, p. 165

260 *a woman in her late sixties:* Felman, Shoshana and Dori Laub, *Testimony: Crises of Witnessing in Literature, Psychoanalysis, and History,* Routledge, 1991, p. 51

261 *"Historians Gary Minkley and Ciraj Rassool:* Minkley, Gary, and Rassool, Ciraj, "Orality, Memory, and Social History in South Africa," in Nuttall, pp. 94–95

Many a time, visitors from outside": Pallo Jordan, quoted in Paton, Carol, "South Africa: the truth in black and white," Johannesburg *Sunday Times,* September 3, 2000 (*www.suntimes.co.za/2000/09/03/ news/news17/htm.*)

31. Hazard Lights

Page

264 *What is she selling you:* Private correspondence

32. The Rainbow Tuck Shop

Page

279 *went to see the official:* described in personal correspondence from Karien van der Merwe and Elize Lötter, and by Sandra in telephone conversations.

33. Yesterday, Today, Tomorrow

282 *"boundary crosser" who "works in the joints":* Hyde, Lewis, *Trickster Makes This World.* New York: Farrar, Straus, and Giroux, 1998, p. 270. I cannot praise this book enough.

lethal anomaly: Hyde, p. 271

285 *in order to cope with abuse:* Herman, p. 103

three thousand pages of statutes: Lelyveld, p. 82

286 *thousands of squatters . . . 45 percent more people have safe clean water:* Wines, Michael, "Shantytown Dwellers in South Africa Protest

the Sluggish Pace of Change," *New York Times*, December 25. 2005, p. 10. "Since 1994, South Africa's government has built 1.8 million basic houses, often to shanty town dwellers," and "more than 10 million people have gained access to clean water."

when the Federation Internationale de Football: Bridgland, Fred, "Crime hurts South Africa's plan to host World Cup," *The Scotsman*, August 9, 2006 (*thescotsman.scotsman.com*)

Four members of the ANC cabinet: "ANC's Year of Shame," *Mail & Guardian*, Nov. 21, 2006

One of the world's highest AIDS rates: 5.4 million people in South Africa are living with HIV/AIDS, out of a population of 47.4 million (nearly 12 percent), according to UNAIDS' "2006 Report on the Global AIDS epidemic: Executive summary *www.unaids.org/en/HIV_data/2006GlobalReport/default.asp*. See also "Latest HIV Indicators Report Released (November 2006), Actuarial Society of South Africa, *www.assa.org.za* (news)

five years of freedom: Gordimer, Nadine, "Five Years Into Freedom," Johannesburg *Sunday Times*, June 27, 1999

287 *"We're supposed to have*: "Beyond the Miracle: Ten Years After Apartheid," Radio National, April 4, 2004. Transcript at *www.abc.net.au/rn/bigidea/stories/s1077245.htm*

forgiveness made headlines: "Vlok kneels at feet of Chikane," Johannesburg Sunday Times, August 27, 2006

three basic ways: "Why Vlok's act just won't wash," [editorial] Sept. 2006

Johannesburg *Sunday Times*; "Former deputy says Vlok apology a watershed moment," *Mail and Guardian Online (www.mg.co.za)*, August 27, 2006

288 *Madam and Eve*: Cartoon number 003278, August 30, 2006, *www.madamandeve.co.za./archive*

Reconciliation isn't a one-time thing: "Many Feet to Wash," *South Africa: The Good News*, Sept. 8, 2006 (*www.sagoodnews.co.za*)